History of the United States Mint and Its Coinage

David W. Lange

First United States Mint by Natalie Hause is a re-creation of Edwin Lamasure Jr.'s painting of the nation's first mint buildings.

Additional Research by Mary Jo Mead

AMERICAN
NUMISMATIC
ASSOCIATION

www.whitmanbooks.com

3101 Clairmont Road, Suite C, Atlanta GA 30329

ISBN: 079481972-9

Printed in China

The Official RED BOOK® **Series includes:**

- *A Guide Book of Morgan Silver Dollars*
- *A Guide Book of Double Eagle Gold Coins*
- *A Guide Book of United States Type Coins*
- *A Guide Book of Modern United States Proof Coin Sets*
- *A Guide Book of United States Nickel Five-Cent Pieces*
- *A Guide Book of Flying Eagle and Indian Cents*
- *A Guide Book of United States Commemorative Coins*
- *A Guide Book of United States Barber Silver Coins*
- *A Guide Book of United States Liberty Seated Silver Coins*

For Amanda,
who is interested in other things right now.

About the Author

A lifelong collector of coins and related items, David W. Lange is a former president of the California State Numismatic Association, the Pacific Coast Numismatic Society, and the New Jersey Numismatic Society.

Highly regarded as one the foremost educators in the field of numismatics, he is a frequent speaker at numismatic conventions and has taught for many years at the American Numismatic Association's Annual Summer Seminar in Colorado Springs, Colorado.

Lange holds life memberships in the American Numismatic Association (ANA) and the Numismatic Literary Guild, both of which have presented him with numerous awards for his writing. He has been a columnist for the ANA's monthly journal, *Numismatist*, since 1988, and has contributed countless feature articles on United States coinage to that and many other publications. He also serves as a consultant and guest for a number of radio and television programs covering numismatic subjects.

David W. Lange

Employed by Numismatic Guaranty Corporation since 1994, Lange is NGC's Director of Research. His responsibilities there include variety attribution, counterfeit detection, research and writing, as well as the maintenance of NGC's coin Census Report and Certified Collectors Registry. He attends most major coin shows on behalf of the company and is always ready to meet coin enthusiasts.

History of the United States Mint and its Coinage is Lange's sixth book. His other titles include *The Complete Guide to Lincoln Cents, The Complete Guide to Buffalo Nickels,* and *The Complete Guide to Mercury Dimes,* each recognized as the standard reference for its series. Another of his recent Whitman titles is the *Guide Book of Modern United States Proof Coin Sets.*

A native of San Francisco, David W. Lange now lives in Florida with wife Alba and daughter Amanda.

Acknowledgments

I would like to express my gratitude to Thomas K. DeLorey, R.W. Julian, and John Kraljevich, Jr. for reviewing the manuscript and providing valuable additions and corrections.

David W. Lange

Foreword
by Q. David Bowers

Today, millions of people pursue what has been called "the world's greatest hobby"—the collecting of rare coins. Included are casual dabblers who set aside a few quarters from the United States Mint's 50 State Quarters® Program, Kennedy half dollars, or other souvenir issues. More serious are several hundred thousand individuals who methodically collect items of interest such as Uncirculated Morgan silver dollars of the 1878 to 1921 era, available from long dispersed Treasury hoards; Lincoln cents by date and mintmark, including the enticing, desirable, rare 1909-S V.D.B.; modern commemoratives from 1982 to date; large copper cents distinguished by minute die variety differences of the years 1793 to 1814; or other distinct types and series of coins.

The natural way to begin coin collecting is to go out and *buy something*. For most, acquisition is the logical beginning step, whether from finding an interesting coin in circulation or buying a coin that sparks an interest because of its history or beauty. From there, coin by coin, collections grow.

While collecting coins, relatively few people have taken the time to learn the background of what they collect—how their coins were minted and where. The present book, *History of the United States Mint and Its Coinage* by David W. Lange, with its attractive design and supplemental research by Mary Jo Meade, offers to remedy that!

In the pages to follow you will "be there" in Philadelphia at the first federal mint when it was being built in 1792. You will be on hand in Lumpkin County, Georgia, where gold was in abundance and a place was needed to mint it (the answer: a federal facility opened in Dahlonega, Georgia, in 1838, which continued in operation to 1861). You will be in those places and more. Many more. Far more than a recitation of dates, people, and events, Dave Lange shares with the reader his love and interest in history, each chapter offering its own morsels and tidbits. And the illustrations compiled by Mary Jo Meade—in a word, outstanding! Even the most dedicated numismatist will appreciate—possibly seeing them for the first time—proposed sketches for coins by James B. Longacre, or photos of the San Francisco Mint in the wake of the 1906 earthquake, to mention but a few tidbits from a memorable smorgasbord.

Social history is a part of coins—indeed, commerce, society, and coinage are all interlinked—and here and again the authors insert items from America's past, not always pleasant, but always informative. Then, of course, there is the twice-told tale of Augustus Saint-Gaudens and his cooperation with President Theodore Roosevelt, along with other accounts—no doubt many of them new to most readers.

In today's world not everyone has time to sit down and spend hours on end with a single book. Instead, the typical reader will probably spend a half hour or an hour, do something else, then come back later. For such readers this book is ideal, as each section is essentially stand-alone—you can begin anywhere, end anywhere, and pick up anywhere. Of course, starting at the beginning and traveling along to the end will give you a better picture of the Mint and its coinage.

My congratulations to David W. Lange and Mary Jo Meade on the creation of such an excellent book. And a special thank you to the American Numismatic Association for the vision and commitment to print and distribute it. May it achieve the circulation and popularity it richly deserves.

Q. David Bowers
Wolfeboro, New Hampshire

Discover and Explore the World of Money

by Christopher Cipoletti

I know that you will enjoy this publication as you learn about the history of United States coinage through the developments of the United States Mint. And as your interest is piqued and you become intrigued with the history, the art, the culture, and the science reflected in the money of the United States Mint, we hope that you will want to further that interest. The American Numismatic Association, headquartered in Colorado Springs, Colorado, exists to help you fulfill your interest as you "Discover and Explore the World of Money."

Founded in 1891, the ANA encourages and educates people to study and collect money and related items. The Association is a nonprofit, educational organization dedicated to preserving culture and history as reflected through money. Money memorializes all that we are as a society. It traces our geographic paths; it reflects political happenings from the reigns of monarchies to the progress of democracies. It is artistic in its design and scientific in its metal and paper content. It touches every aspect of our lives.

In short: the American Numismatic Association is here to help you learn about the important cultural and historical asset that is money.

The ANA Is For Everyone

The ANA promotes studying and collecting money for research, interpretation, and preservation of history and culture from ancient times to the present. Through resources such as our publications, Money Museum, Dwight N. Manley Numismatic Library, and educational programming, the ANA makes a wide range of educational exhibits, services, and seminars available to its members, as well as to students, historians, the academic community, and the general public.

Members enjoy the monthly magazine, *Numismatist*, online newsletters, and a variety of numismatic publications such as correspondence courses and museum catalogs. The Association web site (www.money.org) opens the door to classes and seminars, the library catalog, virtual exhibits, interesting articles, lesson plans for teachers, programs for Scouts, information for young and emerging collectors, as well as information on consumer protection, coin shows, and clubs.

Coin Collecting: A Hobby With a Long History

People have been collecting money since the ancient Greek staters, made of a natural alloy of gold and silver called *electrum*, were introduced in Asia Minor around 600 B.C. In the United States, coin collecting became a thriving hobby in the 19th century, with collectors saving copper large cents by date and carefully arranging them in special velvet-lined mahogany cabinets.

Since the early days of collecting United States Mint coinage, a varied and thriving hobby has developed. This exciting hobby has grown and prospered because it offers so much diversity and so many options to those who become involved in collecting. David W. Lange's *History of the United States Mint and Its Coinage* expands hobbyists' horizons by exploring the manufacturer of America's coinage. There is a rich, untapped history that is a part of the United States Mint. This history is part of our American culture. This great book provides information and education to all who explore its pages.

Today, hobbyists range from schoolchildren searching their lunch money for the newest state quarters to sophisticated and knowledgeable researchers of rare and valuable pieces. By organizing and learning about the history of their coins, how they are made, why designs are used and changed, and the stories and legends surrounding each piece of silver or gold, a collector gains greater satisfaction from the unique assortment that makes up his or her collection.

Looking Into the Future

The American Numismatic Association guides your journey into the world of money. The Association has challenged people in their collecting interests and provided information to its members since 1891. Looking to the future, the ANA is charting a course for collectors and encouraging young and old alike to discover and explore the exciting and educational world of money.

We encourage you to join us on this journey of history, geography, economics, art, science, and culture. Explore money's impact on our politics. See how it teaches math, art, science, economics, and so much more. Discover the excitement of finding a unique coin in your grocery store change. Learn about the minting process and the creativity that is a part of money from the United States and around the world.

Consider becoming a part of this exciting journey—the world of money awaits your involvement. **Discover and Explore the World of Money** with the American Numismatic Association. Join online at www.money.org, or call us at 1-800-514-COIN (2646). We look forward to having you become our newest member.

Christopher Cipoletti
Executive Director,
American Numismatic Association
Colorado Springs, Colorado
April 2005

Contents

BLACK
HAT →

F
E
K
G
E
H
D
C
B
A

Chapter One

The Pre-Colonial and Colonial Eras

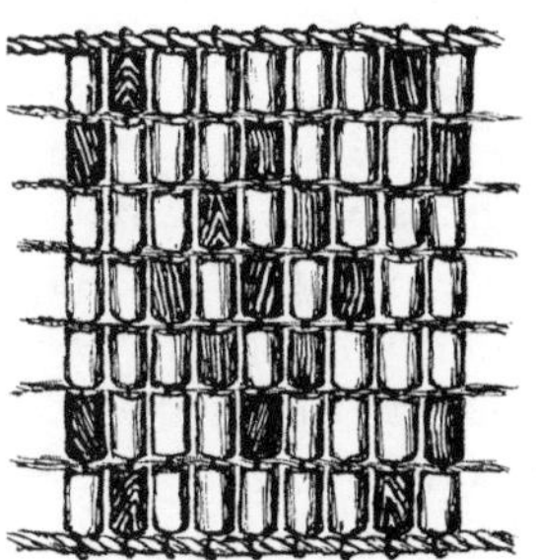

Symbolic designs woven into a wampum belt might hold a tribe's history or record the terms of an alliance. A row of diamond shapes might stand for friendship and squares could signify council fires.

The first Americans settled the land we now know as the United States of America thousands of years ago. Native Americans enjoyed a simple barter economy, trading among themselves for the things they needed. While some of the items they made by hand were of a practical nature, such as sharpened stones for cutting or woven baskets for carrying food, they also made items that were simply desirable for their beauty. These included pieces of jewelry fashioned from polished stones or, in the case of those living near the shore, from seashells.

Maryland settlers bargain with Indians for land on which to build the colony's first capital, St. Mary's City.

Though Native Americans did not use coins of the sort we know today, some of them did have wampum, which was made from seashells. Along the eastern shore of North America, the Indians retrieved small mollusk shells, cutting them down to about the size of a corn kernel and rolling them smooth on sandstone to make beads. In fact, the word "wampum" means "white shell beads" in the language of the Algonquins. Though white beads were the most common, the more valuable wampum was made from mollusk shells of a deep blue or purple color.

Wampum, which was highly prized, was drilled and strung on leather thongs into single strands or woven to make a belt. Using the different colors, pictures could be formed in these belts in the same way that small tiles or stones are still used to form mosaics.

Though the shells were only found along the ocean shore, the wampum made from them was traded between the tribes of the Eastern Woodlands and those of the Plains. These little beads were of no practical use in themselves, but they still represented a known value, so wampum may be thought of as similar to coins in the way it was exchanged for items that were of a more useful nature.

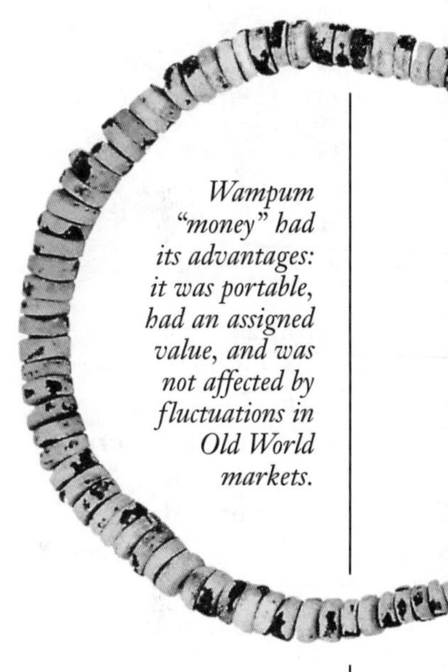

Wampum "money" had its advantages: it was portable, had an assigned value, and was not affected by fluctuations in Old World markets.

◀ *Theodor de Bry's 1590 engraving, "The Village of Secota," shows a Native American village on Roanoke Island.*

Beaver Fur "Money"

There were very few coins circulating in the Colonies, so people usually traded for the items they needed. Native Americans wanted metal tools, kettles, cloth, and other man-made commodities, and European settlers wanted animal skins they could sell for cash or use in trade.

European demand for beaver-fur hats turned beaver pelts into a form of money. On the price bulletin seen at right, the cost of trade items and the values of other animal hides are expressed in numbers of beaver pelts *in season.*

The trapper's prize was an adult beaver killed in wintertime, when its fur was thickest. Once the hide had been stretched and dried, it was known as a "made beaver," or a beaver "in season," which became a standard unit of money.

July 14th. 1703.
Prices of Goods
Supplyed to the
Eaſtern Indians,
By the ſeveral Truckmaſters ; and of the Peltry received by the Truckmaſters of the ſaid *Indians.*

ONe yard Broad Cloth, *three* Beaver skins, *in ſeaſon.*
One yard & half Gingerline, *one* Beaver skin, *in ſeaſon*
One yard Red or Blew Kerſey, *two* Beaver skins, *in ſeaſon.*
One yard good Duffels, *one* Beaver skin, *in ſeaſon.*
One yard & half broad fine Cotton, *one* Beaver skin, *in ſeaſon*
Two yards of Cotton, *one* Beaver skin, *in ſeaſon.*
One yard & half of half thicks, *one* Beaver skin, *in ſeaſon.*
Five Pecks Indian Corn, *one* Beaver skin, *in ſeaſon*
Five Pecks Indian Meal, *one* Beaver Skin, *in ſeaſon.*
Four Pecks Peaſe, *one* Beaver skin, *in ſeaſon.*
Two Pints of Powder, *one* Beaver skin, *in ſeaſon.*
One Pint of Shot, *one* Beaver skin, *in ſeaſon.*
Six Fathom of Tobacco, *one* Beaver skin, *in ſeaſon.*
Forty Biskets, *one* Beaver skin, *in ſeaſon.*
Ten Pound of Pork, *one* Beaver skin, *in ſeaſon.*
Six Knives, *one* Beaver skin, *in ſeaſon.*
Six Combes, *one* Beaver skin, *in ſeaſon.*
Twenty Scaines Thread, *one* Beaver skin, *in ſeaſon.*
One Hat, *two* Beaver skins, *in ſeaſon.*
One Hat with Hatband, *three* Beaver skins, *in ſeaſon.*
Two Pound of large Kettles, *one* Beaver skin, *in ſeaſon.*
One Pound & half of ſmall Kettles, *one* Beaver skin, *in ſeaſon*
One Shirt, *one* Beaver skin, *in ſeaſon.*
One Shirt with Ruffels, *two* Beaver skins, *in ſeaſon.*
Two Small Axes, *one* Beaver skin, *in ſeaſon.*
Two Small Hoes, *one* Beaver skin, *in ſeaſon.*
Three Dozen middling Hooks, *one* Beaver skin, *in ſeaſon.*
One Sword Blade, *one & half* Beaver skin, *in ſeaſon.*

What ſhall be accounted in Value equal One Beaver in ſeaſon : *Viz.*

ONe Otter skin in ſeaſon, is one Beaver
One Bear skin in ſeaſon, is one Beaver,
Two Half skins in ſeaſon, is one Beaver
Four Pappcote skins in ſeaſon, is one Beaver
Two Foxes in ſeaſon, is one Beaver.
Two Woodchocks in ſeaſon, is one Beaver.
Four Martins in ſeaſon, is one Beaver.
Eight Mincks in ſeaſon, is one Beaver.
Five Pounds of Feathers, is one Beaver.
Four Raccoones in ſeaſon, is one Beaver.
Four Seil skins large, is one Beaver.
One Mooſe Hide, is two Beavers.
One Pound of Caſtorum, is one Beaver.

The manufacture of beaver hats was among the first colonial industries. The worker shown at left is ironing a nearly finished hat to give the fur a high gloss.

Colonial hatters supplied markets that might otherwise have been served by British manufacturers, so Parliament passed the Hat Act of 1732, which restricted colonial production and export. The act was part of Britain's mercantile policy, designed to keep the colonial economy dependent on the mother country.

The Colonial Era

When Europeans first began to settle in America during the 1500s, there was little use for coins. Where would you spend them in a complete wilderness? Coins meant nothing to the native people, yet the Europeans found that they needed to trade with the Indians in order to survive, particularly during winter. Whites soon adopted the native practice of exchanging wampum for food, animal skins, and other necessities. As the natives acquired a taste for items of European manufacture, this trading increased.

Wampum was one of several items found in nature to serve as a form of money during the Colonial era. Another highly prized commodity, especially in Europe, was a plant native to America called tobacco. Both were so commonly exchanged that the English Colonies of the Atlantic coast actually passed laws regulating their values by weight or count.

These values fluctuated according to the availability of each item, and when a particular product became too common, its value as measured by other goods would fall. When such commodities were in short supply, people were willing to pay more of some other valued item to acquire them. This illustrates the law of supply and demand, which is crucial to understanding the role of money in early America.

The colonists soon learned how to manipulate the supply of wampum in their favor. By using manufacturing techniques unknown to the native people, they produced finished wampum from natural shells at such a high rate that its trade value declined. By the end of the 1600s, wampum was no longer prized as a form of wealth, though its use as jewelry and for ceremonial purposes continued.

The simple barter economy of the early colonists eventually gave way to a system of commerce that resembled those of the cities and towns they had left behind in Europe. With craftsmen and merchants setting up shops in villages up and down the Atlantic coast, the need for a more sophisticated medium of exchange demanded that coins be made available. With no mints in the American Colonies to manufacture coins, the colonists relied on whatever supply arrived with new immigrants.

England and the other European nations limited the amount of gold and silver coins that could be taken out of their countries by departing colonists, and these coins remained in such short supply that once spent by the newcomers, they rarely returned to circulation. More often they were hoarded as a store of wealth. There were no banks in the early years of colonial America, and most people would not have trusted them with their money if they had existed.

There was a critical need for coins, since the main source of income for colonial governments was in the form of customs duties, taxes paid on goods that were imported from outside the Colonies. These fees had to be paid in lawful money, and in those days that

Tobacco and other crops were called "country money" or "country pay" and functioned as cash in colonial America. "Tobacco notes," certificates representing tobacco deposited in public warehouses, were an early form of paper money.

◀ *The hard-working colonists seen at left illustrate a maxim from Benjamin Franklin's* Almanack: *"He that hath a trade hath an estate."*

Obverse of a 1652 "New England" Massachusetts shilling. The value in pence, XII, is punched into the reverse. (25-28 mm)

Massachusetts Bay Colony Pine Tree shilling, dated 1652 (25-28 mm)

William Wood's 1722 Rosa Americana penny (25-29 mm)

meant coins – and only gold or silver coins. In addition, coins were needed to purchase the goods themselves from Europe. The lack of coins restricted trade and kept the American economies from growing.

With the exception of the Massachusetts silver coinage of 1652-1682, Cecil Calvert's Maryland issues of circa 1659 (see shilling on page 15), William Wood's Rosa Americana issues of 1722-1724, Higley's coppers of 1737-1739, and the 1773 Virginia halfpennies, there are few uniquely American coins from the colonial era.

Other small issues of coins and tokens were made from time to time during this period (1587-1776), but these were isolated productions that saw little circulation and were restricted to use in small areas. It may be seen from these mostly unsuccessful attempts at coinage that the needs of the American colonists were not being met. This attitude of disregard on the part of England toward its countrymen overseas would eventually lead to rebellion and American independence.

Higley copper threepence, circa 1737 (28.6 mm)

1773 Virginia half penny (25 mm)

For the most part, the real money of the colonial era consisted of paper currency notes issued by the Colonies, as well as a broad mixture of foreign coins. While we tend to think of the colonists as British, several of the American colonies were populated primarily by those whose origins lay elsewhere in Europe. New York was originally New Netherland, a Dutch colony. Delaware, too, was settled by Dutch immigrants, as well as by Swedes. Many Pennsylvanians were German by birth. Trade between Europe and these new Americans resulted in the coins of many countries circulating side-by-side in what is now the United States of America. Among the more common gold and silver pieces were those of England, France, Portugal, and Spain.

Of all these countries, Spain had the greatest influence on the money supply of the American colonists. With its vast colonial empire, including Mexico and most of Central and South America, Spain dominated the world's supply of both gold and silver for centuries. The majority of coins circulating in the American colonies at the time of the War of Independence were Spanish pieces minted at Mexico City; Lima, Peru; or Potosí, Bolivia. While gold issues were important to bankers and those engaged in international trade, the coins handled by the average American were most likely to be the Spanish silver 8-*reales* piece and its various fractions.

The 8-*reales* coin, or Spanish Milled dollar as it was described in financial documents, is best known today for the frequent references to "pieces of eight" found in pirate tales. As its name implies, this silver dollar-size coin was valued at 8 *reales*, each *real*, or "bit," being worth 12½ cents. From this value still survives the expression "two bits," meaning 25 cents.

Spanish dollars and their silver fractions were minted in huge numbers throughout the 1700s and 1800s in Spain and its American colonies. Early types displayed on their obverse the Pillars of Hercules, a symbolic representation of the Strait of Gibraltar

COINS.	Weights. OZ	dwt	Gr	Value OLD TENOR £ s d	Lawfull Money s
Guinea	0	5	9	10.10.–	28/–
Half D°.		2	16½	5.5 –	14/–
Moidore		6	22½	13.10 –	36/–
Half D°.		3	11	6.15 –	18/–
Dubloon or Pistole Piece		17	8	33. –	88/–
Half D°.		8	16	16.10 –	44/–
Pistole		4	8	8.5. –	22/–
Half D°.		2	4	4.2.6	11/–
Double Joannes or £3 12 Sterl. Piece		18	10	36. –	96/–
Single Joannes or 36/ Sterl. Piece		9	5	18. –	48/–
Half D°.		4	14½	9. –	24/–
Quarter D°.		2	7¼	4.10 –	12/–

Silver Coins	Weights. OZ	dwt	Gr	Value £ s
Eng Crown	0	19	8½	2.1[illegible]
Half Ditto		9	16¼	1.5[illegible]
Dollar		17	12	2.5[illegible]
Half Ditto		8	18	1.2[illegible]
Quarter D°.		4	9	.11[illegible]

oz. dwt	Gr	GOLD per oz	SIL[illegible]
1. 0	0	£38. 0. 0	2.[illegible]
10	0	19. –	1.[illegible]
5	0	9.10 –	[illegible]
2	0	3.16 –	[illegible]
1	0	1.18 –	[illegible]
0	12	19 –	[illegible]
0	6	9.6	[illegible]

Colonists struggled with a confusing array of coins from foreign countries, and relied on conversion charts such as this to determine values.

In Maryland, Cecil Calvert had silver coins made valued at 1 shilling, 6 pence, and 4 pence. These coins had no date, but they were made around 1659.

that separates Spain from North Africa. Beginning with the coins of King Carlos III in 1772, the Spanish dollar and its fractions carried a portrait of the reigning monarch on their obverse, and the Pillars of Hercules were relocated to the reverse.

While coins became more available to Americans during the 1700s, not everyone used them. They were commonplace in the cities, especially those with seaports, but in rural areas coins were nearly unknown. Farmers and animal trappers living in the interior of the country had little use for them. They either traded with the natives, who did not value coins, or exchanged their own products for food and those few manufactured items they needed. In the cities, most people used whatever copper and small silver coins were available, while the use of larger silver pieces and gold coins was largely restricted to bankers and those engaged in trade with the West Indies, East Asia, or Europe.

The West Indies were a particularly rich source of coins, since so much of the world's trade passed through these islands between Europe, Africa, and the Far East. Sadly, some of this wealth was based on the slave trade, which remained legal in the United States until long after the colonial period.

Lord Baltimore Large Head shilling (27 mm)

1739 Spanish Milled dollar (39 mm)

GOLD AND SILVER FOR MEN AT WAR

[Mass]

In the House of REPRESENTATIVES, Feb. 14, 1776.

WHEREAS the honorable the Continental Congress have desired this Court to make Application to the several Towns in this Colony, to know what Quantity of Silver and Gold can be procured in Exchange for the Continental Bills, as that Sort of Money is greatly wanted to support that Part of the Army gone against Quebec: Therefore,

Resolved, That the Persons hereafter named in each County of this Colony, be a Committee to make Enquiry what Money in Silver and Gold can be procured in Exchange for Continental Bills; and the same Committee are required to obtain Subscriptions in their several Counties, of all Persons that are willing, in this Time of Danger and Distress, to exchange hard Money for said Bills: And that each Person set down against his Name, the Amount of such Sum as he is ready to exchange; and that the said Committee make Report of their Doings therein, on the second Day of the next Sitting of this Court. And that Mr. *Perry*, Col. *Lovell*, and Col. *Davis*, for the County of *Suffolk*; Col. *Orne*, Major *Cross*, Mr. *Hopkins*, and Mr. *Phillips*, for the County of *Essex*; Mr. *Hall*, Col. *Barrett*, and Mr. *Hobart*, for the County of *Middlesex*; Major *Hawley*, Major *Ely*, Col. *Bliss*, Capt. *Goodman*, and Col. *Field*, for the County of *Hampshire*; Mr. *Cushing*, Mr. *Turner*, & Major *White*, for the County of *Plymouth*; Col. *Otis*, and Col. *Doane*, for the County of *Barnstable*; Mr. *Durfey*, Col. *Bowers*, Col. *Godfrey*, and Col. *Carpenter*, for the County of *Bristol*; Capt. *Parker*, Esq; *Caldwell*, Deacon *Rawson*, Mr. *Singletary*, Mr. *Bancroft*, and Mr. *Wheeler*, for the County of *Worcester*; Deacon *Curtis*, Dr. *Whiting*, and Mr. *Dickinson*, for the County of *Berkshire*; Capt. *Bragdon*, Deacon *Hovey*, and Col. *Sayer*, for the County of *York*; Mr. *Freeman*, Brigadier *Thomson*, and Mr. *Fabyan*, for the County of *Cumberland*; Mr. *Rice*, Capt. *Howard*, Major *Sewall*, and Col. *Jones*, for the County of *Lincoln*; Col. *Norton*, for the County of *Duke's County*; and Mr. *Stephen Hussey*, for the County of *Nantucket*, be a Committee for the Purposes aforesaid; and that Esq; *Davis*, give Notice to Mr. *Hussey*, of his being appointed for the Purpose aforesaid. Sent up for Concurrence.

WILLIAM COOPER, Speaker, pro Tem.

In Council, *February* 15, 1776. Read and Concurr'd.

PEREZ MORTON, Dep. Sec'ry.

Consented to,

BENJAMIN GREENLEAF,
WALTER SPOONER,
CALEB CUSHING,
THOMAS CUSHING,
JEDEDIAH FOSTER,
JOSEPH PALMER,
JOHN TAYLOR,
BENJAMIN LINCOLN,
JOHN WHETCOMB,
ELDAD TAYLOR,
JABEZ FISHER,
MICHAEL FARLEY,
SAMUEL HOLTEN,
MOSES GILL,
BENJAMIN WHITE,

A true Copy, Attest. *PEREZ MORTON*, Dep. Sec'ry.

Chapter Two

Independence and the Confederation

◀ *The February 15, 1776, document shown opposite lists county representatives in Massachusetts who were assigned the task of soliciting gold and silver from their neighbors in exchange for Continental paper money. During the Revolutionary War, there was very little precious metal available to pay for military supplies. Massachusetts colonists were working to raise hard money to support the Continental Army, which had been sent to conquer Canada.*

When Britain's American colonies declared their independence in 1776, one of the greatest problems facing the Continental Congress was financing the war effort. Soldiers and seamen needed food, clothing, and weapons, all of which were in very short supply throughout most of the war years.

Britain had been America's primary trading partner. Now that trade was cut off and, along with it, the colonies' principal source of hard money.

Supplies of refined silver and gold, as well as the known sources of raw ore from which these metals were taken, were quite scarce in the American colonies. The great gold and silver discoveries of the 1800s were still decades away, and the only coining metal available from domestic mines in any reasonable amount was copper.

While it would be nice to have some copper coins from the War of Independence (1775 to 1783), the simple fact is that no such coins were made, aside from a few abortive and very rare issues dated 1776. In the initial enthusiasm of that year, several of the new states made plans for their own copper coinage. One state that actually went through with this idea was New Hampshire. In March 1776, its House of Representatives and Council appointed a committee to look into the practicality of minting copper coins. They recommended that William Moulton be assigned to coin 100 pounds of copper into pieces valued at 108 to the Spanish milled dollar.

These fascinating coins, of which fewer than 10 are known today, display on one side a tree and the inscription AMERICAN LIBERTY. The other side features simply a harp. Numis-matic scholar Walter Breen suggested that this device was taken from one of the ContinentalCurrency notes then circulating, which, in addition to the harp, included a Latin inscription that translates to "The bigger blend harmoniously with the smaller." New Hampshire was evidently seen as one

1776 New Hampshire copper (28.6 mm)

1776 Massachusetts copper (31.8 mm)

General Benedict Arnold led Continental troops against Quebec on November 14, 1775, not knowing the city had been reinforced the day before by a division of British soldiers.

The government issued Continental Currency from 1775 to 1779.

Money is justly called the Sinews of War; and if the stipulated Prices are not complied with, it is natural to conclude, the Money will depreciate faster than it has ever done; and should that be unhappily our Case, soon, very soon, it will not be in our Power to support the Army, or even ourselves.

– From the report of a Continental Congress delegates meeting on November 3, 1779, urging towns to fix maximum prices for such commodities as cheese, lumber, and West India rum to protect the value of Continental Currency

of the smaller states, so the motto was quite appropriate. Oddly, however, there is no mention anywhere on these coins that they were issued by New Hampshire!

In that same year of 1776, Massachusetts produced an attractive copper piece of which but a single specimen is known today. Its obverse displays a pine tree, the symbol of a Cambridge, Massachusetts, patriotic society called the Sons of Liberty. Around this is inscribed MASSACHUSETTS STATE. On the reverse is a familiar seated figure similar to Britannia that, while symbolic of the hated Britain, was used here because it was typical of the copper coins in circulation and would ease acceptance. The date 1776 sits below, and the legend LIBERTY AND VIRTUE appears around the border. The great rarity of this historic penny suggests that it was only a pattern, a coin made in small numbers to test the dies. Who prepared the dies and struck this issue remains unknown to this day.

Benjamin Franklin

Aside from these two examples, the grand plans of the individual states to produce their own coinage ultimately came to nothing until after the war's end. The economic uncertainty that typically accompanies wartime led to the hoarding of all coins, so there was simply no point in making new ones. As a consequence, the American war effort was funded almost entirely with paper money. These notes were issued by both the individual colonies and the Continental Congress, and they stated on them that they were redeemable in Spanish Milled dollars. In actual fact, however, most of the notes could not be redeemed by the cash-poor governments that issued them, and they quickly lost their value. This sad situation gave rise to an expression that was long familiar to Americans, though it is mostly forgotten today: "Not worth a Continental" was often used to describe anything of doubtful value.

The hope for an American coinage did produce some experimental coins. Early in the war, Congress anticipated receiving a large loan of silver from France, America's ally in the struggle against Great Britain.

A New Jersey engraver named Elisha Gallaudet was hired to create dies for what would be known as the Continental dollar. Examples of the dollar were coined for circulation in pewter, but their low intrinsic value led to a general rejection by the American people. A few hundred survive today as reminders of a desperate period in United States history, and these are highly prized by collectors.

1776 Continental dollar (40 mm; varies)

Continental dollars are rich in American symbolism, and the designs were created by such important figures as printer and statesman Benjamin Franklin and the scientist and mathematician David Rittenhouse. (Franklin printed some of the Continental Currency paper money, while

Rittenhouse later became the first director of the United States Mint.)

On the obverse of the Continental dollar appeared a sundial, an antique device for measuring the time of day using the sun's shadow projected on a scale. The sun itself is also seen on these coins, along with the words MIND YOUR BUSINESS. This expression did not mean

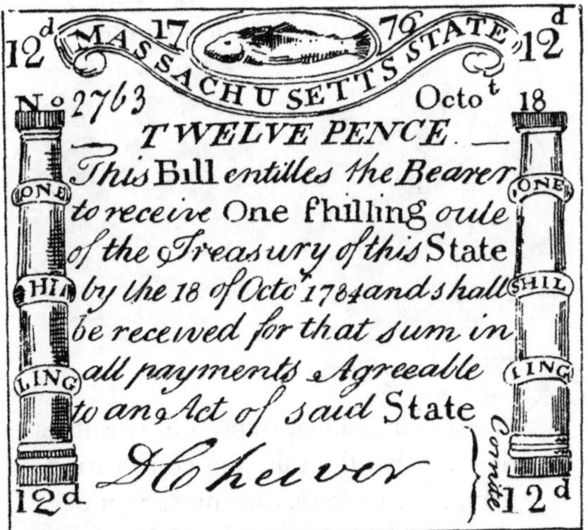

Some states issued paper money redeemable for specie, further confusing the new nation's already muddled monetary situation. This is the front of a 1776 1-shilling codfish note from Massachusetts, a legal-tender bill of credit payable in lawful money from the state treasury by October 18, 1784.

the same thing then that it does today. Two hundred years ago, it was intended to say "Take care of your business, and your business will take care of you." The Latin word FUGIO is also included near the sundial. Since *fugio* means "I fly," its use with the sundial warned that time flies, reinforcing the message that you should take care of business while you can. On the reverse of this fascinating coin are 13 interlocking rings, each of which bears the name of one of the colonies. At the center are the words AMERICAN CONGRESS and WE ARE ONE. This expresses the unity that the American colonies needed to win their independence. The message was particularly important, since most colonists were loyal to their own colony, but did not initially feel much connec-tion to neighboring colonies. Such a feeling of unity would only come from a shared struggle against Britain.

The last major battle of the War of Independence occurred in 1781, and a formal treaty of peace between Great Britain and the new United States of America was signed two years later. Among the pressing issues facing the infant nation were repayment of its war debts and the creation of a new monetary system. Americans still used the English reckoning of pounds, shillings, and pence, an awkward division of the pound into 240 pence that dated from ancient times.

There were a number of financial leaders in America who believed that a decimal system of money, based on multiples and fractions of the number 10, was highly desirable. No nation had yet implemented such a practical system but, as in many aspects of government, Americans would lead the way.

The first to propose a decimal system for American coinage was Gouverneur Morris, the assistant superintendent of finance. In 1782, he came up with an elaborate system based on a unit of value called, simply, the unit.

Its value was set at one-quarter grain of silver (a grain is equal to .0468 gram or .0023 ounce). There would be silver coins valued at 100 units and 1,000 units, as well as a gold coin of 10,000 units. Robert Morris (who was not related to Gouverneur) was the superintendent of finance, and he was so impressed by his assistant's plan that he commissioned engraver Benjamin Dudley to establish a mint. Once again, however, the plans of well-meaning individuals fell through because of America's economic condition at the time. The lack of silver bullion in the United States, plus the government's poor credit rating as a result of its nearly worthless paper money, prevented the minting of coins. Only a few patterns were struck, and these coins are very rare and highly desired by collectors.

The Morris pattern coins feature on their obverse the All-Seeing Eye of God, surrounded by 13 rays and stars, repre-

Robert Morris, a prominent Philadelphia merchant, was superintendent of finance for the Continental Congress. Charged with raising money to supply Revolutionary forces, he was criticized by some for using the "art ... of dazzling the public eye by the same piece of coin, multiplied by a thousand reflectors." Regardless of the smoke and mirrors he relied on to get the job done, he earned the title "Financier of the American Revolution."

Gouverneur Morris

1783 Constellatio Nova pattern coin worth 1,000 units (33 mm)

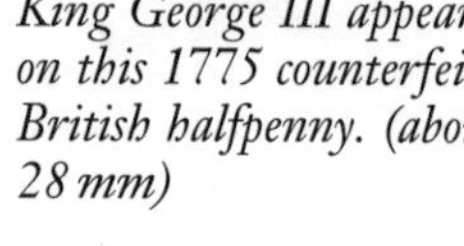

King George III appears on this 1775 counterfeit British halfpenny. (about 28 mm)

senting the 13 states. Around this is the Latin legend CONSTELLATIO NOVA, meaning new constellation, a reference to the new nation. On the reverse are the letters U.S. and the value in units. These elements are surrounded by a wreath and the Latin mottoes LIBERTAS and JUSTITA (liberty and justice). The date 1783 appears at the bottom.

Not one to give up, Gouverneur Morris decided to mint copper coins instead, using the same design but without a stated value. These coins, which are a bit larger than a quarter, were made in England at the Wyon family mint. More than a million were struck and shipped to America, where they were usually valued at one halfpenny. Though not produced by the United States government, the Constellatio Nova pieces were the first circulating coins to bear American imagery and inscriptions. They are also common enough that any collector can own one.

These coins had some competition in everyday circulation. In fact, most of the coins circulating during the 1780s were copper pieces, though an assortment of foreign silver and gold coins were also seen. Of the various coppers circulating, by far the most common were English halfpence. It was almost as though the break with Britain had never occurred, since these coins bore the portrait of England's king. There was a catch, however – nearly all of these halfpence were counterfeit!

King George III

Viewed today, after the passage of more than 200 years, this seems like an intolerable situation, but the truth is that few people of that time cared whether the copper coins were genuine or fake. Copper coins were not legal tender, which means they had no lawful value. They were accepted at a nominal value for the sake of convenience, and their metallic worth was below that figure whether a coin was genuine or counterfeit. In fact, Britain had not made any genuine halfpence for years, and most of those circulating in that country were likewise imitations.

The widespread acceptance of copper coins valued at one halfpenny was inviting to both counterfeiters and legitimate governments. Under the Articles of Confederation, the governing document that guided the United States from 1781 to 1789, Congress had limited power

1787 Massachusetts cent (24 mm)

over the individual states. One result of this was that the values of coins varied from state to state, causing economic chaos. In fact, the Articles of Confederation permitted individual states to mint and issue their own coins. Several of them did so beginning in 1785, and these state-sanctioned coppers only added to the confusion.

Most of the state coppers were struck by private companies under contract to the respective states. As payment, these companies received a fixed percentage of the pieces they produced. While the coins issued by the Commonwealth of Massachusetts remained of fine quality and legal weight, those of the other states and the Republic of Vermont soon became so deficient on both counts that they were frequently discounted by neighboring states. Though the coppers were worth intrinsically only about half their circulating value of one halfpenny, the

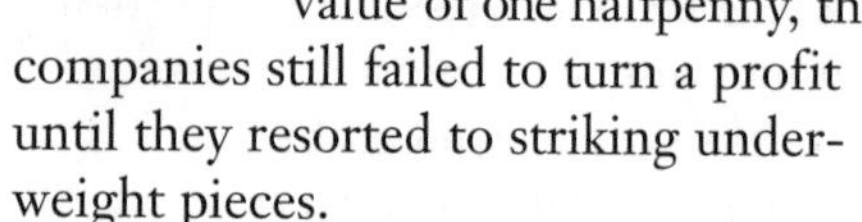

companies still failed to turn a profit until they resorted to striking underweight pieces.

As the states began placing restrictions on the circulation of deficient coppers, a general discrediting of all copper coins created an economic crisis during 1789. Congress had been aware of the coinage problem for some time, and it was determined that the situation not be allowed to persist. For this and other reasons, a constitutional convention was held in Philadelphia beginning in 1787 to draft a more effective government charter. Ratified March 4, 1789, this became the Federal Constitution that we still use today.

The new Constitution directed more power to the central government than it had held under the old Articles of Confederation. One of the powers Congress reserved for itself was the right to coin money and to regulate the value thereof. The states were now forbidden to do this, though individuals were permitted to make money of their own design as late as 1864!

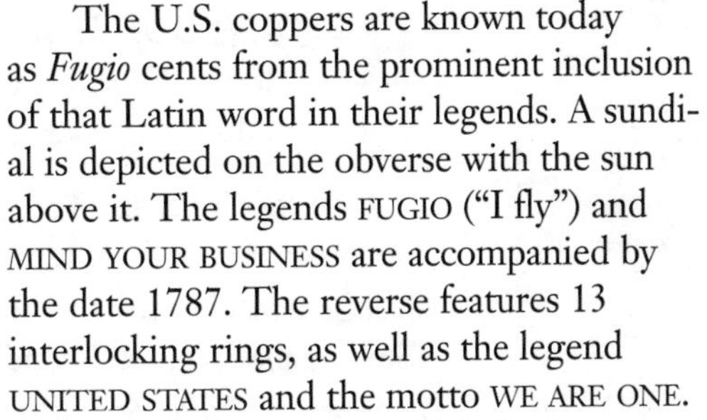

1786 Vermont copper (27 mm)

With a stronger central government, it would be just a matter of time before the United States had its own mint. Even so, private coiners enjoyed one last taste of privilege. The first national coins authorized were actually produced by a private contractor. Congress, still laboring under the Confederation government, voted on April 21, 1787, for a coinage of copper cents.

Among those petitioning for this very desirable contract was Matthias Ogden, who was then engaged in manufacturing New Jersey coppers. He lost his bid to James Jarvis, whose firm Jarvis & Company was given the contract. Jarvis was already coining Connecticut coppers, perhaps the least reputable of the state issues. Only later did it come out that Jarvis had bribed William Duer, head of the Board of Treasury, some $10,000 to swing the contract his way. This shameful act set the stage for the even greater embarrassment that followed.

Jarvis's firm included among its members his father-in-law, Samuel Broome. While Jarvis was in Europe attempting to secure financial backing or perhaps even subcontract the work to a mint there, Broome began using the copper alreadysupplied by the national government to strike Connecticut coins. Since these weighed less, they were more profitable.

It is not certain whether Jarvis knew of this embezzlement, but the government soon found out about it and Congress voided his contract on September 16, 1788. The original authorization was for 345 tons of copper coins (more than 32 million pieces), but only about 2.5 million coins were delivered. The United States sued Jarvis & Company for the value of its embezzled copper, but all the partners had fled and the government received nothing.

The U.S. coppers are known today as *Fugio* cents from the prominent inclusion of that Latin word in their legends. A sundial is depicted on the obverse with the sun above it. The legends FUGIO ("I fly") and MIND YOUR BUSINESS are accompanied by the date 1787. The reverse features 13 interlocking rings, as well as the legend UNITED STATES and the motto WE ARE ONE.

Ultimately, it mattered little that the contract for this coinage went unfulfilled, since the public largely rejected the coppers. Their distinctive design, adapted from the 1776 Continental Currency dollars, was simply unfamiliar. For a largely illiterate population, it was comforting to handle coins that were recognizable. Numismatists treasure these pieces, however, and they are a welcome addition to any collection. They are important in representing the first, albeit ill-fated, coinage of the United States of America.

Ephraim Brasher did not receive a contract to produce copper coins for New York, so he created the Brasher Doubloon to persuade the legislature to reconsider. The only gold coin from this period, it was equal in value to the Spanish doubloon, which was then worth $16. (30 mm)

1787 Fugio cent (28.6 mm)

The Story Begins

Having had under consideration the letter of the Director of the Mint of this day's date, I hereby declare my approbation of the purchase he has made of the house and lot for the Mint; of the employment of Mr. Voight as Coiner; of the procuring fifteen tons of Copper, and proceeding to coin the Cents and half Cents of Copper, and Dimes and half dimes of silver; and I leave to his discretion to have such alterations and additions made to the buildings purchased, as he shall find necessary; satisfied that under his orders no expence will be incurred which reason and necessity will not justify. And I desire that he will make out an Estimate of the sums of money which will be wanting for these purposes, and of the times at which they will be wanting, in order to enable the Treasury to make arrangements for furnishing them with convenience.

– Letter from George Washington to David Rittenhouse concerning funding for the Mint, July 9, 1792

The first United States Mint. (From Illustrated History of the United States Mint *by George G. Evans, 1885)*

The Senate and House of Representatives passed a bill during the third session of the United States Congress creating the young nation's first mint (below). (This is a replica of the original printed by Francis Childs and John Swaine in 1791.)

David Rittenhouse, a noted astronomer, surveyor and instrument maker, was appointed first director of the United States Mint, serving from April 1792 until June 1795.

Congreſs of the United States:

AT THE THIRD SESSION,

Begun and held at the City of Philadelphia, on Monday the ſixth of December, one thouſand ſeven hundred and ninety.

RESOLVED *by the* SENATE *and* HOUSE *of* REPRESENTATIVES *of the United States of America in Congreſs aſſembled,* That a mint ſhall be eſtabliſhed under ſuch regulations as ſhall be directed by law.

Reſolved, That the Preſident of the United States be, and he is hereby authorized to cauſe to be engaged, ſuch principal artiſts as ſhall be neceſſary to carry the preceeding reſolution into effect, and to ſtipulate the terms and conditions of their ſervice, and alſo to cauſe to be procured ſuch apparatus as ſhall be requiſite for the ſame purpoſe.

FREDERICK AUGUSTUS MUHLENBERG,
Speaker of the Houſe of Repreſentatives.

JOHN ADAMS, *Vice-Preſident of the United States, and Preſident of the Senate.*

APPROVED, March the third, 1791.

GEORGE WASHINGTON, *Preſident of the United States.*

DEPOSITED among the ROLLS in the OFFICE of the SECRETARY of STATE.

Th: Jefferson *Secretary of State.*

CHAPTER THREE

Establishing the United States Mint

Thomas Jefferson

I had sealed my letter before I discovered that I had omitted to desire of you, while at Madrid, to procure if possible some account of the dollars of that country from the earliest to the last, stating their dates, places where coined, weight & fineness. Such a statement, if it can be here in time before the next meeting of Congress (Nov. 1) to enable them, before we begin our coinage, to place our unit on a proper footing, will be of great & permanent importance. ...

– Letter from Thomas Jefferson to diplomat William Short, April 24, 1792

Between 1782 and 1790, there was much discussion in Congress about the creation of a national mint, but it was not until the adoption of a new constitution in 1789 that any real progress could be made. If anyone could be called the Father of the United States Mint, it would be Alexander Hamilton, the first person to serve as Secretary of the Treasury. After studying the monetary questions of the day at great length, Hamilton submitted his detailed report to Congress on January 28, 1791. In fairness, it should be noted that some of the groundwork for this study was done by Secretary of State Thomas Jefferson, though it was Hamilton who possessed a more precise understanding of the critical issues.

Alexander Hamilton

Their efforts could not have come at a better moment, as there had been pressure for some time to seek yet another contract coinage with a private mint. The front-runner was Matthew Boulton's Soho Mint near Birmingham, England. In partnership with James Watt, the genius who tamed steam power for use by industry, Boulton enjoyed a profitable business manufacturing copper tokens for various tradesmen in Britain. These tokens were superior in quality to anything being made by the world's mints, and Congress hoped to have coins of such quality for use in America.

Hamilton's report laid the foundation for what would become the United States coinage. Though the most commonly traded coin worldwide was the Spanish silver dollar, he advocated adoption of a bimetallic standard in which gold and silver would enjoy equal status. The prevailing market ratio between the metals was then about 15-to-1, an ounce of gold being worth 15 times as much as an ounce of silver. His plan was to determine the standard weight and fineness of the Spanish dollar, adopt those values for the American dollar, and then apply the 15-to-1 ratio in determining the ideal weights for the gold dollar and its multiples.

Hamilton arrived at the weight of his proposed silver dollar by weighing a random sample of Spanish dollars taken from circulation and averaging these figures. But, since Hamilton's sampling of dollars included many worn pieces, these coins provided him with a figure that was lower than their original average weight as minted.

Jefferson noted this flaw in the plan and advised Hamilton against such a low-weight dollar. In fact, Jefferson was correct, and the importance of this discrepancy became even more apparent when silver's value relative to that of gold began to decline on the international market.

George Washington

A company seeking a contract to produce coins for the United States had John Gregory Hancock design the 1791 Small Eagle cent seen below. The coin was rejected by President Washington, who thought his portrait on U.S. coins would be monarchical and objected to purchasing private contract coinage for the new nation. (32 mm)

The coins to be issued by the United States, as outlined in Hamilton's report, included the following:

> One gold piece equal in weight and value to ten units or dollars.
>
> One gold piece, equal to a tenth part of the former and which shall be a unit or dollar.
>
> One silver piece, which shall also be a unit or dollar.
>
> One silver piece, which shall be, in weight and value, one tenth part of a silver unit or dollar.
>
> One copper piece, which shall be of value of a hundredth part of a dollar.
>
> One copper piece, which shall be half the value of the former.

Though provided for in Hamilton's plan, the inclusion of a gold dollar was rejected at the time of the U.S. Mint's establishment in 1792, but this coin ultimately did appear more than 50 years later. Hamilton included the copper half-cent piece as a coin for the poor, so they would not have to purchase items in quantities exceeding their actual need. He also believed that the availability of such coins would foster competition between merchants by permitting them to price articles in half-cent increments.

Congress received Hamilton's report enthusiastically, but it would be more than a year before legislation creating the U.S. Mint and its coinage system was passed. There was much fine-tuning to perform, as well as several issues pending that led to heated debate. All the while, there were those seeking to obtain a private contract for supplying the nation with its coinage. These proposals were still being received more than a decade after the Mint began issuing coins!

One of the great debates of the coinage bill as originally drafted centered on the selection of designs for the new coins. Though the proposed reverse design of an eagle for the silver and gold issues and a simple statement of value for the copper pieces prompted no objections, the text of this bill included the following passage relating to the obverse design:

> Upon one side of each of the said coins there shall be an impression or representation of the head of the President of the United States for the time being, with an inscription which shall express the initial or first letter of his Christian or first name, and his surname at length, the succession of the Presidency numerically, and the year of the coinage ... .

Americans have since become used to seeing busts of past presidents on their coins, but this was a very controversial issue at the time. The proposed design sounded very reminiscent of Britain's coins, with the use of the current president's portrait seeming just a little too monarchical. It has been said that President George Washington himself strongly opposed the use of his portrait on the coinage. Even so, various pattern coins bearing his likeness were produced by those seeking a coinage contract in an effort to curry favor with either Washington or Congress.

Despite the objections, this bill passed in the Senate on January 12, 1792. It then stalled in the House of Representatives, where an amendment was proposed striking the reference to the president's portrait in favor of an image "Emblematic of Liberty." The debate was extensive and impassioned, with many opponents of presidential portraits reminding their fellow congressmen that such thinking brought about the downfall of the great Roman Republic and condemned it to centuries of corruption and tyranny at the hands of emperors.

Such pleas ultimately had the desired effect, and the House passed the Mint bill with the amendment attached. The Senate, seeing that to disagree would mean failure of the bill, voted its approval of the amendment striking the president's portrait, and the legislation was signed into law by President Washington on April 2, 1792. At long last, the United States of America had its own mint and coinage, at least on paper.

The First Federal Coins

Alexander Hamilton's original lineup of coin denominations had been altered somewhat in the law as actually passed. The coins to be minted included copper cents and half cents, silver dollars, half dollars, quarter dollars, dimes, and half dimes, as well as gold eagles ($10), half eagles ($5), and quarter eagles ($2.50).

Before any production could begin, however, the mint had to be built. Since the seat of the federal government was then located at Philadelphia, this city would host the mint buildings. On July 18, 1792, David Rittenhouse, who had been selected by President Washington to serve as the first director of the United States Mint, purchased two lots for its use. These faced Seventh Street between Market and Arch Streets. A few structures were already in place, but these proved inadequate to the Mint's needs. They were removed and new buildings put up in their place. Modest by later standards, the new structures were deemed suitable for the Mint's operations as they were envisioned in 1792. Work continued throughout the summer and fall of that year, with the first structure ready by early September.

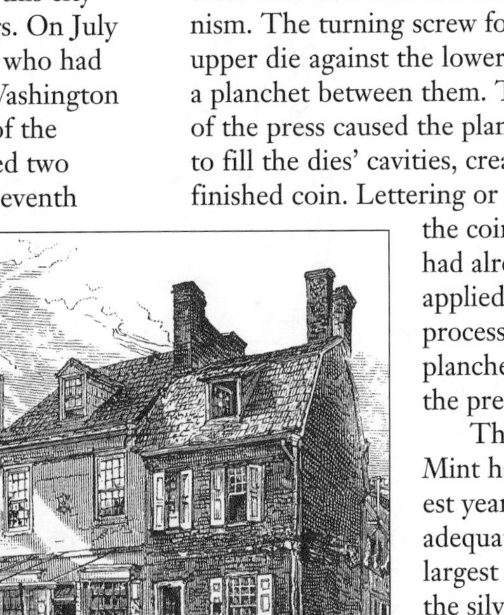

A scene from old Philadelphia

The U.S. Mint began its mission with virtually nothing in the way of equipment. As the Mint acquired its own lathes, saws, and other machine tools, some of its further requirements could be met in-house. One of the most consistent problems for the infant Mint was maintaining suitable rolling machinery for converting metal ingots into the long strips from which coin blanks were punched. The rollers it had were made of copper and easily wore out or broke. Steel rollers came only later. The failure of these vital parts would halt production on many occasions.

Coin presses of that era were of the screw type and were powered by human muscle and horse power. Two to four men were required to swing the heavy cross-arm that turned a screw mechanism. The turning screw forced the upper die against the lower one, with a planchet between them. The blow of the press caused the planchet metal to fill the dies' cavities, creating a finished coin. Lettering or reeding on the coin's edge had already been applied in a separate process before the planchet was fed into the press.

The presses the Mint had in its earliest years were not adequate to strike the largest coins, such as the silver dollar. As it turned out, the Mint's officers would not discover this until 1794, because they were prohibited by law from coining silver and gold until they had posted the security bonds demanded by the Mint Act. The Mint's first assayer was Albion Cox, and its chief coiner was Henry Voigt, who possessed some previous experience in the German mint of Saxe-Gotha. Both men were required to post bonds of $10,000 before being permitted to accept deposits of silver and gold for coining. This was an almost

David Rittenhouse

Tho' a long continued state of ill health has left me little relish for the usual pursuits of Interest and Ambition, I am extremely sensible of the honor you have done me by appointing me, unsolicited, Director of the Mint. ... I have purchased on account of the United States, a House & Lot which I hope will be found convenient for the mint, but considerable alterations must be made, and some small new buildings erected.

– Letter from David Rittenhouse to President Washington, July 9, 1792

1792 silver half disme (17.5 mm)

In execution of the Authority given by the legislature, measures have been taken for engaging some artists from abroad to aid in the establishment of our mint; others have been employed at home. Provision has been made for the requisite buildings, and these are now putting into proper condition for the purposes of the establishment. There has also been a small beginning in the coinage of half-dismes; the want of small coins in circulation calling the first attention to them.

– From President Washington's address to Congress, November 6, 1792

unimaginable sum in 1793 and one that neither man had any hope of raising. It was not until March 3, 1794, that Congress finally acted to lower the chief coiner's bond to $5,000 and that of the assayer to $1,000. At these figures, Mint Director David Rittenhouse paid for Voigt's security bond, and the money required of Cox was posted by Charles Gilchrist. The latter was "a dealer in buttons, buckles, watches and clocks" and one of the Mint's earliest depositors of silver bullion. Ironically, a year later Gilchrist applied for the position of assayer as Cox's successor, only to be rejected.

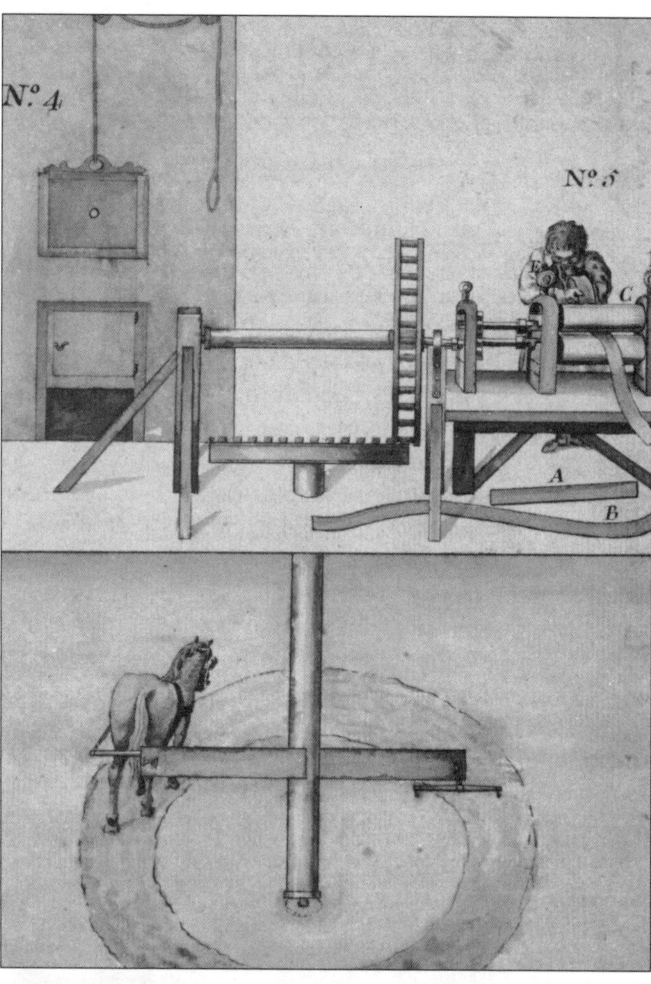

A horse-powered rolling mill; an annealing furnace is seen at left. (From An Essay on Coining *by Samuel Thompson, 1783)*

In actuality, a small coinage of silver had already been undertaken in the summer of 1792. As the Mint structures were not ready, this coining occurred in the cellar of Philadelphia saw-maker John Harper. It is believed that the dies for these half dismes (as their name was spelled on the coins) were engraved by William Russell Birch. Several Mint employees gathered in Harper's shop on July 13, where they struck 1,500 of the coins, these being made to the exact standards specified by the Mint Act of April 2, 1792.

These rare coins, the first produced by the United States Mint, were delivered directly to Secretary of State Thomas Jefferson. As the cabinet member with jurisdiction over the Mint, Jefferson had to assume responsibility for the coins, since the Mint's own officers were not yet bonded! The secretary was given instructions to distribute them to important individuals both in the U.S. and abroad. Many later found their way into general circulation, becoming heavily worn. So desirable are these historic pieces that even the worn ones are worth quite a bit of money to collectors.

An old legend has it that President and Mrs. Washington donated some of their silverware to be melted as a supply of bullion for these first coins. Though this wonderful tale cannot be confirmed, it is more believable than it may seem. The president took a very personal interest in the affairs of the Mint, recognizing that coins bearing the imprint of the United States were an unquestionable mark of national sovereignty and prestige. In fact, he frequently stopped by the Mint on his daily walk to work! In his annual address to the nation in November, Washington, alluding to the silver half dismes, mentioned that "a small beginning" had been made in the matter of coinage.

Other pattern coins were made as tests of potential new designs but, with the exception of the 1792 half dismes, none were produced in numbers large enough to qualify as regular production. Until the bonds of Cox and Voigt were posted in 1794, the Mint had to content itself with producing just cents and half cents. The first cents were minted in late February 1793 and delivered March 1. Like those that would follow for the next 64 years, these early cents were made of pure copper and were quite large, nearly the size of our modern half dollar.

The design selected for the first cents shows a youthful bust of Liberty facing right with long, flowing hair. The motto LIBERTY is above and the date below. On the reverse is a circular chain of 15 links, representing the number of states in the Union following the admission of Vermont in 1791 and Kentucky a year later. Within the chain is the value expressed as both ONE CENT and 1/100. The legend UNITED STATES OF AMERICA is inscribed around the border, though on one variety the abbreviation AMERI. is used, the engraver having evidently miscalculated his spacing.

Screw-action presses were slow and labor-intensive. (From An Essay on Coining *by Samuel Thompson, 1783)*

That individual must have been Chief Coiner Henry Voigt, as the Mint did not yet have an official engraver, and Voigt is known to have served as engraver pro-tem until the fall of 1794.

These coins, known to collectors as Chain cents, were not popular with the public. A Philadelphia newspaper ran the following account in its issue of March 18, 1793:

> The American cents do not answer our expectations. The chain on the reverse is but a bad omen for liberty, and Liberty herself appears to be in a fright. May she not justly cry out in the words of the Apostle, "Alexander the coppersmith hath done me much evil: the Lord reward him according to his works!"

Despite a needless slur against Alexander Hamilton, who was closely associated with the federal coinage, this criticism was valid. The Chain cents, of which just 36,103 pieces were minted, are not especially attractive and did not wear well in circulation. Many surviving examples are barely identifiable, their distinctive chain often being the only element still visible.

This design was quickly replaced by one featuring a somewhat similar head of Liberty, but with the addition of a sprig of some uncertain plant beneath the bust. A similarly unidentifiable wreath appears on the reverse in place of the misunderstood chain links. As on the Chain cent, the value is expressed as both ONE CENT and 1/100, but with the fraction appearing below the wreath. The Wreath cents also include an inscription on their edge reading ONE HUNDRED FOR A DOLLAR. Adam Eckfeldt has been credited by some writers as the engraver of the revised cents, though they were more likely the work of

Continued on page 36

1793 Flowing Hair Chain cent, AMERICA reverse (26 mm)

1793 Flowing Hair, Wreath cent (28 mm)

The U.S. Mint at Philadelphia

In many ways, the history of the Philadelphia Mint as an individual facility is the story of the United States Mint as an institution. For more than 40 years it was the only U.S. mint, and all of the various people employed in making coins for the young republic occupied offices there. This included the director of the Mint, a position since relocated to Washington, D.C. As the U.S. Mint of the late 18th and early 19th centuries struggled to remain in operation, despite continual threats of obliteration from Congress, it was inconceivable that there would ever be additional branches spreading from Atlantic to Pacific.

Edwin Lamasure Jr., who once worked as an engraver at the Bureau of Engraving and Printing, was most famous as a landscape painter. Included among his subjects was this view of the original United States Mint buildings at Philadelphia, painted in watercolor.

Philadelphia is still the place where all new coins are developed by the U.S. Mint's staff of sculptors and engravers, even though the designs may be supplied by outside artists. For generations the Philadelphia Mint was also the exclusive manufacturer of dies for coining, though this monopoly ended in 1996 with the opening of the Denver Mint's die shop. The process of minting, once more a craft than an industry, is now almost totally automated, yet Philadelphia remains the spiritual center of the United States Mint.

The story of how the U.S. Mint as an institution came into existence is told elsewhere in this volume, so the present study will focus on the construction and operation of the Mint facility. As related in the main text, the federal government purchased a lot for the purpose of building a mint in 1792. At that time the U.S. Mint was under the direction of the State Department. Writing to Secretary of State Thomas Jefferson on June 9, President Washington expressed his views on the matter:

> I am in sentiment with you and the Director of the Mint [David Rittenhouse], respecting the purchase of the lots and houses which are offered for sale, in preference to renting – as the latter will certainly exceed the interest of the former.

Exactly one month later Washington approved Rittenhouse's purchase of the lot in question, upon which stood a vacant distillery formerly operated by Michael Shubert. The land comprised two lots, Numbers 37 and 39 North Seventh Street, being contiguous with 631 Filbert Street (then known as Sugar Alley). It was purchased July 18, 1792, from then owner Frederick Hailer for $4,266.67, and destruction of the existing structures commenced the following day.

Construction of the new Mint buildings began July 31, this date being celebrated with a round of punch for the workmen financed by Rittenhouse's sale of debris from the old distillery. Progress was rapid in that era of 11-hour workdays and no safety regulations, and the roof of the first structure was raised August 25. Completed on September 7, the building housed the rolling and drawing mills on its first floor and the smelting furnace above. Built subsequently was the main Mint structure, where the public was received and deposits were taken. The three-story brick building fronted on Seventh Street and contained the Mint's various offices, a basement vault, and the gold-coining room.

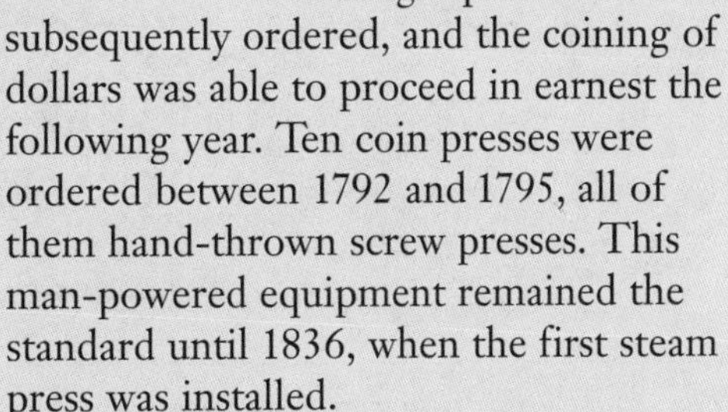

The first mintages of United States coins were produced on a small screw press similar to the one seen here.

The two lots owned by the U.S. Mint formed an L-shaped area with a frontage of approximately 37 feet on Seventh Street and 17 feet on Filbert, though both lots extended from the street for much greater lengths. It soon became evident that the existing structures were not large enough for all of the Mint's operations. Thus, on October 4, 1794, the government purchased William Hamilton's lot at 629 Filbert Street, this having a frontage of 20 feet, 6 inches, and being separated from 631 Filbert by a narrow path called Bone Alley. Copper and silver coins were produced in small structures extending back from Filbert Street and connecting to one another along this alley. Both Filbert Street lots were subject to annual rentals payable in Spanish Milled dollars, the famous "pieces of eight" that then comprised the primary specie in circulation.

At various times between 1794 and the vacation of this site in 1833, the U.S. Mint rented adjacent properties for storage and miscellaneous operations. Of course, it would have been desirable from a security standpoint for the Mint to own the entire block, but Congress was so undecided over the Mint's future that it continually declined to allocate the necessary funds. In desperation, Chief Coiner Adam Eckfeldt actually purchased one of the adjoining lots in 1828 and rented it to the Mint himself!

Furnishing the Mint's machinery was an even greater challenge, one that seemed to be little understood at the outset. The Mint's first presses were adequate only for coining copper and small silver pieces, as evidenced by the incomplete impressions on the first silver dollar coinage of 1794. Larger presses were subsequently ordered, and the coining of dollars was able to proceed in earnest the following year. Ten coin presses were ordered between 1792 and 1795, all of them hand-thrown screw presses. This man-powered equipment remained the standard until 1836, when the first steam press was installed.

When the Philadelphia Mint began production early in 1793, its officers included Director David Rittenhouse, Treasurer Tristam Dalton, and Coiner Henry Voigt. Assayer Albion Cox came aboard shortly after coinage commenced. The position of melter and refiner, so important to any mint, was not officially filled until 1797, when Joseph Cloud was appointed by President Washington. David Ott had performed these duties previously, though his employment dated only to November 1794. Before that time, Albion Cox filled the role of melter

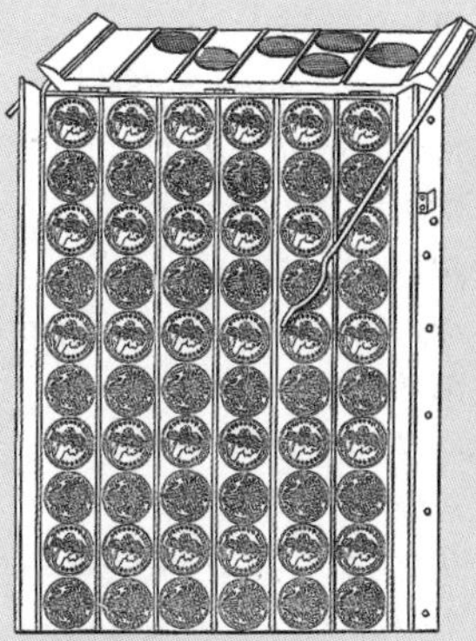

The invention of the counting board allowed a Mint worker to quickly count silver and small gold coins. Copper partitions sectioned the boards according to coin size, and the pieces were slipped into place until the board was full. From there, the coins slid off the board and into a drawer, which was then emptied into a bag for shipment. Twenty-five dollars' worth of 5-cent pieces could be counted in under a minute. (From Illustrated History of the United States Mint *by George G. Evans, 1890)*

I also send, by this mail, some copper pieces struck at the mint today on our new press by steam. They are the first ever struck by this power in America. We must consider this day, therefore, as marking an epoch in our coinage.

– Mint Director Robert M. Patterson, writing to Treasury Secretary Levi Woodbury, March 23, 1836

and refiner on an informal basis.

The critical position of Mint engraver was likewise a troublesome one. Secretary of State Jefferson attempted repeatedly to secure the services of Jean-Pierre Droz but found the renowned Swiss engraver to be coy and quite vain. His negotiations proved fruitless. In the absence of native talent, Director Rittenhouse was forced to rely on the primitive engraving skills of Coiner Voigt until a true engraver was finally hired in late June or early July of 1793. Joseph Wright was a fine artist. His Liberty Cap cent of that year, while it did not hold up well in circulation, is a very attractive piece when unworn. Wright, however, succumbed to the dreaded yellow fever later that same summer. His replacement was Robert Scot, a skilled engraver indeed, but a person who had little experience in relief work and evidently none in die-sinking.

The second U.S. Mint was designed with a courtyard to allow sunlight to illuminate the space inside. (From Harper's Magazine)

The U.S. Mint's woes in fighting off the double threat of imminent closure and would-be contract coiners is documented in the main text and will not be repeated here. Over the 41 years of its operation, the first Mint facility redeemed itself in the eyes of its detractors. A catastrophic fire in January 1816 consumed the structure housing its rolling and drawing mills and its melting room. This suspended the coining of gold and silver until well into the following year. The Mint rebuilt the lost wooden structures in brick. By the late 1820s, whatever improvements were possible within the constraints of the existing property had been made, and it became evident that continued growth would require a complete rebuilding.

On March 2, 1829, Congress finally appropriated money for an entirely new structure that would house all of the Mint's operations under one roof. A lot fronting on Juniper Street at Chestnut was purchased April 30 from Ann Poyntell and Mr. and Mrs. R.A. Caldcleugh, and the new building's cornerstone was laid with much fanfare on July 4. The coining of half dimes, suspended since 1805, resumed that very day with a new design. Proofs of these first coins are said to have been distributed to various dignitaries gathered for the occasion, and it is possible that some were even sealed in the cornerstone.

The new Mint building was in the Greek Revival style so popular during the 1830s. Designed by architect William Strickland, it had a frontage of 150 feet and extended back from the street some 204 feet. Faced in white marble, the structure enclosed a courtyard, this layout being common to several Mint buildings erected during that era before electric lighting reduced the need for natural sunlight.

As the new structure neared completion, the old Mint property was put up for sale. The buildings, less their contents, ultimately received a winning bid of just $10,100 on October 8, 1835. The buyer was Michael Kates, in whose family the property remained until being purchased by Frank H. Stewart early in

This Greek Revival building, the Mint's second home, was replaced in 1901.

the 20th century. Recognizing the historic value of these structures, Stewart attempted to have either the city or the federal government purchase them for rebuilding on another site, but both entities declined. Needing the lot for a new building to house his electrical supply company, Stewart had no choice but to demolish the first structures built by the federal government. He did record their current state in a series of photographs, including them in his superb book, *History of the First United States Mint*.

The old Mint's machinery was relocated to the new facility in January 1833, and used there for another two years. At that time new machinery was installed, some of it incorporating technical improvements brought back by Assistant Assayer Franklin Peale from his fact-finding tour of various European mints. Peale ultimately rose to the position of chief coiner in 1839, only to be fired for malfeasance 15 years later.

His most important discovery while in Europe during 1833 to 1835 was the French Thonnelier coin press. Driven by steam, it supplied a lever action for striking coins, and this improved both the quality and quantity of the U.S. Mint's output. Also new to the Mint was the Contamin Portrait Lathe, which permitted the reproduction of hubs in any desired size from a single model.

Mint officers at the time the new facility was occupied in 1833 included Director Samuel Moore, Chief Coiner Adam Eckfeldt, and Assayer Jacob Eckfeldt. The

This March 23, 1836, medal, struck on cent planchets, was the first piece made on the new steam press (left). Daily production on the press was 40,000 coins, a significant improvement over the 13,000 coins struck on the old screw-action presses. (27 mm)

The delicate trust reposed in all persons employed in the Mint, presupposes that their character is free from all suspicion, but the director feels it his duty nevertheless, in order that none may plead ignorance on the subject, to warn them of the dangers of violating so high a trust. Such a crime as embezzlement of any of the coins struck at the Mint, or of any of the metals brought to the Mint for coinage, would be punished under the laws of Pennsylvania, by a fine and penitentiary imprisonment at hard labor. The punishment annexed to this crime by the laws of the United States enacted for the special protection of deposits made at the Mint is DEATH.

– From Director Samuel Moore's rules and regulations of the Mint, January 1, 1825

Workers display $100,000 in newly minted double eagles in the coiners counting room at the Philadelphia Mint, January 1894.

prominence of the Eckfeldt family in Mint affairs would last some 130 years, before the last employee bearing this name finally retired in 1924. Moore was soon replaced by Robert Maskell Patterson, under whose direction three new branch mints were established in the South. While the Philadelphia Mint was no longer the only coining facility after 1838, it was the sole manufacturer of dies until 1996. It also retained the U.S. Mint's Engraving Department and, of course, the director still maintained his office there and oversaw the operations of the various branches. This changed in 1873, when sweeping new Mint legislation moved the director to Washington, D.C., replacing him at Philadelphia with a superintendent equal in status to those at the other mints and answerable to the director.

The second Philadelphia Mint operated from 1833 until 1901, when it was replaced by a still larger structure. This period witnessed some of the more dramatic events in U.S. Mint history, including the outpouring of gold from California in 1849 and Colorado in 1858 and of silver from Nevada in 1859. A suspension of specie payments during the 1860s and '70s led to a reduction in work that was relieved only by the tremendous demand for minor coins of various new types. The vast coining of fractional silver pieces beginning in the mid-1870s drew to a close and was followed by even larger mintages of unneeded silver dollars beginning in 1878. Further gold strikes in the Cripple

A transfer lathe converted the design on an artist's 6-inch model for use on a coin. (From Illustrated History of the United States Mint *by George G. Evans, 1888)*

Creek region of Colorado and in Alaska and the Yukon during the 1890s brought another surge in gold coinage just as the nation's growing population prompted increases in the number of fractional and minor coins needed to maintain daily commerce.

This pressure to produce ever more coins prompted calls for the creation of a new Mint building. Giving weight to this argument were the conditions evident in the existing structure as described by Montana Senator Thomas Carter, who declared, "there does not exist on this continent today an intelligent and prudent businessman who would ask free-born American citizens to spend their lives and perform their duties in the cold, damp, subterranean passages in which our fellow citizens are compelled to work in the Mint at Philadelphia."

Treasury Secretary William Windom requested that Congress act to approve a new Mint in January 1891, but his proposal was soon mired in pork-barrel politics. Though the Senate passed such a bill just one month after Windom's plea, the House held up approval of the new Philadelphia Mint while its members squabbled over its cost and location. The latter issue was raised by congressmen who sought to favor their own districts with this lucrative federal plum, and there was debate over whether to move the Mint to New York or St. Louis. Reason ultimately prevailed, and the bill was passed in the House on March 2, 1891. Money for the new Mint was appropriated the following year, and construction began soon afterward.

The new Philadelphia Mint was completed in June 1901. Fronting on Spring Garden Street, this splendid Beaux Arts edifice occupied the entire block between 16th and 17th Streets. The old building was soon vacated and sold, remaining just a few years before being demolished.

Among the developments that led to construction of a new Mint was the superiority of electricity as a motive power source. While the old Mint had been powered by large steam engines that transmitted their energy by means of pulleys, the new Mint used individual electric motors to drive each of the various machines, including the coin presses. Another vast improvement was the introduction of electrolytic refining, which saved tremendously on the number of steps involved in processing metals and, like most such advances, reduced manpower needs.

The third Philadelphia Mint helped meet the nation's demand for coinage throughout much of the 20th century. Though it lost its exclusive role in supplying copper coins after the San Francisco Mint coined its first cents in 1908, Philadelphia still bore the brunt of this work. The demand for cents in particular rose to previously inconceivable levels during World War I. The Philadelphia Mint produced a record 392,021,000 "pennies" in 1919, this figure not being equaled again until 1940. While the demand for coins tapered off during the early 1920s, the Mint was still kept busy producing service medals for military veterans. To this was added the recoining of more than 270 million silver dollars melted under the Pittman Act of 1918. While all three mints participated in this massive effort from 1921 to 1928, over 50 percent of the new dollars were struck at Philadelphia, which also had the task of providing dies for each mint.

One activity unique to Philadelphia among the various U.S. mints at that time was the development of new

Mint Director Robert Maskell Patterson

The Philadelphia Mint of 1901 to 1969 now serves as a community college.

minting technology. This included experiments with new coinage alloys, proposed new varieties of die steel and the heat treatment thereof, the implementation of improved machinery, and other advances designed to extend the useful life of minting equipment and reduce manpower needs. The onset of World War II led to such a tremendous demand for additional coins to serve the vigorous wartime economy that the shortcomings of the existing mint facilities and techniques became increasingly apparent. The record number of cents coined at the Philadelphia Mint in 1919 was more than tripled in 1944, when it struck nearly 1.5 billion cents. To this increased workload was added the immense number of medals needed to recognize America's men and women in the military. While some of this work was undertaken by the other mints, furnishing dies was still the responsibility of the Philadelphia Mint.

A coil of metal destined to become coins at the United States Mint

Even after the war, when the demand for fresh coins declined to more manageable levels, the Treasury Department sought to improve efficiency at the same time Congress was slashing the U.S. Mint's annual appropriation. In keeping with a popular business practice of the time, the Mint employed industrial filmmakers to undertake motion studies that determined where time was being lost to unnecessary movements. As a result, the layout of machinery in the Philadelphia and Denver Mints was rearranged to minimize steps, but the small size of the San Francisco Mint's structure precluded such measures, dooming it to closure in 1955. At the two remaining mints, however, the cost per unit for producing coins was lowered dramatically during the late 1940s and early '50s. But there was one cost the bureaucrats failed to measure, and it was evident in the declining quality of U.S. coins during this period. Their soft, ill-defined details clearly revealed that dies were being used too long in a misguided effort at economy.

Even with improvements in efficiency, there were signs that the Philadelphia Mint was outgrowing its home. As early as 1945 the Bureau of the Mint requested that Congress approve a new Mint building. This request was repeated a number of times through the 1950s but fell on deaf ears. Only the nationwide coin shortage that began in the early 1960s prompted Congress to approve a new building. Public Law 88-102, passed August 20, 1963, provided for a new Philadelphia Mint. Scheduled to open in 1967, it was only partially occupied in 1968 and was not fully operational until the following year. The American Numismatic Association's 1969 convention was held in the City of Brotherly Love, and a tour of the nation's newest Mint was among its highlights. Mint Director Eva Adams had spearheaded the project and saw it through to completion, though her term ended shortly thereafter.

The new structure is in the Modern style and occupies an entire block in downtown Philadelphia. Fronting on Fifth Street and facing Independence Mall, it is bounded by Market, Arch, and Fourth Streets. Much of its machinery was new when the Mint opened, though many of the older presses remained in use for some years thereafter. The 1901 mint building was sold and remains in place today, now occupied by a community college. The wonderful stained-glass scenes of historic minting techniques, commissioned in 1899 from Louis Comfort Tiffany, were carefully removed and reinstalled in the new structure, where they may still be enjoyed today. Also still on view is Peter the eagle, mascot of the second Philadelphia Mint, who was killed in 1835 when he alighted upon a flywheel that shortly thereafter began turning.

In anticipation of the opening of its new facility, the Philadelphia Mint began experimenting in 1967-68 with a unique, ultra-high-speed coin press for cents. Designed and manufactured by General Motors, the roller press worked on the same principle as a web printing press – the reciprocating motion of a conventional press was replaced with a rotary motion employing rollers in continual contact with one another.

Long strips of metal were passed between the first and second rollers, which punched out the planchets and simultaneously positioned them in die receptacles mounted on the second roller. They were then carried by the motion of the second roller until they came into contact with the third roller, upon which were mounted a series of mating dies. In this one continual motion, dozens of coins could be struck every second.

Though a brilliant invention, the roller press proved to be a monster to maintain. It dripped lubricating oil onto the dies and planchets, spoiling the cents. Furthermore, each time a single die failed, the entire press had to be shut down while the die was replaced. By the time the new Mint opened in 1969, the roller press had already been declared an expensive flop, one of the few setbacks the U.S. Mint has experienced in its quest for the latest technology.

Though its coining capacity is equaled by that of Denver, the Philadelphia Mint is still the source of new coin designs, and it is thought of by numismatists as the U.S. Mint's home. Until recent years its coins never bore mintmarks, since these letters were thought of as distinguishing the products of branch mints from those of the mother mint, Philadelphia. The sole exceptions prior to 1979 were the wartime alloy five-cent pieces of 1942 through 1945, which bore a large P mintmark to facilitate their anticipated withdrawal after the war, and various issues struck for other nations.

The ill-fated Anthony dollar, introduced in 1979, was the first United States coin to carry a P mintmark on a regular basis, a feature extended to all other denominations beginning in 1980, save for the cent. This omission was due to the fact that cents were also being struck without mintmarks at the San Francisco and West Point mints. To prevent the hoarding of these other cents, which had much smaller mintages, it was decided to not distinguish the Philadelphia coins in any way. Since no cents have been coined at the smaller mints since 1984, it would now be permissible to place a P mintmark on those issued by Philadelphia, but it seems that the Treasury Department has simply overlooked this possibility.

Until recently, the Philadelphia Mint was one of that city's principal tourist attractions. Tours were conducted regularly, though this activity was suspended after the September 11, 2001, terrorist attacks. As this is written in 2005, tours are once again available by appointment only. They are limited to student groups, military and veterans organizations, and congressionally sponsored groups of six or fewer persons.

The mint should be able to serve the nation's coinage needs for decades to come, until it, too, is ultimately replaced by a state-of-the-art facility. Given the trend in world mints, this will most likely be situated in a suburb of Philadelphia to take advantage of lower real estate prices and the greater availability of large lots.

1979-P Susan B. Anthony dollar (26.5 mm)

Although the fourth Philadelphia Mint lacks the majesty of its predecessors, it does have necessary highway access and sophisticated security systems.

A workman at the drawing bench, circa 1885

The time of work and Labour in the Mint, shall be understood by all employed therein, to be Eleven Hours in each Day – and shall from the 10th of November, begin at 6 o'clock in the morning and continue till 7 o'clock in the Evening allowing from 8 to 9 o'clock for Breakfast, and from 1 till 2 o'clock for dinner.

– From the Mint's rules and regulations for 1795

1795 Liberty Cap cent (29 mm)

Continued from page 27

engraver pro-tem Henry Voigt. As with so many facts of the early U.S. Mint, the coins themselves offer the best and sometimes only clues. These Wreath cents were produced from April to July of 1793.

The United States Mint did not seem to offer very promising employment to skilled people in its early days, and Secretary of State Jefferson had little success in securing a qualified engraver from Europe. (The Mint was then a division of the State Department; it was moved to the Treasury Department some years later.) Success came in the summer of 1793 with the appointment of superb engraver Joseph Wright. Sadly, Wright succumbed to the dreaded yellow fever just a few months later. This disease ravaged Philadelphia nearly every year between August and November, causing the mint to be closed for months at a time.

Before he died, however, Wright created a fine portrait of Liberty that was used by his successor over the next few years. This popular design is known as the Liberty Cap cent, since resting upon Liberty's shoulder is a staff bearing the Phrygian cap, worn by freed slaves in ancient times. Cents of this type were minted from 1793 to 1796, and their reverse is similar to that of the Wreath cent. Like the Wreath cents, the early issues have a beaded border around both sides, while the later pieces have toothed, or denticulated, borders. In

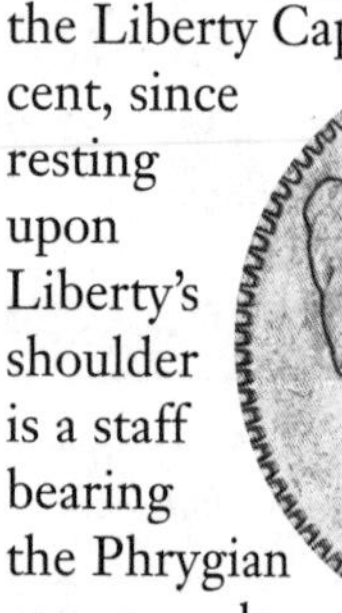

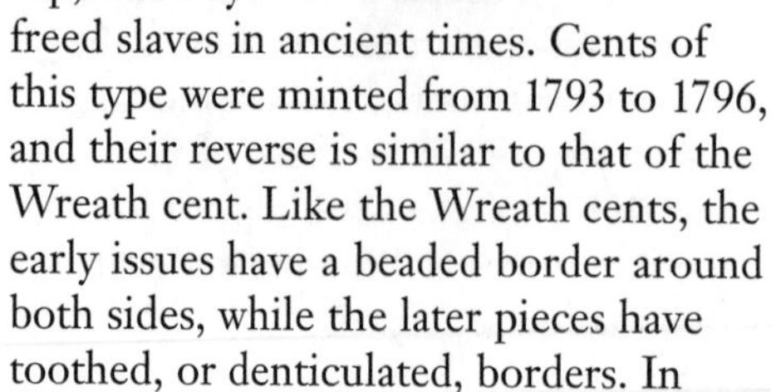

1793 Liberty Cap half cent (22 mm)

1794 Liberty Cap half cent (23.5 mm)

1795, the weight and thickness of the cent and half cent were reduced, and these coins no longer had lettered edges. Instead, their edges were plain.

The Liberty Cap design was copied from a medal conceived by Benjamin Franklin and struck at the Paris Mint in 1783. This charming medal, *Libertas Americana*, was engraved by Augustin Dupré. Its obverse bust of Liberty also served as the model for the first federal half cents, the obverse of which as been attributed to Wright. The reverse of the Liberty Cap half cents of 1793 features a wreath enclosing the value HALF CENT. This is also expressed on the reverse as 1/200 and on the edge as TWO HUNDRED FOR A DOLLAR. It is believed that Henry Voigt engraved the reverse for these half cents. They were minted only from July 20 to September 18, 1793, when the mint closed due to the yellow fever epidemic. A mere 35,334 examples were produced, and the several hundred surviving pieces are typically quite worn.

Wright's original Liberty Cap bust was revised in 1794 by Robert Scot, who had been hired for the position of engraver the previous November. In the process, Scot turned Liberty's face from left to right so it conformed to the portrait on the cents. John Smith Gardner further revised this bust for the cent late in 1794, lowering its relief to provide fuller strikes and to extend die life. His revised Liberty Cap design was extended to the half cent the following year.

By the summer of 1794, the security bonds of Chief Coiner Henry Voigt and Assayer Albion Cox had been posted, and the Philadelphia Mint was ready to coin silver, with gold to follow a bit later. As the most prestigious of the silver denominations, the dollar was selected to come first, and dies for it were engraved by Robert Scot. Though Scot was actually a plate engraver and not at all experienced in die cutting, he learned that specialized skill on the job. His obverse for the dollar features a youthful bust of Liberty facing right with flowing hair, with LIBERTY above and the date below. Fifteen stars around the border represent the number of states in the Union. The reverse depicts a small, facing eagle perched atop a rock, its wings partially raised. The eagle is enclosed in a wreath formed by two olive branches that are secured at their intersection by a bow. UNITED STATES OF AMERICA appears around the border, while the value HUNDRED CENTS ONE DOLLAR OR UNIT is inscribed on the edge, accompanied by curious geometric figures.

1795 Flowing Hair silver dollar (39-40 mm)

In addition to its technical and financial hurdles, the United States Mint was burdened with a procedural handicap. It could coin silver and gold only in response to deposits of these metals by individuals or businesses. Since no coined money was on hand to make immediate payment for deposits, there was always a delay of from several days to several weeks before the transaction was complete. This awkward arrangement remained in effect until 1837, when the U.S. Mint finally received a bullion fund to purchase metals for its own account in advance of deposits.

The first to deposit silver for coining was the Bank of Maryland. It brought to the mint on July 18, 1794, some 94,532 ounces of silver in the form of French coins. These were duly melted and the resulting bullion brought to the desired fineness. The actual coining did not occur until October 15, when 2,000 new silver dollars were struck from ingots deposited by Director Rittenhouse himself. Since the Mint lacked a press of sufficient power, these coins are a bit indistinct in places. In fact, quite a few were unfit to release, and just 1,758 pieces were issued. These coins are extremely desirable to collectors as the first United States silver dollars. Only about 100 to 130 examples are known today, most of them heavily worn.

It was not until May 1795 that the Mint finally obtained a press large enough to coin silver dollars properly, and production resumed at that time. Most of the silver dollars minted that year, more than 160,000 of them, were of the same Flowing Hair design as the 1794 pieces. This fortunate circumstance has enabled collectors to own one of these beautiful and historic pieces.

In October, a new type of silver dollar was first minted, the glorious Draped

The reverse of Augustin Dupré's Libertas Americana *medal displays an allegorical scene in which the infant Hercules represents America. The new nation is being shielded from the British Lion by the goddess Minerva, personifying France. (47.5 mm)*

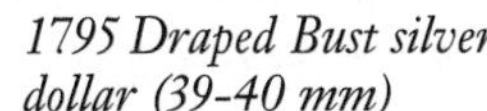

1795 Draped Bust silver dollar (39-40 mm)

1795 Draped Bust half eagle with the small eagle reverse (25 mm)

1805 Draped Bust half eagle with the heraldic eagle reverse (25 mm)

Bust Liberty. The design for this coin was reportedly furnished by famed American painter Gilbert Stuart, whose portrait of George Washington appears on our current one dollar note. Unfortunately, no correspondence exists to confirm this appealing tale. It is known that Robert Scot engraved the master punches and dies based on a relief model of Stuart's design prepared by John Eckstein. Aside from the different portrait used, the obverse of this coin is similar to the preceding type. On the reverse, however, the eagle is now perched atop clouds, with the enclosing wreath formed by branches of olive to the left and palm to the right.

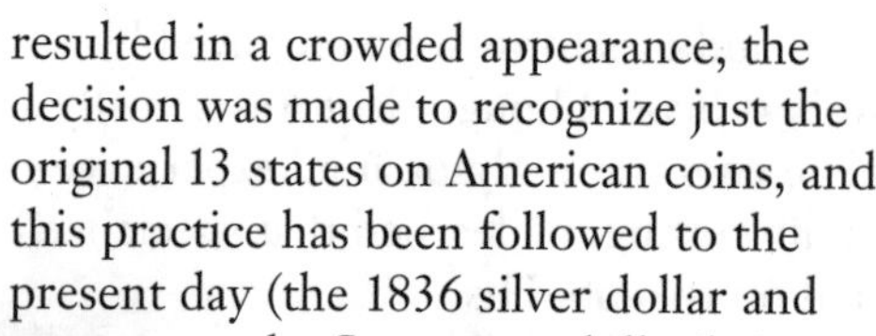

Gilbert Stuart

Draped Bust silver dollars displayed this reverse from 1795 to 1798, when a new reverse was introduced featuring the Great Seal of the United States. This remained in use on the dollar through 1803 and on the other silver coins as late as 1807. The Great Seal was adopted in 1782. It shows a facing eagle with upraised wings, the national shield on its breast. The eagle grasps an olive branch in its right, or dexter, claw and a bundle of 13 arrows in its left, or sinister, claw. (On these early U.S. coins, the elements are transposed, reversing their emphasis of peace over war.) A banner reading E PLURIBUS UNUM is held in the eagle's beak, and a constellation of 13 stars appears over its head. On the dollar, an arc of clouds sits above the stars, with the inscription UNITED STATES OF AMERICA surrounding all.

During its first few years of production, the Draped Bust silver dollar featured as many as 16 stars on its obverse, since engraver Scot was attempting to keep up with the new states (Tennessee became the 16th in 1796). When this resulted in a crowded appearance, the decision was made to recognize just the original 13 states on American coins, and this practice has been followed to the present day (the 1836 silver dollar and the Sacagawea dollar being the exceptions).

Shortly after the first silver dollars were minted, other denominations began to appear as demand warranted. The half dollar debuted in November 1794, followed by half dimes the following March. These bore the Flowing Hair design until it was replaced by the Draped Bust type in 1796. Draped Bust dimes debuted in January 1796, with similar quarter dollars following in April.

The half dollar's edge featured the inscription FIFTY CENTS OR HALF DOLLAR, alternating with geometric figures as on the dollar. The edges of the lesser silver coins were reeded.

(It is interesting to note that the designs of the fractional silver coins copied those of the dollar until 1878, when a distinctive silver dollar type first appeared. The fractional silver coins, however, kept their matching designs as late as 1916. Since then, unique imagery has been used for all new coin types produced by the U.S. Mint.)

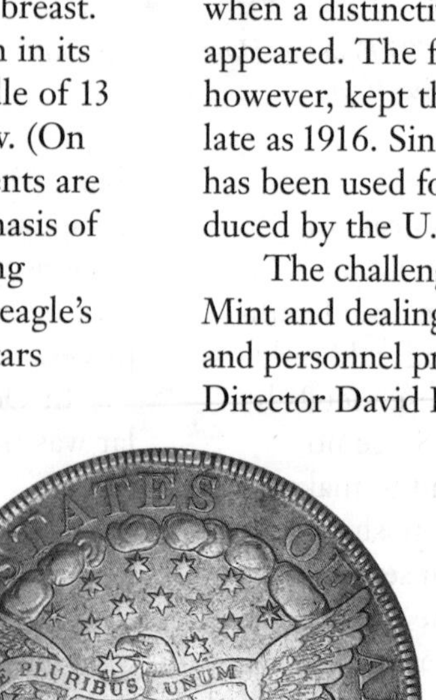

The challenge of establishing the Mint and dealing with all of its equipment and personnel problems exhausted Director David Rittenhouse, and he stepped down from office in June 1795. His successor was Henry William DeSaussure, who reluctantly assumed the position at the urging of President Washington. One of his first tasks was to initiate the production of gold coins. Though authorized by the Mint Act of 1792, no such coins had been produced. Robert Scot

Heraldic reverse of a 1799 Draped Bust silver dollar (39-40 mm)

had begun work on dies for the half eagle during the Rittenhouse administration. These were now ready, and the first delivery of gold coins from the Mint's coiner to its treasurer occurred on July 31, 1795.

These early half eagles feature a beautiful profile of the goddess Liberty with long, flowing curls. She wears a loose gown and a tall, peaked hat known as a mobcap. This was in fashion at the time, and it does not carry the symbolic reference of the Phrygian cap seen on the copper coins. Half eagles of this first type have either 15 or 16 stars, depending on whether the obverse die was prepared before or after Tennessee's admission to the Union on June 1, 1796. The reverse displays a facing eagle perched on a palm branch and grasping an olive wreath in its beak. Beginning in 1798, the half eagle featured a new reverse design bearing the Great Seal of the United States, which served to make it consistent with the other silver and gold denominations. The edge of this coin type is reeded, a feature common to all U.S. gold coins until 1907.

Though some half eagles dated as early as 1795 have this new reverse, these were coined after 1798 using leftover obverse dies. The Mint was thrifty in its early years, and dies were not taken out of service until they were no longer usable. This bit of economy was prompted by the difficulty and expense of making dies at the time. When their manufacture became more practical and standardized, the old habit of using outdated dies was eliminated.

DeSaussure was determined to produce all denominations called for in the Mint Act of 1792. The eagle was first coined on September 22, 1795, its design matching that of the half eagle. The first quarter eagles were not delivered to the Mint's treasurer until September of the following year. These featured the same design as the other gold coins, but included the Great Seal reverse from the outset. Two major varieties were produced with the date 1796. The first had no stars on its obverse, perhaps because of the uncertainty caused by the rapid addition of new states. The second variety of that year and subsequent years did include the stars.

The Mint Is Threatened

Henry William DeSaussure did not remain in office long enough to witness the quarter eagle coinage. He quit in October 1795, after just a few months as director. In tendering his resignation, DeSaussure confided his concerns about the unhealthy climate of Philadelphia, a reasonable consideration given that the two previous summers had been attended by withering epidemics of yellow fever. It was a disappointing administration in any case, as Congress, frustrated with the Mint's small output of coins, had been unwilling to listen to the director's reports of inadequate equipment and funding. DeSaussure was succeeded as director by Elias Boudinot, a distinguished statesman from New Jersey who had been president of the Continental Congress during 1781 and 1782.

Boudinot had also served on a congressional committee investigating the U.S. Mint in 1795, and his keen assessment of its problems made him the ideal figure to oversee operations. He was an energetic and dedicated public servant, and held the office of Mint Director for 10 years. These were difficult years indeed for the United States Mint. Due to the poor quality of its machinery and the lack of both raw materials and

Elias Boudinot

The appearance of a malignant Fever in the City again threatens dispersion of the Citizens, and the probable Shutting up of the Mint ... .

– Mint Director Elias Boudinot, preparing for the 1803 outbreak of yellow fever in Philadelphia

In this situation a great part of the inhabitants fled to the country in every direction ... . Those who staid, were cautious how they went about the streets, so that the city appeared in a degree to be depopulated; business of almost every kind was suspended, inward bound ships came to at the villages down the river; and for nearly two months our streets were deserted by all ... .

– Philadelphia residents Samuel and Miles Fisher describing a yellow fever outbreak, November 18, 1793

skilled personnel to replace this equipment, the Mint's struggle to produce enough coins to meet public demand was an exhausting one.

It should be noted, however, that the Mint shared a problem faced by all American industries at that time. The United States was not a large producer of copper, iron, and the other metals needed for industrial growth; this would come much later. In addition, there were very few individuals living in this country who possessed specialized skills such as engraving and die-cutting, so crucial to manufacturing industries. Skilled artisans and mechanics could earn a better living in Europe, especially in England, which was then leading the world in technical advancements.

Though the U.S. Mint was in nearly continual operation from 1793 onward (excluding the annual closures for the settling of accounts and the periodic outbreaks of yellow fever), it was unable to make enough coins to have a real impact on the money supply. The American people, outside of those living in the largest cities of the Northeast, rarely saw United States coins. In 1800, nearly all of the coins to be found in circulation were still of foreign origin. Congress had been compelled to establish legal-tender values for these alien issues again and again, and its patience was growing thin.

Many U.S. silver coins were shipped overseas, where they circulated more freely than at home. U.S. gold coins proved to be worth more than their equivalent face value in silver coins, a legacy of Hamilton's original miscalculation in 1791, and they were often exported as just so much bullion. Nearly all of the exported gold coins were quickly melted. Only the copper cents circulated to any extent, and their higher mintages reflect this pattern.

One of the reasons that United States fractional silver coins remained so scarce is that each depositor had the right to specify how he was to receive his payment. Since most silver bullion deposits came from banks, the depositors typically requested the largest denominations possible, which eased the process of counting coins. It was simply more convenient to get paid in silver dollars than in dimes or other small coins. It was also easier and more cost-effective for the Mint to make 100 silver dollars than 1,000 dimes, so the public was rarely provided with enough small change in American coins to drive out the countless foreign pieces.

In time, all of these problems were addressed and solved, but that did not occur until the 1830s. Before then, the average American had to contend with a dizzying array of foreign coins and tokens, as well as with paper money issued by commercial banks and local governments.

The late 1700s and early 1800s were the United States Mint's dark-

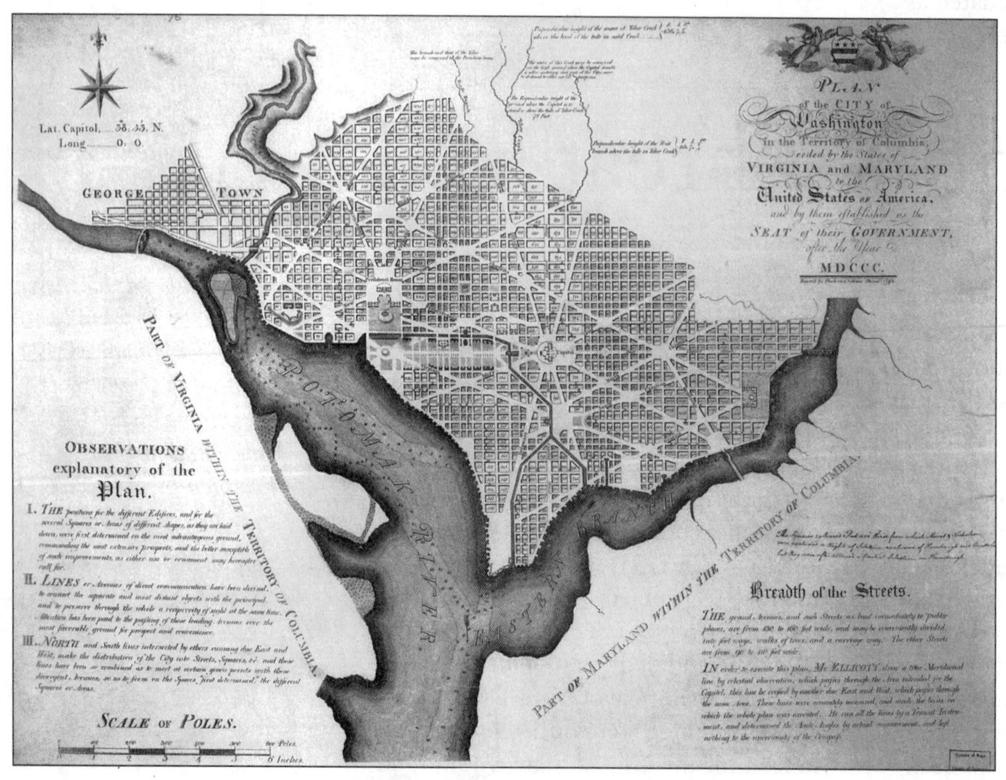

President Washington selected 23-year-old French engineer Pierre L'Enfant to create a plan for the City of Washington. This 1792 engraving is based on L'Enfant's original drawing.

est days, and it seemed that the end was near. Declaring the Mint a failure, many in Congress wanted to abolish it. Director Boudinot, in an attempt to salvage the beleaguered institution, wrote to innovative coiner Matthew Boulton in 1799. Boudinot inquired of Boulton the cost of furnishing the United States with entirely new mint machinery that would employ the steam power used at his Soho Mint near Birmingham, England. Nothing came of this proposal, but it does reveal the degree of desperation felt by supporters of the U.S. Mint.

In 1801, bullion deposits dropped off dramatically, and the Mint again was threatened with extinction. Only the previous year, the Senate had passed a resolution that called for abolishing the U.S. Mint and placing a contract for coining with the Bank of the United States. The lack of federal coinage was blamed on inefficiency and incompetence, while the real reasons were little understood by Congress. Under the Democratic administration of President Jefferson, the Mint was viewed as a costly luxury perpetrated on the American people by his Federalist predecessors. Such uncertainty over the Mint's future is what kept this institution in Philadelphia, when the other federal agencies moved to the new capital at Washington, D.C.

While the Mint continued to produce coins as supplies of copper and bullion deposits permitted, those bearing the U.S. imprint remained a rare sight in circulation. Cents, which now featured the Draped Bust of Liberty taken from the silver pieces, were coined in fairly large numbers, yet they rarely passed more than a few hundred miles from Philadelphia. Half cents were oftentimes minted only when planchets for cents were unavailable. In fact, defective cent planchets or mis-struck cents were often salvaged for use in coining half cents!

Silver dollars were likewise minted in quantity, but they were quickly shipped overseas, falling victim to a revolving scheme in which they were exchanged at par for Spanish dollars. Because Asian merchants placed a premium on Spanish dollars over other silver coins of similar intrinsic value, the Spanish pieces comprised the primary trade coins of the Far East. Some U.S. silver dollars also found their way to the treaty ports of southern China, where they fed that region's insatiable demand for silver. There the dollars that were not immediately rendered into bullion were circulated as international trade coins, effectively lost to domestic commerce.

While gold coins were also produced in somewhat lesser numbers, these were either exported as bullion or held in banks as reserve assets. Due to depositors' demonstrated preference for the largest denomination of each metal, the quantities of all other coins produced were so small as to be meaningless.

Learned individuals outside of the Mint talked of improved machinery as a solution, never realizing that the lack of deposits brought on by the obsolete legal ratio of gold to silver had left Mint workmen idle much of the time. It was inevitable that the small number of coins produced under such conditions would not be cost-effective, but the Mint's opponents failed to take this into consideration.

Bills calling for elimination of the U.S. Mint and/or for a contract coinage from the Bank of the United States were drafted, debated, revised and debated again throughout the years 1800 to 1802. On April 26, 1802, a bill for abolishing the Mint actually passed in the House of Representatives, but was disregarded by the Senate, which curiously moved to extend the Mint's lease on life. After nearly a year of continued political wrangling, the House finally concurred with this motion. The bill became law on March 3, 1803, and it called for a renewal of the Mint's operations for a period of five years. Similar extensions were repeatedly made over the next 20 years. Finally, on May 19, 1828, the Mint was granted a permanent lease to remain "in force and operation, until otherwise provided by law."

Be it enacted *by the Senate and House of Representatives of the United States of America, in Congress assembled, That from, and after the ____ day of ____ so much of the acts; the one, intituled, "An act establishing a mint; and regulating the coins of the United States," the other, intituled "An act supplementary to the act establishing a mint; and regulating the coins of the United states," as relate to the establishing a mint, be, and the same are hereby repealed.*

Sec. 2. And be it further enacted, *That all the property, both real and personal, belonging to the United States, which is now used for the purposes of carrying on the said mint establishment, be sold for the best price that can be obtained for the same, under the direction of the secretary of the treasury; and that the monies arising from such sales be placed in the treasury of the United States, to be accounted for in like manner with other public monies … .*

– Bill discussed in the House of Representatives on April 2, 1802

Obverse of an "I Take the Responsibility" token (28.5 mm)

Reverse of a "Running Boar" token (28-29 mm)

Martin Van Buren token (28.5 mm)

Many Hard Times Tokens bore satirical images and mottoes critical of the monetary policies of Andrew Jackson and Martin Van Buren. The top token shows Jackson in a bank, holding a purse and a sword, reflecting people's fear of presidential power over both the nation's money and military. The middle token criticizes Jackson's experimentation with the country's funds. The bottom token, from Van Buren's administration, shows the ship of state foundering on the rocks.

Renewed Hopes

Though it was no longer under continual scrutiny by Congress, the U.S. Mint still faced numerous obstacles to carrying out its mission. Bullion supplies remained erratic, fluctuating with the changing economic scene. Disruptions were particularly common during Europe's Napoleonic Wars (circa 1800 to 1815), when the values of silver and gold were subject to abrupt adjustments. The overall trend, however, was toward a reduction in the value of silver as measured against gold, and U.S. gold coins were driven ever farther toward annihilation. Coining of the eagle was suspended in 1804, but the half eagle and quarter eagle seemed just as scarce to the American people.

After 1804, production of the silver dollar was likewise discontinued, President Jefferson having halted its coinage when it became obvious that it had become merely an item for export. Nearly all of the Mint's output of silver coinage was now in the form of half dollars, and this denomination, along with the copper cent, was to dominate United States coinage for the next 30 years. During this time, Americans suffered through a bewildering array of coins and paper currency.

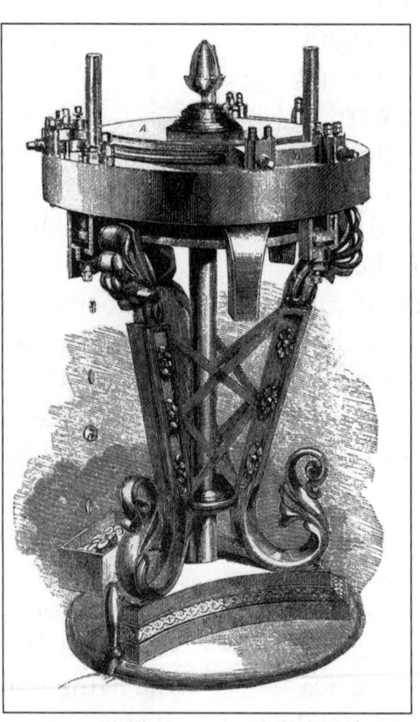

A steam-powered milling machine was installed in 1836 to raise, or "upset," a rim around each coin. This circa 1885 model performed the same function. (From Illustrated History of the United States Mint *by George G. Evans, 1885)*

The money in circulation before the mid-1830s typically consisted of the following: currency notes issued by state-chartered private banks accounted for the denominations above one dollar; Spanish colonial coins from the mints at Mexico City and Lima, Peru, made up most of the dollars and fractional silver to be found; and U.S. cents and half cents were used for making small change. Supplementing these currencies were paper notes valued from 6 1/4¢ (one-half Spanish *real*) through 75¢ (6 *reales*). These notes were issued by both commercial banks and merchants, the latter also circulating copper tokens from time to time that were readily accepted as cents. Token issues were produced in especially large numbers between 1834 and 1844, and many of these combined advertising with political themes, usually criticisms of President Andrew Jackson and his successor, Martin Van Buren.

Very popular with today's collectors, the commercial and political tokens of this period are grouped together under the catchall banner Hard Times tokens, and they offer a rich array of amusing images and inscriptions.

Though America's leaders gradually became aware of the problems that prevented the Mint from fulfilling its destiny, it was not until the 1830s that Congress finally began to address these issues, specifically with respect to gold coins. The fact that gold was legally undervalued in relation to silver had long been a poorly kept secret, but it was not until 1834 that legislation was finally passed to rectify this imbalance by reducing the weights of each gold denomination. Following several years of debate over the correct ratio between these two metals, the Act of June 28, 1834, reset the legal ratio in U.S. coins from 15-to-1 to 16.002-to-1, meaning that a dollar's worth of coined silver would weigh slightly more than 16 times as much as a dollar in gold. The gold coins, now reduced in both size and weight, received slightly altered designs, the most obvious change being the elimination of the legend E PLURIBUS UNUM, which Mint Director Samuel Moore considered to be redundant with UNITED STATES OF AMERICA.

The silver-to-gold ratio was a bit of overcompensation, since the actual market ratio was somewhere between 15.8-to-1 and 15.9-to-l. Though in theory this now threatened the circulation of U.S. silver coins, it also assured that the Mint's output of gold coinage would function as a tool of commerce.

Evidently, market forces were such that silver was not driven from circulation. The Mint's output of silver coins had become so much greater beginning in 1829 to 1831 that it seemed to actually force their circulation. For the first time in the young nation's history, United States coins circulated freely alongside their foreign competitors, though the latter still held a considerable edge in numbers.

The minting of both gold and silver coins rose dramatically during the 1830s, aided in part by some long-overdue advances in minting technology. The first of these was the introduction of the collar die, or "close collar" as it was known in U.S. Mint parlance. Prior to 1828, all federal coins were struck without collars, their reeded or lettered edges being applied separately in a previous operation. With the new collars, these edge patterns were imparted during the coining process, saving much labor and giving the finished coins uniform diameters and sharply raised rims. This technology was introduced for the dime in 1828, with the other denominations following over the next few years.

A second important milestone was the erection of a new and much larger mint structure in Philadelphia that opened in 1833. This replaced horse and human power with steam-driven machines for virtually all of its operations. The lone holdout was the coining process itself, the Mint's aging screw presses still being set in motion by the might of two or more brawny men. The third major improvement was thus the introduction of steam into the coining operation.

Steam power to run Mint machinery came from this circa 1830 steeple engine. (From Gleason's Pictorial Drawing Room Companion, *July 17, 1852)*

Driven indirectly by long belts linked to a central steam engine, the new coin presses were copied from the French Thonnelier model, which the Mint's melter and refiner, Franklin Peale, had observed and sketched during his fact-finding tour of European mints. The first steam-driven press went into operation in March 1836, signaling the impending end of a romantic but labor-intensive era in the U.S. Mint's history.

We have just completed under the superintendence of Mr. Peale, a model of a coining press, formed from plans which he saw in successful operation in France and in Germany, and possessing many very manifest advantages over the Screw press now employed at the Mint. Among these one of the most important is that [it] admits the immediate and easy application of steam power. At present our larger presses require the operation of three men each, while I am sure that one man could attend two of the new presses. The work too may be done much more rapidly – a desideratum of which we now feel the necessity.

– Letter from Mint Director Robert M. Patterson to Secretary of the Treasury Levi Woodbury, September 26, 1835

1807 Capped Bust half dollar (32.5 mm)

Though largely unseen by Americans at the time, several new coin designs were employed in the years before 1836. Chief Engraver Robert Scot was joined by a second engraver in 1807, a German immigrant named John Reich. Skeptical of Scot's abilities, Mint Director Robert Patterson had hired Reich specifically to redesign all of the nation's coins. New silver half dollars and gold half eagles bearing Reich's portrait of Liberty appeared in 1807 and were a radical departure from previous types.

1808 Classic Head cent (29 mm)

On both coins, Liberty faces left, wearing a cap that is hemmed by a band inscribed with her name. Thirteen stars are arranged around the periphery, with the date below. On the reverse of both coins is the facing figure of an eagle clutching three arrows and an olive branch, the Union shield superimposed upon its breast. The eagle's wings are upraised on the gold coin and partially folded on the half dollar. A banner inscribed E PLURIBUS UNUM sits above the eagle, and the coin's value is below in abbreviated form. The legend UNITED STATES OF AMERICA appears around the periphery of each coin.

John Reich's beautiful design, known to coin collectors as the Capped Bust, was extended to each of the remaining denominations over the next few years. In keeping with tradition, however, the copper cent and half cent bore simple wreath reverses with a statement of value and national origin, rather than the splendid eagle motif. In addition, Liberty's head was bare, aside from a headband inscribed with her name. The copper coins are thus distinguished by the name Classic Head. Reich's designs were modified slightly over the next 30 years, but his basic themes continued until the general redesign of 1837 to 1840, when all of our coins were given new imagery.

The same steam engine that powered Mint equipment in the 1830s was still on the job more than 40 years later, providing much of the power needed to run heavy machinery. The presses seen in this circa 1885 view of the coining room were essentially the same as the first steam press installed in 1836. (From Visitor's Guide and History of the United States Mint, *published by A.M. Smith, 1885)*

CHAPTER FOUR

Mint Expansion and New Designs

With coinage increasing during the 1830s, the existing problems in transporting bullion to the Philadelphia Mint were exacerbated. While there was very little silver mined in the United States before 1859, native deposits of gold were discovered in Georgia and North Carolina as early as the 1790s. This bullion was of little practical value until it had been refined and formed into bars or coins, but in the era before railroads the cost and risk of transporting it to Philadelphia were great. Seeing both a need and an opportunity, local assayers took to coining this gold within a few miles of its source. Templeton Reid began striking coins in Georgia in 1830, and in 1831 the Bechtler family inaugurated its North Carolina minting operation. Both produced gold coins in denominations that mirrored those of federal coinage. The Bechtlers took matters a step further, introducing a new denomination in the form of a gold dollar coin.

The creation of these privately run mints (then permissible under law) awakened Congress to the need for regional branches of the United States Mint. On March 3, 1835, a bill was passed establishing three branch facilities. The new mint at New Orleans was permitted to coin gold and silver, while those at Charlotte, North Carolina, and Dahlonega, Georgia, were to coin gold only. By 1838, all three were in operation, though only the New Orleans Mint ever produced coins in large numbers, since it was a major receiving port for bullion arriving from Latin America and the Caribbean islands.

To distinguish coins of the branch mints from those struck in Philadelphia, each piece from the Southern mints carried its own mintmark in the form of a letter: C for Charlotte, D for Dahlonega and O for New Orleans. In 1861, all three mints were seized by their rebellious state governments and later turned over to the Confederate States of America. Coining ceased at each facility that same year, as soon as existing bullion supplies were exhausted. Only the New Orleans Mint resumed operations as a United States Mint following the war.

◄ *Miners launched flat-bottom boats onto north Georgia's Chestatee and Etowah Rivers to bring up gold from the gravels below. Two men in a boat about 10 feet long worked together with specially designed shovels. One man gathered a shovel full of gravel, then the other pulled up a rope connected to the shovel's head and dumped the material into the boat. While the gravel was being brought to the surface, the first man began filling another shovel. The pair filled and emptied the boat about five times a day, and a good day's yield was between a half-ounce and an ounce, worth $10 to $20. (From "Essay on the Georgia Gold Mines" by William Phillips, 1833)*

The widespread circulation of United States coins after 1834 prompted newly appointed Mint Director Robert M. Patterson to seek fresh designs. Chief Engraver William Kneass, who succeeded Robert Scot in 1824, had already made modifications to the various denominations to reflect the changing technology that was just

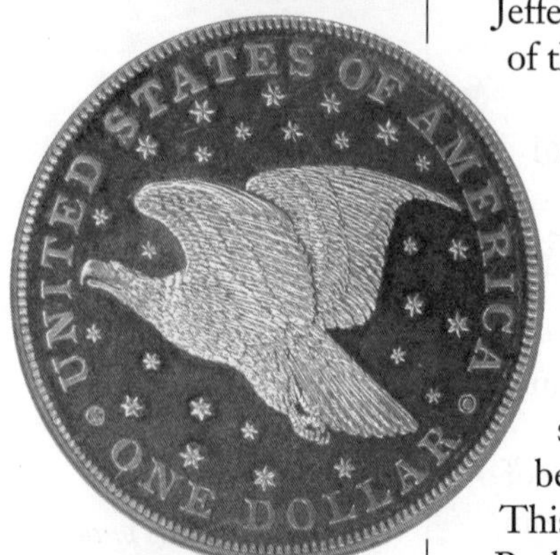

1836 Gobrecht silver dollar (38.1 mm)

1847 Liberty Seated half dollar (30.6 mm)

becoming available. Even so, Patterson sought a clean break with the past, so he commissioned renowned Philadelphia artists Thomas Sully and Titian Peale to prepare designs for a new issue of silver dollars. These would be the first coins of this denomination minted since President Jefferson's suspension of dollar coinage 30 years earlier. Their coinage had been made possible when, in 1831, President Andrew Jackson rescinded Jefferson's earlier suspension at the request of then-director Samuel Moore.

Sully's obverse drawing was derived from Patterson's fondness for the figure of Britannia, a familiar allegorical image on the coins of Great Britain. As translated by Sully, Liberty is seen seated upon a rock, while supporting the Union shield with her right hand and a staff bearing the Liberty Cap with her left. This image was then painted by Titian Peale, who also designed a soaring eagle for the reverse of the new dollar. Legend has it that this eagle was modeled after Peter, the Mint's mascot, who came and went freely until one day running afoul of a flywheel and losing his life. (Mounted and preserved, this handsome bird remains on display at the Philadelphia Mint to the present day.)

About this same time, William Kneass was partially paralyzed by a stroke, and superb plate engraver Christian Gobrecht was hired as the second engraver. Despite his nominally subordinate role, it was Gobrecht who performed the greater part of the Mint's engraving work until Kneass died in 1840. From then until his own death four years later, Gobrecht held the position of chief engraver.

It is not always certain whose work is reflected in the many modifications made to the existing designs between 1835 and 1839, but the new coin types are attributed solely to Gobrecht. He executed the master hubs and dies for the new Liberty Seated silver dollar that debuted in a limited coinage dated 1836. A number of slight variations of this basic design were produced, these bearing the dates 1836, 1838, and 1839. Though all of the original impressions (later restrikes are known) were coined as proofs at the specific request of Director Patterson, it is now widely accepted that one of the 1836 varieties (Judd-60) was actually issued as a circulating dollar. This is the variety reading C. GOBRECHT F. on the base of the Liberty figure (the letter "F" is for the Latin word *fecit*, meaning "he made it"). On each of the Gobrecht dollars, Titian Peale's eagle is shown on the reverse. The circulating issue of 1836, as well as several other varieties, feature 26 stars arranged randomly around the eagle and representing the number of states at that time. Other varieties lack these stars.

Gobrecht was assisted in his undertaking by the addition of a new machine copied from one Franklin Peale had observed at the Paris Mint. This was the *Tour à Portrait* lathe. It permitted the reduction of an artist's oversized model to the size of the desired hub. This operated on the pantograph principle, a tracer being mechanically linked to a sharpened graver. As the tracer rose and fell in response to the contours of the rotating model, its motions were mimicked by the graver on the hub face. With a bit of hand-finishing, this hub was then suitable for sinking a master die from which working hubs and working dies were ultimately produced. The size of the reproduction could be varied by changing the distance between tracer and graver, permitting the transfer of a single model to hubs of several denominations. The U.S. Mint's portrait lathe arrived in the spring of 1837, too late for the first emission of dollars. It did, however, aid in the reduction of hubs for the fractional Liberty Seated coins, which made their debut that same year.

The adoption of this machine and several other innovations were the result of the two years Franklin Peale spent in Europe, the same exploration that had brought the Mint its first steam presses. The son of famed portrait painter

Charles Willson Peale and brother of Titian Peale, noted above in connection with the Liberty Seated design, Franklin became a key figure in the Mint's activities. He succeeded the stalwart Adam Eckfeldt as chief coiner in 1839 and remained in this post for the next 15 years until being fired under accusations of using his position for private gain. In 1835, however, he was the bearer of many innovations devised in the mints of Europe and now made available to the United States Mint at Philadelphia.

The combination of new personnel and new technology resulted in a total rebirth of U.S. coinage between 1836 and 1840. Gobrecht's Liberty Seated silver dollar was not mass-produced until 1840, but the design was adapted to the fractional silver pieces during 1837 to 1839. Sadly, Titian Peale's beautiful soaring eagle was not used. In its place appeared an updated version of the old Reich/Kneass bird, whose shield-on-breast motif has prompted some numismatists to condemn it as the "sandwich board eagle." Presumably, this substitution was made so the dollar would conform to the Liberty Seated quarter dollar and half dollar, introduced in 1838 and 1839, respectively. Why Peale's flying eagle was not used from the outset for the fractional pieces remains a mystery. On the smaller silver coins, the dime and half dime, the eagle was dropped altogether in favor of a simple wreath, as used on the copper pieces.

At about this same time, Gobrecht's new portrait bust of Liberty debuted on the 1838 eagle, the first coinage of this denomination since 1804. Extended to the half eagle in 1839 and the quarter eagle in 1840, this design would remain in production until the early years of the 20th century. Known as the Coronet Head of Liberty, the goddess wears a small crown, or coronet, inscribed with her name. Surrounded by the traditional 13 stars and with the date below, this obverse design was paired with a reverse nearly identical to that of the Reich/Kneass model that preceded it.

The cent was revised in a series of modifications during the years 1835 to 1839, but the design that lasted was Christian Gobrecht's adaptation of his own Coronet Head from the gold issues. Introduced in 1839, it was modified only slightly in 1843 and continued in production until coinage of the large copper cent was discontinued altogether in 1857. The half cent, the total coinage of which never amounted to much, was not issued for circulation with this design until 1849, but its production continued on a small scale until the denomination was abolished along with the large cent in 1857. In its final years, the half cent was reportedly coined almost solely for the use of federal post offices, which evidently made change in half-cent amounts.

The fact that United States coins were finally circulating in large numbers prompted a re-evaluation of the Mint statutes. So many aspects of the existing laws were obsolete or ineffective that a sweeping new bill was enacted on January 18, 1837. This law completely restated the operations of the Mint and the roles of its officers and workers. In addition, it eliminated the awkward standards for silver and gold coins imposed by the Act of 1792, replacing both with a more easily calculated fineness of nine parts precious metal to one part alloy. The fine weights of our gold coins, which had been reduced too much in 1834, were increased slightly to bring gold to a true bimetallic standard with silver.

Also of great value to the Mint was the provision for an advance of up to $1 million in silver and gold bullion from the Treasury. This allowed a suitable supply of coins to be minted ahead of deposits so depositors could be paid just as quickly as their bullion was weighed and assayed. It also permitted coining to be performed in an orderly and efficient manner, rather than being done at the whim of depositors. The net result was a more economical operation than had ever existed.

1843 Petite Head large cent (27.5 mm)

1859 Coronet Head quarter eagle (18 mm)

1838 Liberty Seated half dime (15.5 mm)

Be it enacted by the Senate and House of Representatives of the United States of America in Congress assembled, That branches of the Mint of the United States shall be established as follows: one branch at the city of New Orleans for the coinage of gold and silver; one branch at the town of Charlotte, in Mecklenburg County in the state of North Carolina, for the coinage of gold only; and one branch at or near Dahlonega, in Lumpkin County, in the state of Georgia, also for the coining of gold only ... .

– Senate Bill 155, 23rd Congress, February 10, 1835

North Carolina

The U.S. Mint at Charlotte

The story of the Charlotte Mint begins with the discovery of gold in that part of the country. Colonial-era America had precious few domestic mines, leading to a general shortage of metals of all kinds. This situation persisted throughout the Revolution and the early years of the republic. Though fur trappers and others moving deep into the North American interior brought back tales of gold nuggets found in creek beds, the remoteness of such places weighed against their exploitation. In fact, it was not until the 1790s that the first discovery of native gold occurred in a settled part of the country. The first significant gold find was that of young Conrad Reed in 1799. In the company of his sister and younger brother, 12-year-old Conrad discovered a sizable gold nugget in Little Meadow Creek, which ran through their father's farmland in Cabarrus County, North Carolina. Not recognizing that it was gold ore, the family reportedly used the heavy lump as a doorstop for several years!

In 1802 Conrad's father, John Reed, sensing that the metal might have some value after all, took it to a jeweler in Fayetteville who soon identified it as gold. Reed, unaware of the price of gold, asked for and received just $3.50 for the nugget, which was rumored to have weighed some 17 pounds. Pleased with himself, Reed explored the creek further and, one year later, discovered another nugget weighing 28 pounds. Though this was the largest single find ever made in the region, Reed's explorations revealed that the creek was studded with gold flakes and nuggets for the length of about one mile.

Other discoveries followed those of the Reed family, mostly in Mecklenburg County, North Carolina. This touched off the nation's first gold rush, and the addition of so many miners only increased the rate at

NOTICE
TO GOLD MINERS & OTHERS.

C. BECHTLER, informs all interested in the gold mines and in assaying and bringing the gold of the mines into ingots or pieces of a standard value, that he is now prepared to assay and stamp gold, to any amount, to a standard of 20 carats, making it into pieces of $2.50 and $5.00 value, at his establishment 3½ miles north of Rutherfordton, on the road leading from Rutherfordton to Jeanstown. The following are his prices:

For simply fluxing rough gold,	¾ per cent.
For fluxing gold—to be stamped,	½ per cent.
For assaying gold, any quantity less than 3 lbs.,	$1.00
For stamping,	2½ per cent.

July 2, 1831. 20tf

Christopher Bechtler announced the opening of his business in the July 2, 1831, edition of the North Carolina Spectator and Western Advertiser.

which gold discoveries were made. Things reached a fever pitch during the 1820s and '30s. Soon, a private mint was established in Rutherfordton, North Carolina, by a German immigrant named Christopher Bechtler. The business included his sons Augustus and Charles and a nephew, Christopher. From 1831 to about 1850, the Bechtlers minted gold coins valued at $1, $2.50, and $5.

In fact, the Bechtlers preceded the federal government in the making of gold dollars by some 19 years. Though highly distinctive in design, the Bechtler coins proved to be of full value and were widely circulated in the region.

It was, in part, the success of Christopher Bechtler that led the United States to establish a branch mint at Charlotte.

Building the Mint

As the area grew in both wealth and prestige, there was soon agitation on the part of North Carolina's congressional delegation to establish a branch of the United States Mint at Charlotte, the Mecklenburg County seat. Though not specifically stated, it was expected that such a mint would put the Bechtlers out of business. Legislation creating the Charlotte branch of the U.S. Mint was signed into law by President Andrew Jackson on March 3, 1835. Coinage at the new mint was limited to gold, since that metal provided the sole reason for its creation.

Included in the same bill were provisions for branch mints at New Orleans and at Dahlonega, the county seat of Georgia's Lumpkin County. Like the Charlotte Mint, that of Dahlonega was restricted to coining gold. Given the geographical proximity of Charlotte and Dahlonega, it seems that one mint would have been sufficient to serve the Piedmont region. Politics won out, however, and each goldfield received its own facility.

While the Charlotte Mint now

Bechtler $5 coin made from Carolina gold (24 mm)

A postcard view of the United States Assay Office at Charlotte, circa 1930

existed on paper, it was another matter altogether to build the structure and install its machinery. This task was assigned to Major Samuel McComb, who accepted his commission only after President Jackson's first appointee, James M. Hutchison, declined on political grounds. McComb met with architect William Strickland in June 1835, receiving the plans and cost estimates for the structure. The sum of $1,500 was approved for purchase of the site, and an estimated construction cost of $33,000 was agreed to by Treasury Secretary Levi Woodbury.

McComb encountered a number of delays during the construction process. In November 1835, the contractor declared that Strickland's plans for the structure were unsuitable, and new ones had to be drawn. There were also a few problems to be resolved with the deeds for the various lots acquired for the building's site. Finally, the cornerstone was laid with great ceremony on January 8, 1836. Work continued throughout that year and, on June 24, 1837, Major McComb notified Secretary Woodbury that the building would be completed within two to three weeks.

Wealthier mining companies dug tunnels 7 feet square with timber reinforcements, but most miners settled for the cheaper, but more dangerous, option – tunnels 4 or 5 feet square without wooden braces. (From "Essay on the Georgia Gold Mines" by William Phillips, 1833)

The mint's machinery was arriving at about the same time. The coin presses and milling machines were furnished by Merrick, Agnew and Tyler, while much of the supporting equipment, such as boilers, furnaces, and rolling mills, came from Coleman and Sellers of Philadelphia. These machines were sent by sea, usually arriving at the ports of Charleston and Camden in South Carolina. All of the equipment received by the Charlotte Mint was state-of-the-art. The fact-finding journey of Philadelphia Mint Melter and Refiner Franklin Peale through the mints of Europe in 1833 to 1835 assured that United States coins would be second to none in terms of technology.

It was Peale, in fact, who supervised the final installation of the Charlotte Mint's machinery. He arrived there with his daughter Anna in the early fall of 1837. By November 13 all connections had been made, and the mint was essentially ready for business. The final cost of building the mint came in at $56,412.20 – an overrun of just 13 percent. This was due to flaws in the original and revised plans that only on-site judgments could correct. All parties seemed satisfied with the job as completed, with the possible exception of Samuel McComb, who received a mere $668.87 for more than two years' work. A bill was introduced in Congress to grant him additional compensation for his excellent performance, but it failed to pass.

With all installations completed, it was expected that coining operations could commence before the year ended. The mint's first superintendent, John H. Wheeler, furnished a press release to area newspapers on December 4, 1837, announcing that the mint was ready to begin receiving deposits of gold bullion. Nearly three months later, however, no coins had yet been produced.

On February 23, 1838, Superintendent Wheeler wrote a letter to Coiner John R. Bolton inquiring as to the delay. Bolton notified Wheeler that he had not yet received any ingots from Assayer Dr. J.H. Gibbon. (At the Philadelphia Mint, the roles of assayer and melter-refiner were separated, but at the Charlotte Mint Gibbon was overwhelmed by both tasks and simply could not do all the work himself.) Investigating further, Superintendent Wheeler discovered that a similar situation was holding up production at the Dahlonega Mint.

Coining Begins

No solution was at hand, however, and it was not until March 27, 1838, that the first coins were struck at Charlotte. These consisted of half eagles, valued at $5 apiece.

Unfortunately, due to a curious practice imposed on the new Southern mints by U.S. Mint Director Patterson, the fresh coins could not be paid out until duplicate assays of each gold deposit had been performed at the Philadelphia Mint, a process that could easily take weeks. It was not until May 2 that the first Charlotte coins were finally transferred from the coiner to the treasurer for payment to depositors. The minting of quarter eagles followed later in the year. A total of 7,880 quarter eagles were eventually added to the 17,179 half eagles dated 1838, and these coins comprised the entire output of the Charlotte Mint during its first year of operation. All bore a mintmark letter C indicating their place of manufacture.

An early view of the Charlotte Mint

Quarter eagles were struck at Charlotte for every date from 1838 through 1860, with the exception of 1845, 1853, 1857, and 1859. The annual totals varied from a low of just 3,677 pieces in 1855 to as many as 26,064 in 1843. In an era when the Philadelphia Mint might produce more than a million quarter eagles in a single year, it is obvious that all such coins from the Charlotte Mint are scarce to rare.

Half eagles were likewise coined at Charlotte in nearly every year of operation. The sole exception was 1845, when the mint was still under repair after a catastrophic fire had nearly destroyed it the year before. The greater utility of the half eagle and its more widespread popularity with depositors resulted in generally higher mint-ages than for quarter eagles. The production record was set in 1847, when 84,151 $5 pieces were coined. Mintages rarely fell below 10,000 pieces annually, though a mere 6,879 half eagles were struck in 1861, the final year of operation.

The Charlotte Mint never produced eagles or double eagles, nor did it strike the curious $3 pieces, but Charlotte did contribute to the coining of gold dollars.

Authorized by the Act of March 3, 1849, this diminutive coin debuted that same year. Coined in part to utilize the vast amounts of gold coming from new discoveries in California, the gold dollar was also belated recognition of the Bechtler family's success with this useful denomination.

Charlotte struck gold dollars from 1849 through 1859, with the exception of 1854, 1856, and 1858. Mintages averaged over 10,000 pieces per year, though several years saw output below that figure. The lowest production occurred in 1859, when just 5,235 gold dollars were coined. The highest figure was the 1851 mintage of 41,267 pieces.

John Hill Wheeler, first superintendent of the Charlotte Mint

1855-C Indian Head gold dollar (15 mm)

At the present day the surface gold is very scarce, and the precious ore is found principally in veins of quartz, bedded in the hardest black slate.

– From a *Harper's Magazine* article on mining in North Carolina, August 1857

Disaster at the Mint

One of the most significant events in the history of the Charlotte Mint occurred early on the morning of Saturday, July 27, 1844. Superintendent Green W. Caldwell had been ill on Friday and was not present when a fire was discovered. Small and contained to a single room, the fire could have been extinguished by the reservoir of water used to supply the boilers, but no one took the initiative to do this. Nearly the entire structure was destroyed and much of the machinery damaged. Fortunately, the mint's bullion supply had been removed for safekeeping to the branch bank of the State of North Carolina, and the treasurer's account books had been spared destruction.

Inventor Thomas Edison (left) at the Haile Gold Mine south of Charlotte in 1913. After most of the area's gold deposits were played out, the Haile Mine continued to supply the federal assay office. In 1901 Edison had a laboratory in the old Charlotte Mint building, where he worked to find a method of using electricity to extract gold from ore.

There were many recriminations following this costly fire, though no satisfactory explanation for its cause was ever proved. Superintendent Caldwell maintained that his quarters had been robbed and that the fire was set by the thief to cover his tracks. A black servant named Calvin was briefly held as the suspected thief, but he was later released.

The issue of rebuilding the mint was not a straightforward one. There had been many opponents to its creation in 1835, and the question once again became a political football. The patience of the region's miners wore thin when no action had been taken even months after the fire. A miners' convention was held in Charlotte on October 8, 1844, to present a united front in advocating reconstruction of the mint. It was not until after the general election of that year, however, that the climate was finally right for taking action. Appropriate estimates for repairing the structure and machinery were prepared, which resulted in several more months of debate. The expenditure was not authorized until March 1845, and the construction contract was awarded April 16. One curious provision of the appropriations bill specified that the Charlotte Mint could have just a single coining press!

All machinery had been sent from Philadelphia by December 1845, and George Eckfeldt was dispatched to Charlotte to oversee its installation the following spring. Though the structure was still incomplete, all that was delaying the resumption of coining at that point was the absence of bricks for the furnace; these arrived on May 11. A new coiner had to be appointed, too, since John Bolton had died the previous July 4. Emmor Graham succeeded Bolton in August 1846, and coining resumed in October using deposits received shortly before the fire.

A few years later, on December 7, 1854, another fire broke out on the mint's roof. Fortunately, this blaze was quickly contained, and the mint was saved. Since it was a spark alighting on the structure's shingled roof that had started the fire, Superintendent Caldwell took this opportunity to petition Mint Director James R. Snowden for a fire-resistant metal roof. Ultimately, however, it was a tremendous conflagration of an entirely different kind that determined the last role the Charlotte Mint would play – war was coming.

Wartime Operations

1861-C Coronet Head half eagle (21.6 mm)

The election of Abraham Lincoln to the presidency in November 1860 set off a chain reaction among the Southern states. Beginning the following month with South Carolina, each one seceded from the Union, turning its back on the federal government. North Carolina did not officially secede until May 20, 1861, though it was evident early on that its destiny lay with the South.

For a time it was business as usual at the Charlotte Mint. The dies for 1861's coinage were shipped from Philadelphia on December 13, and Superintendent Caldwell continued to submit his monthly reports. Funds for the mint's operation were forwarded to Charlotte through March 1861, after which all formal communications ceased. When war broke out on April 12, it was just a matter of time before the Charlotte Mint would fall into Confederate hands. A detachment of North Carolina militiamen arrived eight days later under the leadership of Colonel John Y. Bryce. Bearing orders from Governor John Ellis, Bryce demanded that Caldwell surrender the mint and all its assets and deposits to the State of North Carolina.

Despite their support for the Southern cause, North Carolina's business and banking community petitioned the governor to permit the mint's trained personnel to continue operations. In this they were joined by Superintendent Caldwell, who advised Governor Ellis that much of the mint's bullion fund was not in a state of refined metal and could be lost if handled by unskilled persons. The governor saw the wisdom of these views and the value of the mint to the community, and replied to Caldwell on April 2, 1861, "Reposing every confidence in your well known devotion to the cause of the South, and the interest of North Carolina, I request that you will take charge of the Mint at Charlotte."

Though one of the North Carolina troops was posted as a sentry, the mint otherwise resumed normal operations. The first deposits of gold under the new state authority were received May 1, 1861. The final deposits were taken just three weeks later, on May 21. It is not known whether depositors simply stopped bringing bullion to the mint or Caldwell declined to receive any more. In any case, nearly all depositors had been paid off by the end of that month. As the fiscal year came to a close on June 30, the mint held just over $4,000 in gold coin, and this was in reserve to provide for employee salaries and the few remaining depositors. The mint had been turned over to the Confederate States of America (CSA) three days earlier, and it was redesignated an assay office on August 24.

The employees were paid through the third quarter of 1861, when the mint officially ceased to exist as such. On October 12, CSA Treasurer Christopher Memminger instructed

Although none of the three Southern branch mints was the scene of fighting, the coming of the Civil War meant mint employees worked, temporarily at least, for the Confederate States of America. (From Leslie's Weekly)

Superintendent Caldwell to relinquish all gold and silver assets of the former Charlotte Mint. These were to be tendered to Assistant Treasurer B.C. Pressley in Charleston. Thus, the mint served as an assay office in name only, evidently taking no further deposits.

The structure was used early in the Civil War to roll copper sheets for the manufacture of percussion caps, and the mint's basement and outbuildings were used during the war to store naval supplies shipped there from Norfolk, Virginia. Local citizens used the mint for various social functions, the building being one of the grandest in Charlotte. Only a skeleton crew remained to man the facility, though Superintendent Caldwell continued to run it under the CSA until his death on July 10, 1864.

An Ending and a New Beginning

The city of tomorrow will justly censure the careless waste of such a useful and historic landmark.

– Architect Martin Boyer commenting on the potential loss to Charlotte of the historic mint building, circa 1932

After the war ended in 1865, the mint building was used for about two years as a United States military post. It reopened as a federal assay office in 1867 with Dr. Isaac W. Jones as its superintendent. The General Assembly of North Carolina petitioned Congress to resume coining at Charlotte in 1873, but it was already evident that the regional mines were playing out. The former United States Mint at Charlotte never again produced a single coin.

As gold deposits continued to dwindle, the Treasury Department ordered the closure of the Charlotte Assay Office in 1913. It stood vacant for four years and was then used as a meeting place for the Charlotte Woman's Club from 1917 to 1919 and as a Red Cross station during World War I. It also saw some use as a federal courthouse, but later plans to convert it to a public school fell through.

Lying in the way of a proposed expansion of the city's post office, the venerable building was slated for demolition in 1932. The subcontractor asked a mere $1,500 for all of the bricks and stones that comprised the mint building, provided the purchaser could also pay for the cost of hauling them away to the new site. Coming during the very greatest depth of the Depression, however, even the modest sum required was not easily had. After considerable pleading by local citizens the contractor, W.R. Hart, accepted their counteroffer of $950. The mint building was thus saved.

After debating several possible sites for rebuilding the structure, a lot measuring three acres was generously donated by E.C. Griffith. The contractor fulfilled his part of the bargain, numbering the various components as they were taken down and then quite literally dumping them at the new site. The task of reassembling the building was funded through a grant from the Federal Emergency Relief Administration, which assigned this undertaking to the Civil Works Administration, part of President Franklin D. Roosevelt's "alphabet soup" of make-work programs. Martin E. Boyer donated his services as supervising architect, and the mint structure was slowly rebuilt between 1933 and 1936.

The formal opening of the Mint Museum of Art took place October 22, 1936. Since then, it has served the City of Charlotte well as a major cultural institution. Of interest to numismatists is its collection of gold coins produced by the Charlotte Mint between 1838 and 1861.

The U.S. Mint at Dahlonega

1830 $10 gold piece struck by Templeton Reid (33.7 mm)

The town of Dahlonega is the Lumpkin County seat, located in north-central Georgia, not far from the modern metropolis of Atlanta. In the early 1830s, however, there was no city of Atlanta, and there was just barely what could be described as a town at Dahlonega.

What prompted construction of a U.S. branch mint in this sleepy hamlet was the 1828 discovery of gold – vast amounts of gold – in northeastern Georgia. The yellow metal had been found in large deposits in parts of North Carolina some years earlier, and together these events led to America's first gold rush during the 1820s and early '30s. This development furnished millions of dollars' worth of gold to the young nation, though sadly it also resulted in the expulsion of the Cherokee people from their ancestral lands.

Just as the California miners would discover 20 years later, gold nuggets and dust do not make for a practical medium of exchange, and their use in transactions often led to heated arguments over value. The solution to this problem was to have the gold coined so it came back to its owner in units of recognized value. In the era before railroads, however, this meant slow and uncertain transportation via wagon and canal boat to the U.S. Mint at Philadelphia. Not only was such a route risky, it was also quite expensive and time-consuming.

The first to coin gold in Georgia was not the federal government but a jeweler

1830 Templeton Reid $5 gold piece (25 mm)

"The Trail of Tears" by Robert Lindneux depicts the removal of the Cherokee from their homelands.

It is a much more complicated and massive concern than we had expected. The entire Machinery necessary for coining, weighs upward of ***fifty thousand pounds,*** *and cost the Government for its transportation from Augusta [Georgia] to this place, upwards of one thousand dollars.*

– From an article in the *Dahlonega Recorder* describing the arrival of 10 wagons carrying 15 crates of mint machinery valued at over $15,000

and metalsmith named Templeton Reid. First in the town of Milledgeville, then later in Gainesville, Reid minted gold coins having declared values the same as those of the United States Mint: $2.50, $5, and $10. These coins were similar to the federal issues only in size and value, their designs being highly distinctive. A unique specimen of the $25 denomination once held in the U.S. Mint's coin collection was stolen in 1858 and never seen again.

Reid's mint operated only from about July to October of 1830, when he evidently ceased coining due to claims that his issues were worth less than their stated values. Assays performed at the Philadelphia Mint, however, revealed that while the Reid coins were slightly lower in weight than the federal issues, their higher fineness made them equal or greater in gold content. Despite this endorsement, nearly all of the Templeton Reid coins were ultimately sent to Philadelphia for recoining into federal issues. Surviving pieces are exceedingly rare, the $10 denomination being unique.

A New Mint

As far as the miners were concerned, the real solution to their lack of coined money was for the United States Mint to establish a branch facility in the mining region. Their goal was initially expressed as the need for a federal assay office but, as the pleas of Georgia's congressional delegation went unanswered year after year, this desire eventually became a demand for a U.S. minting facility. Both Louisiana and North Carolina were likewise seeking branch mints during the 1830s.

This was the Jacksonian Era, however, and debate raged continually in Congress over the merits of hard money and stability versus paper currency and the more lenient credit that its issuance prompted. There were forces opposed to expanding the coinage of gold, especially after August 1, 1834, when the standard of United States gold coins was lowered to permit their unrestricted circulation. Leading this opposition was the influential senator Henry Clay of Kentucky. In support of the bill calling for three new Southern mints was the equally persuasive South Carolina senator John C. Calhoun. With his endorsement and continued campaigning, the bill was passed first in the House of Representatives and then in the Senate. It was signed into law by President Andrew Jackson on March 3, 1835.

In addition to authorizing mints at New Orleans for the coining of gold and silver and at Charlotte, North Carolina, for coining gold only, this legislation provided for "one branch at or near Dahlonega, Lumpkin County, in the State of Georgia, also for the coinage of gold only." The United States branch mint at Dahlonega now existed on paper, but there was as yet no facility to house it. The actual construction of the mint and the installation of its machinery would prove to be an even greater obstacle than merely providing for its authorization.

At the instigation of President Jackson, on March 13, 1835, Treasury Secretary Levi Woodbury appointed Ignatius A. Few as commissioner of the Dahlonega Mint's construction. Mint Director Samuel Moore advised Few by letter to visit the Philadelphia Mint before undertaking this task, as it would be beneficial to see what such an operation entailed. Instead, Few remained in Georgia, anticipating

This photo of the Dahlonega Mint building was taken between January 1877, when it was being used as the main building of North Georgia Agricultural College, and December 20, 1878, when it burned down. The long-lost image was discovered on October 15, 1997, in a file marked "Old Photographs" in the office of the president of North Georgia College and State University, as the school is now known.

the arrival of building plans before proceeding to Dahlonega. When they failed to materialize, he went ahead to examine proposed building sites in Dahlonega, returning to Athens, Georgia, a week or two later. Few wrote to Moore on May 21, bemoaning that, "those most immediately interested in the establishment of the Branch Mint at Dahlonega are already disposed to complain of what they consider tardiness in carrying the law establishing it into effect." Moore responded that he had taken no action on supplying plans because he anticipated Few's arrival in Philadelphia, as requested. This sort of misunderstanding was typical in the protracted construction of the Dahlonega Mint that would lead to so much frustration at both ends.

Commissioner Few, distrusting Moore, began to correspond directly with Treasury Secretary Woodbury, notifying the secretary of the various proposed lots on which the mint could be built. Moore shortly thereafter advised Woodbury that he had written Few to find out what was delaying work on the new mint. He added that he saw no reason why the plans for the Charlotte Mint, already drawn by architect William Strickland and approved by the Treasury Department, would not suffice for the Dahlonega Mint. Moore expressed some urgency in his letter, as he was soon to be succeeded as Mint Director by Robert M. Patterson. In subsequent correspondence, Patterson seconded Moore, suggesting that both the plans and the budget for the Charlotte Mint be approved for Dahlonega.

In the meantime, there was growing concern in Lumpkin County, as the miners and prominent figures in the

Working a "hollow gum" rocker (above), miners used flowing water to move sand and gravel over riffle bars that trapped gold particles. The sluice box at right had a perforated iron plate through which particles of gold fell, landing in a box below. (From "Essay on the Georgia Gold Mines" by William Phillips, 1833)

The buildings at Charlotte have been faithfully executed according to the designs and contracts, made and furnished for that purpose. ... I regret that I cannot report so favorably of the building at Dahlonega, it has not been executed with the care and skill which the contract calls for, and it appears ... that the commissioner Col. I. Few has not by his presence or attention, sufficiently protected the interests of the Government.

– Report from Franklin Peale on construction progress at Charlotte and Dahlonega, December 23, 1837

community saw no progress being made. In July, a committee formed from their ranks petitioned Secretary Woodbury to expedite construction of the mint, so crucial to the regional economy. The committee also took exception to Ignatius Few, citing his poor health and his reluctance to relocate to remote Dahlonega. Indeed, Few had remained in the more genteel Gainesville and had visited the proposed mint site only once since his appointment. They urged his replacement with a local businessman who, it was assumed, would be more attentive to the task.

Commissioner Few defended his inaction. Learning of the Treasury Department's intention to use the Charlotte building plans, he questioned why they had not been sent to him sooner so he could have proceeded with the work. In actuality, Few had been making progress. He purchased 10 acres from William J. Worley, though it would later be revealed that lots had been trading so quickly and without formal recording that it was not certain who actually held title to the site. Once the plans arrived, the commissioner contracted with Benjamin Towns to build the mint at a cost of $33,450. The estimated completion date of March 22, 1837, did not sit well with the Treasury Department, though Few and the contractor understood (certainly better than those in Philadelphia) the challenge of completing a building in what was then still a semi-wilderness.

Work did indeed proceed slowly. By April 1836 only the foundation was laid, though the materials for erecting walls had already been acquired. Commissioner Few offered a variety of explanations for the delay. He cited inadequacies in the furnished plans that necessitated some on-site changes. The area was experiencing unusually heavy rainfall that year, Few added. As a final touch, even an Indian uprising of the local Creeks was included as a cause for the slow progress. By September 1836 only the basement and a portion of the first story had been completed.

It was soon discovered that not only was the work slow, but it was sloppy as well. The mint's newly appointed superintendent-treasurer, Dr. Joseph J. Singleton, arrived in Dahlonega in March 1837 to assume his duties, expecting to find the mint nearly ready for the installation of its machinery. Instead, he found an engineering catastrophe. Masonry arches had been designed as a support for the mint's floor, but these caused a lateral thrust that the poorly constructed walls were unable to withstand. Thus, further work had come to a standstill, and extensive changes would have to be made. In addition, no water supply had been furnished for the mint's boilers, and Commissioner Few had been unsuccessful in locating a supply of zinc for the building's roof.

When Singleton became more fully aware of the scope of the problem, he informed Mint Director Patterson on August 6 of the weakness of the structure's walls. With the new mint's machinery having already arrived in Dahlonega on May 29, the Treasury Department was thrown into a panic. Concluding that neither Few nor Singleton were really up to the task, Director Patterson ordered Franklin Peale to report to Dahlonega and act as an adviser. Peale was the Philadelphia Mint's melter and refiner, and he would later succeed Adam Eckfeldt as chief coiner in 1839. Also sent to Dahlonega was David H. Mason, who had been appointed the new mint's coiner and was already impressing his superiors with his skill and resourcefulness.

With four men – Few, Singleton, Peale, and Mason – now held accountable for the mint's progress, things came together quickly. Mason was able to return to Philadelphia on November 10, accompanied by William Baker, who had supervised installation of the machinery. Having been delayed at the Charlotte Mint, Peale arrived in Dahlonega 10 days after Mason's departure. He and his men were there just a week, installing the furnaces, refineries, and boilerworks, and Peale left for Philadelphia on November 27.

The machinery for the mint was furnished at a contracted cost of $14,987. The firm of Coleman & Sellers provided much of this, including the steam engines, rolling mills, and milling machines. The coin presses were supplied by Merrick & Agnew and were of the very latest design. Franklin Peale had toured European mints on a fact-finding mission in 1833 to 1835, and his discoveries were perfectly timed for building the Southern mints and upgrading the Philadelphia mint.

Coining Commences

On February 12, 1838, Superintendent Singleton announced in a letter, "This is the day of commencement of Branch Mint operations," referring to the mint's readiness to accept bullion deposits for coining. The actual manufacture of coins would come a bit later. Commissioner Few, in whom no one had much faith at this point, had not been present since the previous summer and would play no further role in the mint's history.

There were yet some obstacles to coining. The roles of assayer versus melter and refiner, separate duties at the Philadelphia Mint, had been combined into a single position at the branch mints. This responsibility fell on Dr. Joseph W. Farnum, and it was simply too much work for him. A similar situation existed at the Charlotte Mint and was likewise causing delays. It was suggested that the melting and refining portion of Farnum's job be transferred to Coiner David H. Mason, but Mason objected to assuming Farnum's duties, as the two were on bad terms. At least one technical problem further delayed coining, when the mint was unable to raise sufficient steam pressure to operate its machinery.

Bullion depositors did not immediately receive their payment in gold coin. They could accept a certificate

The Dahlonega Mint would have had a room for melting and refining similar to this one at the Philadelphia Mint. (From Visitor's Guide and History of the United States Mint *by A.M. Smith, 1885)*

redeemable in coin at Philadelphia, or they could come back to Dahlonega to collect in coin after their deposit had been assayed and minted, usually a delay of two to three weeks. So, while bullion was received almost immediately after the mint's opening, the first coins were not struck until April 21, 1838. A total of

Using a combination gum rocker and sluice box exploited the benefits of both, but also moved water through a perforated trough that reduced the amount of gold that might otherwise be washed out and lost. (From "Essay on the Georgia Gold Mines" by William Phillips, 1833)

80 half eagles were struck that day. Singleton, furnishing a sample for the U.S. Mint's annual assay, wrote to Director Patterson, "You may possibly consider it presumptuous in me to say that I believe our coin equal to any made in the world both for its beauty and accuracy in its legal parts."

Only half eagles were coined at Dahlonega in 1838, these being the coins most desired by depositors and the most useful in general circulation. A total of 20,583 pieces was minted there in the first year of operation. Quarter eagles followed in 1839. All of these bore a D mintmark denoting their place of manufacture.

The Dahlonega Mint struck quarter eagles annually through 1859, with the sole exception of 1858. Mintages were generally small, especially in comparison to the output of the Philadelphia Mint, which would sometimes produce a million or more strikes in a single year. The largest quarter eagle coinage recorded for the Dahlonega Mint was in 1843, when 36,209 pieces were struck. This was the exception, however, and the absurdly small mintage of just 874 1856-D quarter eagles reveals how rare these coins really are. Half eagle mintages were typically greater, ranging from a high of 98,452 in 1843 to a mere 1,597 pieces in 1861, the final year of production.

In addition to quarter and half eagles, the mint struck gold dollars beginning in 1849. Some 21,588 examples were coined there that first year. Production of this denomination continued annually through 1861, but the high figure of 1849 was never again achieved. The smallest recorded mintage occurred in 1856, when just 1,460 pieces were made.

Troubled Times

The personnel problems at the Dahlonega Mint, alluded to earlier in reference to the feud between Coiner David Mason and Assayer Joseph Farnum, were widespread during the early years of operation. Things settled down with Farnum's resignation in 1843 and the replacement that same year of Superintendent-Treasurer Joseph Singleton with a new appointee, Major James F. Cooper. Singleton had actually done a fine job, all things considered, and his termination was merely a political consequence of the Whig Party's presidential victory. There would be others following Cooper, and the mint's history continued to offer some minor dramas, but these pale in comparison to the events that would unfold in 1861 and ultimately close the mint.

When Abraham Lincoln, an avowed defender of the Union, was elected to the presidency in 1860, it was just a matter of time before conflict developed with the Southern states. South Carolina was the first to defect in December, seceding from the Union and turning its back on the federal government. Others followed, Georgia joining the rebellion on January 19, 1861. As a property and installation of the United States, one possessing a wealth of bullion and machinery, the mint was essentially indefensible in the State of Georgia. The coming of civil war in April 1861 between the United States of America and the Confederate States of America (CSA) made its surrender seem inevitable.

Initially, there was little change in the mint's routine. The new superintendent-treasurer, George Kellogg, had assumed office only months before, in October 1860. He maintained a normal correspondence with Mint Director James R. Snowden, and both the receipt of bullion and the manufacture of coins continued at their usual pace. Though Kellogg was himself a Georgian, he did not initially seem disposed to join the Southern cause. This sentiment was confirmed by Director Snowden to Treasury Secretary Salmon P. Chase: "... notwithstanding the revolutionary proceedings in the State of Georgia, the Branch Mint at Dahlonega continues to recognize itself as a Branch of the Mint of the United States ... ."

Still, uncertainty clouded the mint's future following Georgia's secession and its subsequent admission to the Confederate States of America. Perhaps Snowden and Chase were not aware that the Georgia Secession Convention had already claimed jurisdiction over all property of the U.S. government in that state. Lumpkin County's delegate, a Mr. Hamilton, moved to have the Foreign Relations Committee contemplate a change in the devices on coins being struck at Dahlonega, as well as possible changes in the mint's management.

Perhaps sensing this shift in political winds, Superintendent Kellogg informed the CSA of his willingness to "resign at any time and be commissioned under the Southern Confederacy." Kellogg also appealed to CSA Treasury Secretary Christopher Memminger to retain his position. He formally resigned from office with the U.S. Treasury Department on April 25, 1861, to be effective May 15. In taking this action, it was clear that Kellogg anticipated being renamed to

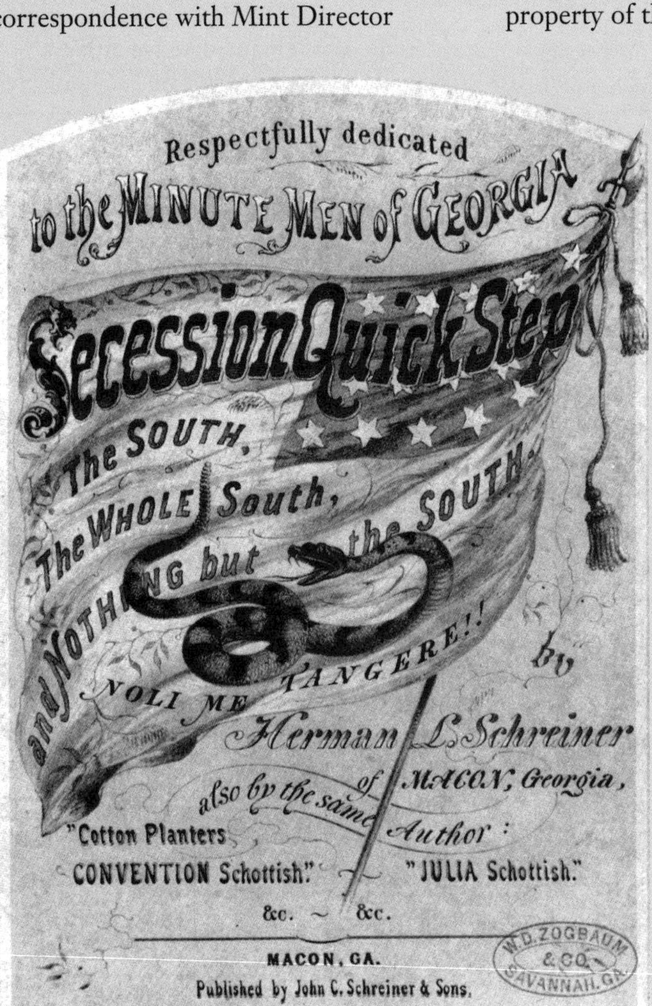

Herman L. Schreiner, a songwriter from Macon, Georgia, wrote his "Secession Quick Step" to celebrate his state's decision to join forces with the South in its fight against the Union.

1839-D Classic Head quarter eagle (18.2 mm)

1851-D Coronet Head half eagle (21.6 mm)

A Bill To establish a national school of mines in the North Georgia Agricultural College, at Dahlonega, Georgia ...

The [College], formerly the United States branch-mint, located in a region abounding in rich and valuable mines of gold, copper, iron, and other ores, will go into operation in January, eighteen hundred and seventy-three ... . It is the duty of the Government, while providing schemes for the promotion and development of the interests of agriculture and the mechanic arts, to provide, at the same time, the means for the ready development of the immense hidden wealth of the United States, which can be done in no other way so well as by imparting to the youths of the country a knowledge of those sciences which tend directly to the proper development of our immense mineral resources ... .

– Bill from the House of Representatives referred to the Committee on Mines and Mining, December 9, 1872

the same position by the Confederate government and that mint operations would continue.

The business community of Lumpkin County and its environs likewise urged that the mint be kept in operation, even if this entailed a change in the imagery of its coins. Both parties were to be disappointed, however, as the CSA government, meeting in its capital, Montgomery, Alabama, decided instead to close the facility. A dejected George Kellogg then informed Secretary Memminger that he would see to the mint's closure by June 1 and discharge all employees. There was some hope of maintaining an assay office at the site, but Kellogg reported to Memminger that this would not be cost-effective, and he held out for an actual mint.

Christopher Memminger, CSA Treasurer (From Harper's Magazine*)*

The last financial report of the Dahlonega Mint was prepared on June 26 by Henry Kellogg, the superintendent's son and clerk. As directed, all the mint's bullion assets were transmitted to Benjamin Pressley, the Confederacy's assistant treasurer in Charleston. The total, $23,716.06, included $4,937.00 in gold and silver coins. The production at Dahlonega that year had been limited to 1,597 half eagles and an unrecorded but small number of gold dollars.

Responding to continued appeals from the residents of northern Georgia, the CSA did finally approve the operation of an assay office in the former Dahlonega Mint on August 24, 1861. In this capacity, the structure remained active at least through the first quarter of 1864, all subsequent records having been lost. Regardless of the official closing date, it is likely that the South's collapsing economy would have led to a cessation of bullion deposits around that time anyway.

The Final Years

At the war's end in 1865, there was a strong desire among Georgians to see the mint reopened. In its constitutional convention that year, a necessary step in Georgia's readmission to the Union, one of the platforms presented was for the resumption of coinage at Dahlonega. When this failed in Congress, an attempt was made to reopen the former mint as a federal assay office, but this too was rejected. The government seemed to have no further use for the old mint, and the structure and its 10-acre plot were deeded to North Georgia Agricultural College. It was serving in this role when the building burned on the night of December 19-20, 1878. The superstructure was razed, and a new college building was erected on the old foundation.

In 1997 a photograph surfaced that provided the first overall view of the original mint building (see page 47). Taken between 1877 and December 20, 1878, when the structure burned, this photograph shows the front elevation of the former mint building during its use as part of North Georgia Agricultural College. No such view had been known to exist previously, despite the fact that the mint's founding nearly coincided with the invention of photography. Such an anomaly seems in keeping with this most mysterious of United States branch mints.

The U.S. Mint at New Orleans

New Orleans was the site of a United States mint that struck coins from 1838 to 1909 and continued to function as a federal assay office for another 22 years afterward. Despite the importance of this facility to American numismatics, there is a surprising lack of published information about it. Entire books have been dedicated to the other Southern branch mints at Charlotte and Dahlonega, yet no such volumes have appeared to tell the tale of the far more significant New Orleans mint. Only a few episodes from its long history have been chronicled in numismatic literature. Today, the structure serves as the Louisiana State Museum.

All three Southern branch mints were created by a single piece of legislation, signed into law by President Andrew Jackson on March 3, 1835. The Jackson administration and its supporters in Congress advocated the creation of new mints to further the long-term expansion of western economic development, but there were also more immediate reasons. Gold had been discovered in

For the purpose of purchasing sites, erecting suitable buildings, and completing the necessary combinations of machinery for the several branches aforesaid, the following sums [are] to be paid out of any money in the Treasury, not otherwise appropriated, [and] shall be, and hereby are appropriated: for the branch at New Orleans the sum of two hundred thousand dollars; for the branch at Charlotte, fifty thousand dollars; for the branch at Dahlonega, fifty thousand dollars.

– Proposed spending for three branch mints, 23rd Congress, February 10, 1835

An 1858 view of the New Orleans Mint as seen in Ballou's Pictorial Magazine

1839-O Capped Bust half dollar (30 mm)

Georgia and North Carolina as early as 1799, though this wealth was not really exploited until the 1820s. Given the crude state of America's transportation system at the time, it made sense to assay and coin the gold closer to its source, and federal mints were thus established at Dahlonega and Charlotte to provide these services.

New Orleans presented a different situation. Though Louisiana lacked such mineral wealth, the city was then one of the United States' most important ports, being second perhaps only to New York City in the value of goods that passed through it. Among its principal imports were silver and gold bullion extracted from the mines of South America. This arrived in the form of both bars and coins. The former were often forwarded intact to such Eastern cities as New York and Boston, while the coins would frequently be circulated in the United States. Such pieces comprised much of our circulating precious-metal coinage until the middle of the 19th century. The mint at New Orleans was established to assay and coin this foreign bullion at a time when domestic production of gold and silver was quite limited.

The creation of three new U.S. Mint branches was vigorously opposed by Whig Party opponents of President Jackson and by the Mint's own director, Samuel Moore. Perhaps as a consequence of his view, Moore resigned soon after passage of this legislation and was replaced by his brother-in-law, Robert M. Patterson. The latter, while similarly skeptical of the need for branch mints, dutifully attended to their construction and staffing.

The Mint Takes Shape

The French Quarter in New Orleans as it looked in December 1862 (From Harper's Magazine*)*

Excited by the prospect of a United States mint in its city, on June 19, 1835, the municipal government of New Orleans provided a plot of land to the federal government for construction of the mint building. Situated at one end of the area known today as the French Quarter, the site was near the Mississippi riverfront and adjacent to Jackson Square.

This name was quite appropriate, as the land had formerly been the site of Fort St. Charles, where Andrew Jackson reviewed his troops prior to the 1815 Battle of New Orleans. Actually fought at nearby Chalmette, this action took place a few weeks after the war between Great Britain and the United States had been ended by treaty. News traveled slowly in those days, and neither side had as yet been informed of the war's end!

The block on which the mint was to be built was bounded by Barracks

Street and Bayou Road, while the building's front faced Esplanade Avenue. Under the terms of the original agreement, the land was to revert to the City of New Orleans should the mint ever cease to operate. Architect William Strickland, who had previously designed the new Philadelphia mint that opened in 1833, was selected to prepare the plans and supervise construction. The mint's cornerstone was laid in September 1835. Due to the oppressive climate that promoted disease, resulting in numerous delays, the building was not completed until 1838.

Massively built for its time, the New Orleans Mint was twice as large as those in Charlotte and Dahlonega. In keeping with the fashion of the time, it was designed in the Greek Revival style. Its main pavilion had a frontage of 282 feet and was 108 feet deep, the entryway being framed with Ionic columns. Two wings, each measuring 81 by 29 feet, completed the three-story structure. Built entirely of brick, this was cemented over, then scored and painted to resemble granite.

1843-O quarter eagle (18 mm)

First Coinage

Assaying operations began on March 8, but coining had to await the arrival of dies from the Philadelphia Mint. Two pairs each of dies for the dime and half dime were shipped April 9 and arrived May 3. Dimes were coined first, on May 7. The first 10 pieces were placed in the cornerstone of the New American Theatre, then under construction, while the next 20 coins were presented to various officials of the mint and the city. Each coin bore the distinguishing letter "O" to indicate its place of manufacture, such mintmarks being new to United States coinage. Coining dimes for general circulation began in June, and enough 1838-O dimes were made that year and early in 1839 to make this a collectible issue.

The first production of half dimes dated 1838-O went unrecorded, but a mere 70,000 pieces were ultimately produced early in 1839, making this a scarce coin in any condition. The extremely rare 1838-O half dollars, all of which were made as Proofs for presentation purposes, were also not coined until early in 1839. Quarter dollars were first produced in April 1840, while the New Orleans Mint did not coin any silver dol-

Mint worker Andrew Berrett pours molten silver into a rotary ingot mold, circa 1890.

1851-O gold dollar (13 mm)

lars until 1846. In 1851, it produced the only mintage of silver three-cent pieces to come from a branch mint, and the experiment was not repeated.

The first emission of gold coins came in 1839, when quarter eagles were struck from dies shipped to the mint on March 14. Half eagles followed in 1840, and the first eagles were struck a year later. Gold dollars were coined at New Orleans from their inception in 1849, through 1855 (excepting 1854), while the $3 piece was produced there only during its first year of issue, 1854. Double eagles were minted at New Orleans annually from 1850 onward, but their production fell to very low levels in some years, such as 1854 (3,250 pieces) and 1856 (2,250). Until 1906, the New Orleans Mint was authorized to coin only gold and silver, so no minor coins were struck there.

It has been reported in a number of reference books that the mint's first presses were hand-thrown screw presses left over from the Philadelphia Mint. This is extremely unlikely, as the other two Southern mints were equipped with steam-driven lever presses from the outset. Clearly the most important of the three facilities, the New Orleans Mint, would have received equipment that was fully equal in quality and performance. The source of this misinformation is not known, but it has been repeated far too often and may now be laid to rest.

Problems at the Mint

1859-O Liberty Seated silver dollar (38.1 mm)

Though the supply of bullion was fairly steady, there were other factors that caused frequent delays and interruptions in coining. Primary among these was disease. The City of New Orleans lies below sea level, and at the time of the mint's establishment in the 1830s and for decades afterward, New Orleans was surrounded by marshlands known as bayous. These swampy areas furnished the perfect breeding environment for mosquitos that carried malaria and yellow fever. A particularly severe outbreak of yellow fever caused the mint to suspend operations from July 1 to November 30, 1839. This same scourge had caused numerous delays at the Philadelphia Mint in its early years, as residents fled the city for the perceived safety of more rural areas. Another, though less frequent, problem was the weather, as summertime occasionally brought hurricanes that swept away lives and property, leaving the city flooded for days at a time.

While the forces of nature prompted periodic interruptions in production, another more insidious ailment plagued the mint from within. Squabbling among its officers was rampant, as charges and countercharges of incompetence and malfeasance delayed coining for months. Many of the same people responsible for this initial delay remained on hand after the mint went into full operation, due to the system by which they had obtained their positions. The Mint Act of March 3, 1835, which had created the three new mints, also specified the positions each facility would need to fill, the respective salaries of these officers, and the means by which they would be hired. The mint's officers, as it turned out, were to be political appointees rather than career civil servants. While this was typical of government service at that time, it was a system that invited corruption and cronyism, and the three branch mints were scenes of nasty infighting. For the most part these ugly incidents were limited to the first few years of operation. When they became a problem for

New Orleans Mint workers roll strips of metal (left), which are then cut into coin blanks.

the Mint Director in Philadelphia, appropriate steps were taken to remove the offending parties.

The officers at the New Orleans Mint, appointed in 1837, included David Bradford as superintendent at a salary of $2,500 per year. Treasurer Edmund Forstall, Coiner Rufus Tyler, Melter and Refiner James Maxwell, and Assayer William Hort each received $2,000 per annum.

Production was fairly steady during the years leading up to the Civil War. The only significant reduction in output occurred during the early 1850s, when the rising value of silver relative to gold caused hoarding of silver coins and a drop in their production. This was rectified through a weight reduction enacted in 1853, and record numbers of fractional silver coins were produced over the next several years. The silver dollar, however, remained at the former standard and was minted at New Orleans only in 1846, 1850, 1859, and 1860. Relatively large numbers were produced during those final two years.

To the delight of collectors, a few hundred uncirculated examples of the 1859-O and 1860-O silver dollars surfaced in U.S. Treasury vaults during the early 1960s. These were quickly absorbed by the hobby. Another hoard of mixed circulated and Mint State coins of the New Orleans Mint was unearthed in that city during 1982. Workers at a construction site spilled the contents of one or more metal boxes containing a blend of "O" mint U.S. coins and coins of Spain's former New World colonies that were so prevalent in the country at that time. These too were quickly placed with coin dealers and collectors, though many display signs of environmental damage.

Women using delicate scales weigh planchets to determine whether they meet requirements.

A Time of Crisis

The onset of the Civil War in 1861 brought dramatic changes to the City of New Orleans and to the United States mint located there. After Louisiana seceded from the Union, the mint was seized by the state militia on January 31, 1861. The officers and employees continued their regular duties, while their status as servants of the United States government was pondered. Both coining and assaying operations continued as normal, since the bullion on hand prior to the state takeover was still owed to its depositors in the form of bars or coin. Exactly two months later, Louisiana turned the mint over to the Confederate States of America (CSA). Work at the mint lasted until May 31, at which time insufficient bullion remained on hand to continue operation, and the mint was closed. Some of its machinery was relocated to munitions plants supplying the Southern army and navy, and CSA troops were briefly housed there, but otherwise no use was made of the building.

The New Orleans Mint coined only two denominations during 1861, one each in gold and silver. The 17,741 double eagles minted during those five months of operation actually represented an increase over the years immediately preceding, while more than 2.5 million silver half dollars were coined. A mere 330,000 of these were halves issued under federal authority before the mint was seized. Another 1,240,000 were coined for the State of Louisiana. The remaining 962,633 were struck after the mint was taken over by the CSA. In addition, just four examples of the CSA's own half-dollar coinage were minted there, these patterns bearing a regular federal obverse paired to a reverse die displaying the Confederate arms. Ultimately, however,

A January 1862 naval skirmish between a Union war steamer and a Confederate floating battery ram and other steamers at the mouth of the Mississippi River at New Orleans (From Frank Leslie's Illustrated History of the Civil War*)*

the introduction by both North and South of irredeemable paper money drove silver and gold coins from circulation, while a Union blockade of Southern ports cut off the supply of bullion to the Crescent City. These factors precluded the production of any more coins for the Confederacy.

As the largest and most valuable of the Southern port cities, New Orleans was an immediate target of the Union army and navy. In addition to the blockade noted above, an assault against the city was launched by navy gunboats in April 1862. Under the command of David G. Farragut, they managed to fight their way past Forts Jackson and St. Philip, which guarded the Mississippi River's gulf approach to New Orleans. With the forts now cut off from any hope of supplies and reinforcements via the river, they had no choice but to surrender. This left New Orleans effectively defenseless, and federal troops under the command of Benjamin Butler were sent in to occupy the city for the duration of the war. CSA Assistant Treasurer A.J. Guirot had meanwhile fled to Vicksburg, Mississippi, taking with him whatever silver and gold remained on hand.

The mint building was placed under the care of soldiers from the 12th Maine Volunteers, who immediately set about making themselves at home. In a postwar report submitted by Dr. M.F. Bonzano, the mint's melter and refiner, this activity included use of the coin presses as chopping blocks by the regiment's butchers, while the cabinets containing the mint's delicate scales were used as meat lockers. The occupation of the mint lasted for just a short period, from May to July of 1862, after which the building was evidently vacant through the war's end three years later.

Reporting to Mint Director Henry R. Linderman in 1867, Bonzano, who had been appointed a special agent of the Treasury Department to assess the mint's postwar status, recommended that it be restored to full operation. Linderman, however, opted to use the facility merely for the distribution of coins manufactured elsewhere. There were three reasons for his decision. First, the unsettled condition of the former Confederate states during the Reconstruction period of 1865 to 1877 made it difficult to predict the performance of the New Orleans Mint under such circumstances. Second, the continued absence of silver and gold coins from circulation in most of the nation so reduced the need for additional coins that it was all he could do to maintain the Philadelphia Mint at minimum efficiency. Finally, so much of the New Orleans Mint's machinery had been either removed or damaged that a resumption of coining would entail expensive repairs. Linderman's decision not to resume coining should have caused the property to revert to the City of New Orleans under the provisions of the original deed, but the federal government simply chose to disregard this contract while it debated the building's future.

In 1874, Deputy Comptroller of the Currency John J. Knox declared that the New Orleans Mint would not be needed, the nation's existing mints being sufficient to meet the demand for coinage. Despite this assessment, the Mint did reopen as a federal assay office on October 23, 1876, an action taken largely to stave off takeover attempts by the city and state. At that time there was no expectation that coining would ever resume at New Orleans.

Many of the New Orleans Mint's tasks were performed by women. This worker puts blanks into the steam-powered press to create finished coins.

This 1861 Confederate half dollar, one of only four, was taken from CSA President Jefferson Davis when he was captured by Union forces in 1865. (30.6 mm)

Henry Stuart Foote, a former United States senator and governor of Mississippi, was opposed to secession but ultimately represented Tennessee in the Confederate Congress. After the war, Foote was exiled twice by the United States government, which later pardoned him and appointed him superintendent of the New Orleans Mint. He served in that capacity from 1878 until his death in 1880. Part of his tenure was spent overseeing the coining of silver to meet the demands of the Bland-Allison Act.

The Presses Run Again

All this changed, however, with the passage of the Bland-Allison Act in February 1878. This legislation called for the coining of millions of silver dollars monthly, which threatened to overtax the U.S. Mint's capacity. The New Orleans Mint was hastily refurbished and fitted with new coin presses to strike dollars. The matter of ownership of the building and its site was settled once and for all when the federal government extracted an outright donation immediately prior to the resumption of coining operations. Beginning in 1879, the New Orleans Mint carried much of the burden imposed by the Bland-Allison Act. Many millions of silver dollars were struck there through 1904 and, perhaps even more importantly, stored there. The coins were unwanted and unneeded, and all of the U.S. Treasury's facilities were soon overwhelmed with mountains of silver dollars.

Aside from silver dollars, only gold coins were produced by the reopened New Orleans Mint until 1891, when dimes and quarter dollars were issued. These were followed by half dollars the next year. All seemed well with the New Orleans Mint for the next 15 years, until the opening of the huge new mint at Denver threatened its existence. Coming in 1906, just five years after Philadelphia had received a gigantic new mint structure, the combination of these two facilities clearly meant that time was running out for the last remaining Southern mint.

Rather than being officially terminated as a mint, New Orleans simply did not receive an appropriation for coining operations during fiscal year 1910. This meant that no money had been budgeted for coining after the end of the previous fiscal year, June 30, 1909. The only denominations coined during calendar year 1909 were dimes, quarter dollars, half dollars, and half eagles. All were produced in sufficient numbers to be collectable, though the $5 pieces are fairly scarce. While the New Orleans Mint was permitted to strike minor coins (cents and nickels) under a law passed in 1906, it never exercised this option.

1891-O Liberty Seated dime (17.9 mm)

Declining Years

The old mint building continued to house a federal assay office after 1909, but there remained sufficient space to provide for other tenants. Beginning in 1910 part of the mint was used as a training center and supply depot by the U.S. Coast Guard. Following World War I, a local office of the Veterans Bureau was located there in 1919 and remained for the next few years. As the building began to show its age, it was vacated on June 30, 1931, and the New Orleans Assay Office was relocated to the customhouse until it closed for good in 1942. A portion of the mint structure was used as a federal prison starting in 1936, cells being installed for that purpose. During this period the mint's prison was used as the setting for a low-budget movie called "Swamp Woman." The onset of World War II led to the closing of the prison, and the mint building remained largely vacant for the next several decades, only the Coast Guard continuing to maintain a small presence there.

In 1962 the General Services Administration (GSA) declared the building to be government surplus and prepared to sell the structure and land at public auction. Under these circumstances it was almost certain that the building would be razed so its site could be developed. Among the proposals offered up by the numismatic community, which naturally wanted to see the historic mint preserved, was that it become the home of the American Numismatic Association (ANA), which was then seeking to establish a headquarters facility. Unfortunately, the mint building had been allowed to deteriorate for decades, and the cost of restoring the existing structure proved to be prohibitive. For this and other reasons, the ANA declined to pursue the matter.

The city sought to use the structure as a temporary jail while its new police complex was under construction. But, as the building was situated in the popular French Quarter, with its extensive tourist industry, this proposal was obviously unpopular with the business community. After three years of fruitless debate, in 1965 the GSA decided to proceed with auctioning the property.

This announcement galvanized various city and state preservation groups, and the media were brought aboard to champion the cause. A plan was advanced to turn it over to the State of Louisiana, but the federal government had already begun accepting bids for the property. Only when these were rejected as being too low did the GSA strike an agreement with the state. The United States would turn over the mint building and its lot to Louisiana, provided that renovation of the structure begin within 10 years of the exchange. Otherwise the property would revert to the federal government.

1897-O Barber half dollar (30.6 mm)

Rebirth

While the New Orleans Mint was designated a National Historic Landmark in 1975, no real progress had been made in undertaking its restoration. In 1976, as the agreed-upon deadline was reached, the federal government granted a four-year extension. The Louisiana legislature finally budgeted the necessary $3 million in 1977, Governor Edwin Edwards signing the bill on July 14. Restoration and development work began the following year.

Reopened in 1981, the former mint building is now the Louisiana State Museum. It houses a blend of educational and commercial attractions, including collections of jazz and Mardi Gras memorabilia. The museum's third floor hosts the Louisiana Historical Society and its library, as well as the Amistad Research Center for minority studies. The museum's modest tribute to its former role as a United States Mint features a number of coins but is generally unworthy of the subject's importance. As this study goes to press, a campaign is under way to greatly improve the numismatic exhibits.

The New Orleans Mint building has been given a second life as the Louisiana State Museum.

The Language of the Mines

California prospectors washing for gold in the foothills of the Sierras hoped to see ***colors,*** *or promising yellow sparkles in the bottom of their pans. (From* Across the Continent *by S. Bowles, 1853)*

This ***quartz mill*** *had iron bars that were lifted by a camshaft, then allowed to fall into rock in the mill's base. The resulting dust and small rock pieces where processed to extract any gold that might be present. (From* Progress of the United States)

Conversation at California gold fields was peppered with the prospectors' colorful lingo:

Sourdough: A savvy veteran of the goldfields, the kind of man who would always be sure to keep his sourdough starter alive – sometimes even sleeping with it to keep it warm.

Horse: Worthless rock that interrupts a vein of gold or silver ore.

Gallows frame: The scaffold over a mine shaft from which the hoisting rope is suspended.

Borrasca: Finding nothing of value.

Gumbo: Wet, sticky clay.

Toplander: A miner who labors above ground level rather than down the shaft.

Giant powder: Slang for dynamite.

Mucker: The worker who loads ore-bearing material for transportation after it has been revealed by blasting hard rock.

Chapter Five

The California Gold Rush

> *Money confusion was indescribable. The perplexed '49er found himself constantly confronted with Spanish doubloons, shillings, francs, florins, pesetas, guilders and rupees. American eagles and double eagles and a small amount of lesser coins alone represented the Government in this melange.*
>
> **– From a banking retrospective by the *San Francisco Examiner*, October 15, 1935**

The years 1837 to 1849 provided a brief lull in the almost continual conflict between gold and silver. This period may be described as the only time in United States history when the policy of bimetallism, or the dual standard, actually worked, both metals circulating side-by-side in this country. It was not to last, however, as this pleasant scene was upset by the discovery of vast gold deposits in California.

It all began quietly enough. In the foothills of the Sierra Nevada Mountains, on a branch of the American River, foreman James Marshall and his crew of workmen were engaged in building a sawmill for Swiss entrepreneur John Sutter. Marshall noticed some peculiar particles in the mill's tailrace, later finding some flakes and even a nugget, all of which he suspected were gold. Marshall took his discovery to Sutter at his trading post in New Helvetia. Consulting an encyclopedia, the men found instructions that led them to weigh the samples and test them with acid. Their efforts confirmed the presence of gold, and there appeared to be much more of it where these small measures had been found. The date was Monday, January 24, 1848, and California had only just become a part of the United States as a consequence of the Mexican-American War.

Some 230 ounces of Sierra gold were shipped east by California's military governor, Colonel R.B. Mason, to demonstrate the richness of its ore. In

During the wild and woolly days of 1849, all it took to become a California banker was ownership of a strong safe, so merchants often played that role. More legitimate banks, such as the one seen below, were established in the 1850s to protect the deposits of miners, merchants, and gamblers.

1848 quarter eagle reverse with CAL. (18 mm)

commemoration of this significant discovery, the metal was coined into quarter eagles. Each coin was then stamped on its reverse with the letters "CAL." to indicate the origin of its metal. Only 1,389 such coins are believed to have been made, and these historic quarter eagles dated 1848 are among the most prized of United States gold pieces.

News traveled slowly from distant California to the East. It was not until December that President James Polk confirmed the discovery of gold in his annual address to the nation, and the rush was on. Thousands came from around the world in 1849 to try their luck at picking and panning. San Francisco was turned from a little-known village into a metropolis in just a few months' time, as the Forty-Niners filled its bay with abandoned ships.

When anything highly prized is suddenly rendered more common, its value is destined to decline, and so the value of gold dropped as measured against silver. After 1849, the bullion value of United States silver coins exceeded their face value by a few cents, making them worth more than an equivalent face value in gold coins. In other words, 10 silver dollars were worth more as metal than a $10 gold piece. The inevitable consequence was that all U.S. silver coins became the objects of hoarders and speculators. It was profitable to ship American silver coins out of the country and exchange them at bullion value for gold, this metal then being returned to the Mint and deposited for coining. The gold coins struck from such deposits carried a greater aggregate face value than the original silver pieces. Even after deducting expenses, the speculator still realized a worthwhile profit.

A view of a commercial street in San Francisco during the early days of the gold rush. (From The Illustrated London News, *October 19, 1850)*

United States silver coins disappeared rapidly from circulation after 1849, as they fell prey to the profit-takers. Left in circulation were copper cents and half cents, U.S. gold coins, and heavily worn and underweight foreign silver pieces. (Despite the growing abundance of U.S. silver coins after 1830, various foreign coins remained legal tender as late as 1857.) The supply of foreign silver coins was totally inadequate, and the nation's commerce was nearly paralyzed. Purchases made with gold coins often resulted in the customer receiving as change large handfuls of coppers and Spanish or Mexican silver pieces worn to the point of being almost unrecognizable. Making an unwelcome return were the dreaded fractional banknotes of earlier years, whose small size caused them to be known derisively as "shinplasters."

A new coin denomination that appeared just in time to address the growing shortage of small change was the silver three-cent piece. This odd denomination was evidently selected to coincide with the reduction of the postal rate from 5¢ to 3¢. A little sliver of a coin, it was named the "trime" by Mint Director James R. Snowden, though the public was more inclined to describe these tiny pieces as "fish scales." Debuting in 1851, the trime was an innovation in the nation's coinage system, relying totally on the public's faith in the government to establish its value. Made of a silver alloy that was only .750 fine, the three-cent piece contained less than three cents' worth of silver and thus became the first "subsidiary" coin minted by the United States. Its less-than-noble nature was acknowledged by giving it a plain, unreeded edge, unique among silver coins of that time. While the more valuable silver issues were being hoarded or exported, the trime continued to circulate at its legal value alongside the federal coppers and foreign silver coins. Its usefulness to the American public was demonstrated by the huge numbers coined – more than 36 million pieces during 1851 to 1853.

1851 three-cent piece (14 mm)

Prepared by James B. Longacre, who succeeded Christian Gobrecht as the Mint's chief engraver in 1844, the silver three-cent piece bears a simple design. A six-pointed star with a Union shield at its center dominates the obverse. Around the periphery is the legend UNITED STATES OF AMERICA, while the date appears below the star. On the reverse is an ornamented letter C enclosing the Roman numeral III, both elements encircled by 13 stars. All trimes were coined at the Philadelphia Mint, except in 1851, when a small number were also struck at the New Orleans Mint. These bear its O mintmark to the right of the ornamented C.

Congress was slow to recognize the desirability of a subsidiary silver coinage, one in which the bullion value was less than for gold coins of equivalent face value, and continued to fret over the lack of fractional silver coins in circulation. Loath to debase the nation's coinage, it was not until February 21, 1853, that Congress enacted legislation providing for a subsidiary coinage of the other silver denominations from half dime through half dollar, reducing their respective weights by just under 7 percent. Though the fineness of .900 silver established in 1837 was retained, the lower weight of these coins permitted them to circulate freely, as their bullion value no longer exceeded their face value.

Oddly, Congress retained the old standard for the silver dollar, effectively condemning it to total obscurity (silver dollars could still be purchased from the Mint, but only at their higher bullion value of $1.08). The dollar's inclusion at all in the new law seems to have been a misguided bid to maintain the old concept of bimetallism, in which both silver and gold are recognized as standards of value. It is evident that the nature of a subsidiary silver coinage was still not fully understood in 1853.

To distinguish the new coins from the earlier issues, opposed arrowheads were placed at either side of the date. This feature appeared on the half dimes, dimes, quarter dollars, and half dollars issued from April 1, 1853, through the end of 1855. During 1853 only, the quarters and halves also featured a glory of rays around the eagle. (The silver dollar was not marked in any way, since its coinage continued at the old standard.) When it became apparent that the new standard was not going to be revoked anytime soon, the distinguishing arrowheads were dropped after 1855, though the new lower weights were retained. In a separate bill passed March 3, 1853, the weight and fineness of the trime were brought into conformity with those of the other fractional silver coins. Its production was halted until 1854, when the revised standards were finally applied and its coinage resumed.

To absorb some of the excess gold flowing from California, Congress created two new coin denominations, the gold dollar and the double eagle ($20). These debuted in 1849 and 1850, respectively. Only the gold dollar was of much use in relieving the shortage of silver coins, and it was minted in very large numbers. On the other hand, the double eagle was a banker's coin. Intended to simplify transfers of large sums between financial institutions and between nations, it too enjoyed very significant mintages.

Both coin types were designed by James B. Longacre and bear the same bust of Liberty facing left amid a circle of 13 stars. As with Gobrecht's design for the lesser gold pieces, Liberty wears a tiara or coronet inscribed with her

1855-O half dollar with arrows at the date (30.6 mm)

1850 double eagle (34 mm)

1854 $3 gold piece (20.5 mm)

1849 gold dollar (13 mm)

name, but her features and hairstyle are different from those of the Gobrecht Liberty. Longacre opted to sign this work, the first instance of an engraver doing so on a U.S. coin since the abortive issue of Gobrecht's silver dollar in 1836. At the truncation of Liberty's bust is the single letter L on the gold dollar and the initials J.B.L. on the double eagle.

Due to its diminutive size (13 mm), the gold dollar's reverse design is limited to a small wreath encircling the value 1 DOLLAR, with the date below (it appears beneath Liberty's bust on the double eagle). Around the periphery is UNITED STATES OF AMERICA. The reverse of the double eagle features a bold expression of mid-19th century patriotic emblems. A facing American eagle is shown with a large Union shield across its breast. In keeping with tradition, the eagle clutches an olive branch in its right claw and three arrows in its left. Flanking the eagle on either side are scepters and two scrolls inscribed E PLURIBUS UNUM. Above the bird is a glory of rays and an elliptical constellation of 13 stars. UNITED STATES OF AMERICA is inscribed in an arc around the periphery, and the value is abbreviated below the eagle as TWENTY D. Beginning in 1877, this was spelled out in full.

The small size of the gold dollar drew criticism, and the Mint experimented with different ways to enlarge the coin without increasing its value. Patterns survive showing the gold dollar in an annular, or ring, shape, its hollow center permitting a larger planchet to be used. This idea was shelved in favor of simply making the gold dollar thinner to increase its diameter. Coins of this size were transitional with the old type during 1854, and a new design was created by Longacre to go with the new size. It portrays Liberty in an Indian feathered headdress. The olive wreath on the reverse was replaced by a larger one of corn, wheat, cotton, and tobacco. This prompted removal of the legend UNITED STATES OF AMERICA to the obverse and elimination of the stars altogether. Though attractive, coins of this type did not strike up well, and a new rendition of this "Indian Princess" theme was adopted in 1856. Larger overall, the new bust was also much lower in relief, and this greatly lessened the striking problems.

The Act of February 21, 1853, provided for yet another new coin denomination to further absorb some of the newly mined gold. The peculiar $3 gold piece was first minted in 1854, and only small quantities were coined after that first year. While this denomination seems especially strange today, there were actually numerous banknotes of that value in everyday circulation, so the coin would not have been as odd in its own time. The $3 piece bears the same design as the third type of gold dollar, while preceding it by two years. The gold dollar and the $3 piece are distinctive as the only regularly issued United States coins to carry their dates on the reverse.

The $3 piece proved to be a useless and unwanted coin from the outset, as its minuscule annual mintages suggest. The gold dollar, too, was a coin whose initial success proved to be short-lived, once the silver crisis of 1849 to 1853 was overcome. Through Congress' benign neglect, both coins managed to survive until 1889. During the final years of their minting they were produced almost solely for the benefit of coin collectors, gift-givers, and those who manufactured coin jewelry.

Despite the introduction of these new gold pieces, the supply of coined money in distant California was woefully inadequate. Gold in the form of nuggets, flakes, and dust was seemingly everywhere; so common, in fact, that its value was depressed, while the prices of other commodities in the far West were extremely high. Unrefined gold was just barely suitable for ordinary commercial transactions, but taxes and customs duties were payable to the government only in gold coins. The result was an immediate drawing away of whatever federal coins entered circulation in the West.

Californians petitioned Congress for

a local branch of the United States Mint, but what they received instead was a federal assay office. Under the administration of U.S. Assayer Augustus Humbert, in 1851 this authority began issuing octagonal gold ingots valued at $50. Though technically not coins, they served as such for large transactions, and the assay office was, in effect, a provisional United States mint. The coins were actually struck by the private coiner Moffat & Company under contract to Humbert. The obverse hub device of a heraldic eagle was engraved by famous medalist and die engraver Charles Cushing Wright, while Humbert prepared the reverse dies with their simple lathe-work pattern.

Needed for everyday commerce were coins of lesser value, and Humbert was not authorized to produce these. Instead, private firms stepped in to meet this demand, the assayers and bankers of San Francisco and surrounding communities combining their efforts to manufacture gold coins valued from $5 to $50. Some of these issues are in imitation of the federal types, with only the legends reading differently, while others bear their own distinctive designs. Among the many firms that produced gold coins in California between 1849 and 1855 were Moffat & Company; J.S. Ormsby; Baldwin & Company; Dunbar & Company; Pacific Company; Shultz & Company; and Wass, Molitor & Company.

1849 $10 gold piece produced by the Miners Bank (27 mm)

Supplying the demand for even smaller coins were San Francisco's jewelers, who struck tiny gold dollars, half dollars, and quarter dollars. Most of them were Frenchmen, and individuals such as Pierre Frontier, Eugene Deviercy, and Antoine Louis Nouizillet were among the more prolific coiners of fractional gold pieces. The majority of the private gold coin issues were short-lived, while others were produced in large numbers over a period of years.

Triumphant miners often returned to their former homes with their riches, prompting the same need for a regional coinage that existed in California. Gold coins were issued by the Oregon Exchange Company in Oregon City and by the Mormon Deseret colony at Salt Lake City, Utah. These non-California coins typically circulated only within a small geographical area, as they were subject to heavy discounting outside the communities that produced them.

A similar coinage of private manufacture arose in Colorado during that region's 1859 to 1861 gold rush. Gold pieces valued from quarter eagle to double eagle were produced by John Parsons & Company; Clark, Gruber & Company; and J.J. Conway & Company. As in California, some of these coins were near copies of federal types, while others were highly distinctive.

It is interesting to note that none of these privately made issues were illegal, as federal law before 1864 prohibited only the states from coining money, not private individuals or companies. The reliability of these coins was another matter, and assays performed both locally and at the Philadelphia Mint proved some of the coins to be worth less than their stated value. More often than not, however, the pioneer gold coins were worth as much as the federal coins or slightly more, since California gold ore included a high percentage of silver. Not only did this render the coins more intrinsically valuable than federal coins, which were alloyed primarily with copper, but it also gave the Western pieces a distinctive, brassy color.

Witnessing the success of the private gold coins in California, the Treasury

1855 Kellogg & Co. $50 gold piece made in San Francisco (41 mm)

1849 Mormon $10 gold piece (25 mm)

During the past year the coinage at the mint and its branches has exceeded $20,000,000. This has consisted chiefly in converting the coins of foreign countries. The largest amount of foreign coin imported has been at New York; and, if a branch mint were established at that city, all the foreign coin received at that port could at once be converted into our own coin, without the expense, risk, and delay of transporting it to the mint for that purpose, and the amount recoined would be much larger. Experience has proved that foreign coin, and especially foreign gold, will not circulate extensively as a currency among the people. The important measure of extending our specie circulation, both of gold and silver, and of diffusing it among our people, can only be effected by converting such foreign coin into American coin.

– President James K. Polk, addressing Congress in 1846. His support for establishment of a branch mint at New York was noted in an 1850 Senate discussion on the subject.

An existing building was enlarged to house the new mint. (From Annals of San Francisco)

Department relented and permitted Augustus Humbert to issue smaller denominations. As with the octagonal "slugs," these were coined by Moffat & Company, though they bear the imprint of the United States of America. These handsome coins likewise feature on their obverse an attractive eagle in heraldic pose. Engraved by Albert Küner from a design by Charles Cushing Wright, the obverse was paired with very plain reverse dies, which typically bore just a machine-turned pattern of lines, similar to that found on bank notes of the time. Reverse legends were limited to a simple statement of the coin's issuing authority, as well as its date and place of manufacture (SAN FRANCISCO, or simply CALIFORNIA).

In the meantime, the issue of creating a branch of the U.S. Mint at San Francisco was held up in Congress. New York's delegation wanted to have a mint of their own in New York City, and attempts to have this provision included in the San Francisco bill delayed its passage until July 3, 1852 (New York ultimately lost its bid).

The first coins of the San Francisco Mint were not struck until 1854. That year it produced large numbers of eagles and double eagles, a modest number of gold dollars, and only token mintages of quarter eagles and half eagles numbering in the hundreds. A lack of acids necessary for parting gold and silver from ore hampered coinage somewhat during this first year, and no silver coins were struck until 1855. After its first two years of operation, however, the San Francisco Mint's output was sufficient to bring to an end the colorful and historic coin issues by banks and private assayers that were so much a part of the Gold Rush years. While surviving examples are now highly prized by numismatists, most of the pioneer gold coins were deposited as bullion at the mint and melted.

CALIFORNIA

The U.S. Mint at San Francisco

The San Francisco Mint is a survivor. In fact, the mint structures survived serious earthquakes in 1857, 1865, 1906, and 1989. More importantly, perhaps, the San Francisco Mint as an institution survived a cost-cutting program in 1955 that suspended its operations for 10 years. Yet, at the beginning of the 21st century, the San Francisco Mint soldiers on, still producing coins. Of course, its output is now limited to special pieces intended specifically for collectors, but that does not diminish the importance of the historic S mintmark, which is still to be seen on the nation's coinage.

The impetus for establishing a federal mint at San Francisco was California's Gold Rush of 1849 to 1855. California had only just become a property of the United States of America in 1848, and this land was distant and geographically isolated from the rest of the nation. Though California grew rapidly enough to achieve statehood in 1850, in practical terms it was still much like a remote American colony. It took several months to travel there from the East, whether by land or sea. The immensity of the mineral wealth being drawn from California's streams and hillsides, combined with the region's relative isolation, required that local solutions be found to the need for assaying and coining.

Among the many thousands of Forty-Niners who emigrated to California during the first year of the gold rush were several who anticipated the demand for skilled assayers and refiners. In addition to having the necessary tools and chemicals, some of these Easterners decided to advance their services further, bringing with them coining

◀ *Rather than work underground in hard-rock mines, many Forty-Niners did placer mining. Hardrock mining required expensive construction and equipment, but the placer miner needed only a pan. Soil and an equal amount of water were put in the pan and the miner gently shook it to let the heavy gold sink to the bottom. Unwanted material was gradually tipped out, leaving a layer of sand that might contain specks of gold.*

1852 United States Assay Office $10 gold piece (27 mm)

equipment and dies of their own styling.

Establishing offices in and around San Francisco's Portsmouth Square were such assaying and banking firms as Moffat & Company, Baldwin and Company, Miner's Bank, and Dubosq and Company. Other coiners, such as J.S. Ormsby, operated out of Sacramento, that much closer to the source of the Sierra gold. These companies struck mostly half eagles and, to a lesser extent, eagles; some of their coins were in close approximation of the federal types, while others bore highly distinctive designs. Though the majority of these firms produced coins equal in value to the federal pieces, a few did not, and all such privately minted gold coins were generally discredited in an 1851 panic.

Still, the short-term success of these gold coins served to highlight an urgent need for reliable assaying and coining facilities. Whatever coins were carried to California by emigrants seldom circulated beyond one or two transactions. Since federal offices, most notably the U.S. Customs House in San Francisco, required payment in lawful money, most United States coins quickly found their way back to the Treasury in Washington. The supply of such pieces was never adequate to the demand, and the general lack of coined money was a great hardship for everyone in California. Gold dust and nuggets, then so abundant, traded at a sharp discount from the Eastern market price of about $16 per ounce. The cost of transporting raw gold to the mints at Philadelphia or New Orleans for coining greatly reduced the net return to both miners and bankers, while such shipments were also made at the risk of theft and other losses. A state assay office was established by the California legislature on April 20, 1850, to provide some standardization for the payment of gold depositors, but the U.S. Constitution forbade the coining of money by the states.

The Arrival of Augustus Humbert

The solution obvious to everyone in California was that the area should have its own branch of the United States Mint. This, however, was not the simple issue that it may have seemed to San Franciscans. The U.S. Mint's administrators were routinely against the proliferation of branch mints, citing the failure of the Charlotte and Dahlonega mints to live up to expectations as proof that such operations were not cost-effective. The issue of where to locate branch mints was also highly politicized, as congressmen naturally sought to locate these prestigious institutions in their own districts. Specifically, New York City was campaigning vigorously for a branch mint, as was St. Louis to a lesser extent. While these debates raged in Congress, the proposed San Francisco Mint was held hostage for several years.

As an interim solution, Congress authorized establishment of a federal assay office for San Francisco on September 30, 1850. Under the direction of Augustus Humbert, it was empowered to purchase bullion at market rates and process the metal into ingots of fixed values ranging from $50 to $10,000. These ingots, though not officially called coins, were to be coin-like in form and carry the normal statutory inscriptions typical of United States coins. In a thinly veiled subterfuge, Congress had created a de facto mint at San Francisco that would produce a de facto coinage.

Since Humbert lacked the facilities to perform this work himself, the refining and coining work was contracted to [John Little] Moffat & Company, the most respected and trusted of the various assaying/coining firms then operating in San Francisco. Octagonal in shape, the "slugs" that Moffat struck for Humbert were an immediate success, and they quickly prompted calls for coins of lesser value. It was not until January 7, 1852, that Humbert received permission from Washington to strike $10 and $20 pieces, by which time the hardships created by the lack of smaller coins had prompted a resumption of their coining by private firms. As Humbert's coins began to fall from the press that winter, they circulated side-by-side with the privately made gold pieces. Under the law of that time, commercial coins were still permitted, though they enjoyed no legal-tender status.

1872-S Liberty Seated half dime (15.5 mm)

San Francisco Finally Gets Its Mint

Much of the delay Humbert experienced in receiving permission to coin smaller denominations was due to the impending establishment of a federal mint at San Francisco. After months of rancorous debate, this bill was finally passed on July 3, 1852. No action was taken immediately, and when the deadline for submission of construction bids came on March 3, 1853, without a viable proposal, it had to be extended. A commitment to build the mint structure for $239,000 was submitted by a Mr. Butler, and his bid was initially accepted by the government. Further negotiation, however, saw the contract transferred to the firm of Curtis, Perry and Ward, these three being the remaining members of Moffat & Company, their namesake

This engraving shows San Francisco as it appeared about a year after the Gold Rush began. The influx of gold-seekers from around the world added to the town's population, which in turn spurred economic growth. (From the Illustrated London News, *October 19, 1850)*

When the Mint was being completed in 1854 the then superintendent in endeavoring to make a reasonable contract for water supply from a private source, became personally offended at the defy: "You must have water, you can't get it elsewhere, pay our price or do without." There was then about $1,600 of an appropriation for other purposes, unexpended. He proceeded to use this money in seeking water and personal satisfaction at one and the same time. The drillers had been at work for weeks, $1,500 had been spent and no water. Disheartened and wondering how he could "square" himself with the Department for using the money without authority, he left on a vacation, scarcely had he reached his destination, when the news came that water had been struck.

– From "A Jaunt Across the Continent" by Farran Zerbe, published in August 1906 in *The Numismatist.*

having withdrawn from the business.

The partnership of Joseph R. Curtis, Philo H. Perry and Samuel H. Ward agreed to furnish both the structure and equipment for the federal mint. In actual fact, the "new" mint building was just an enlargement of the existing Curtis, Perry and Ward structure, which would quickly prove inadequate to the mint's needs. Since the federal mint would wholly succeed the United States Assay Office in San Francisco, Curtis, Perry and Ward's old contract to coin ingots for that establishment was voided, and the assay office passed into history on December 14, 1853. There then followed a trying period in which the San Francisco Mint existed in name only, unready to actually strike coins.

Completion of the expanded mint building and installation of its machinery delayed production until April 3, 1854, when the first gold double eagles fell from the press. These were, of course, of the regular federal type. Before year's end, large numbers of $10 and $20 gold pieces would be issued bearing the S mintmark, along with a somewhat smaller mintage of gold dollars.

For reasons now uncertain, mere token numbers of the gold half eagle and quarter eagle were struck dated 1854-S. These were probably intended as souvenirs of the new mint, though the worn condition of the few known survivors tends to refute this notion. The first gold $3 pieces struck at the San Francisco Mint were dated 1855, and this denomination was never produced in large numbers.

A shortage of the acids necessary to fully refine silver prevented the coining of this metal until the following year. Silver half dollars and quarter dollars were struck at the mint in 1855, followed by the first dimes in 1856, silver dollars in 1859, and half dimes in 1863. Of these, only the half dollars were struck in quantity during the early years of the mint.

A Difficult Job at Best

That any coins could be produced in numbers sufficient to meet the demand seems miraculous, given the inadequate space the mint offered. Just 60 feet square, the building was further burdened by its location. Commercial Street, despite its grand name, was and remains today little more than an alley in downtown San Francisco. An 1856 article documented a visit to the infant mint, in which a writer for *Hutchings' California Magazine* expressed astonishment "at the aggregate amount of coin produced in so short a time, in such a small and very inconvenient building." The reporter further observed that, "every man was more or less in the other's way."

The mint's first superintendent was Dr. Lewis Aiken Birdsall, who had no previous experience in coining matters and was evidently appointed through the influence of his son-in-law, California Congressman Milton S. Latham. Of greater usefulness were the new mint's melter and refiner, John Hewston Jr., late of the Philadelphia Mint, and its chief coiner, John M. Eckfeldt. The Eckfeldt family had by then become something of a dynasty in U.S. Mint service, one or more members serving the Mint in some capacity from 1796 into the 1920s! Appointed assayer was Hungarian expatriate Agoston Haraszthy. Though the latter was charged with embezzlement in 1857, a sensational trial ultimately proved that the missing metal had wafted up through the mint's chimneys and been deposited on neighboring streets and rooftops. Haraszthy was cleared of all wrongdoing, and the mint's chimneys were fitted with screens.

The insufficient size of the mint building became even more evident as production increased during the 1860s. The Comstock Lode of 1859 and subsequent silver discoveries in Nevada and the surrounding states more than compensated for the drop-off in California's gold production. Approval for a new mint structure was given in 1869, and the cornerstone was laid the following year. It took another four years to complete the mint building at the corner of Fifth and Mission Streets, but the great effort clearly showed. A truly grand edifice, the new San Francisco Mint was a large structure in the Greek Revival style. Three stories tall, it also included an attic and a basement with walls six feet thick. Built of brick and finished in granite, the new mint was an imposing figure on the San Francisco skyline. At the time of its opening in November 1874, it was the largest mint in the world, easily dwarfing the main mint at Philadelphia. So great was the capacity of this new facility that its construction allowed the U.S. Mint to accept coining orders from other countries. This was authorized under a law passed January 29, 1874, in anticipation of the new mint's completion.

Construction of the second San Francisco mint (above) as seen from the south, circa 1870. Below is an image of the coiner's weighing room in the completed building, circa 1882 to 1885.

A Structure Sound and Mighty

The opening of the expanded San Francisco Mint came just in time, as economic conditions finally permitted the reintroduction of silver coinage to general circulation. Though both silver and gold had never ceased circulating in the West, the reappearance of silver in the East was expedited by the greater coining capacity of the new San Francisco Mint. This facility also assumed the lion's share of Trade dollar coinage, a logical move in view of the fact that these coins were intended for shipment to Asia. When the standard silver dollar was revived in 1878, San Francisco was one of the biggest producers of these unneeded coins, though that burden was largely shifted to the Philadelphia and New Orleans Mints after 1882.

The production of gold coins at San Francisco was also increased following the opening of the new mint, and this work accelerated during the 1890s when gold was discovered in the Cripple Creek area of Colorado. Vastly greater amounts spewed forth later in that decade from Alaska and the Klondike, and the San Francisco Mint was the coiner of choice for most of this bullion. The greater part of the mint's gold production was in the form of bullion bars, a fact often overlooked by numismatists. While these seldom survive to be collected as numismatic items, they are an integral part of this mint's history, as they are for the other U.S. mints.

The San Francisco Mint of 1874 lost its title as world's largest when the new Philadelphia Mint opened in 1901, and its percentage of the nation's total

The second San Francisco Mint as it looked in 1958. Because the mint's basement had a high ceiling, the building's main floor sat about 12 feet above street level. Inside, most of the woodwork was made of golden mahogany. The building's cornerstone reportedly contained a copper box full of coins, photographs, and newspapers, and mementos from the celebration on the day it was put in place.

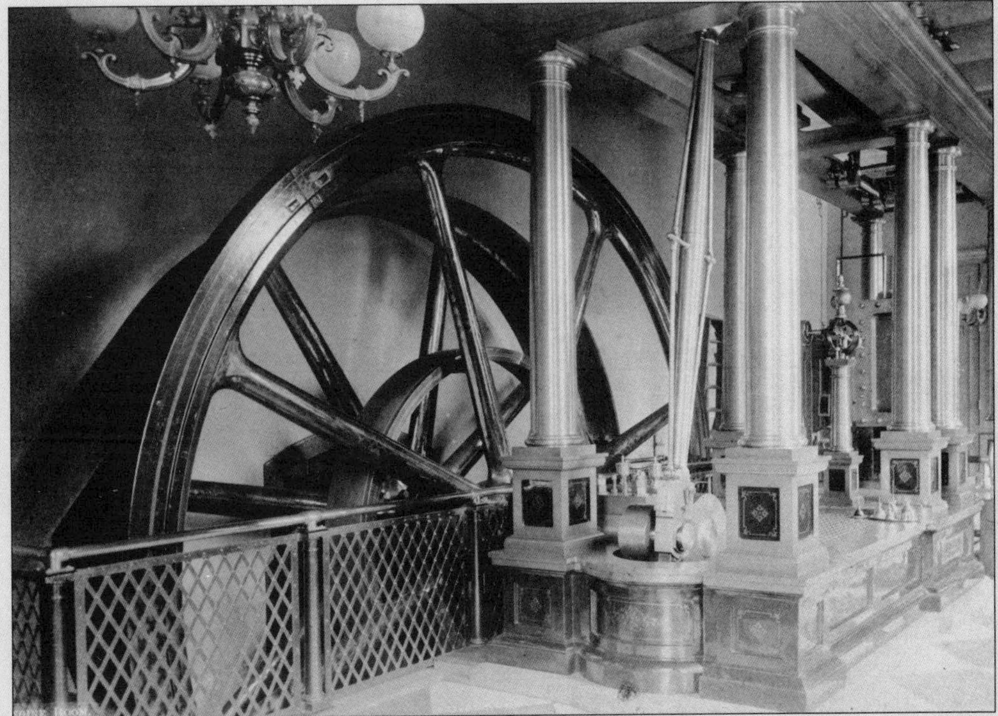

The engine room in the second San Francisco Mint, circa 1882 to 1885

coin production diminished over the next few decades. Throughout this time, however, it maintained an enviable reputation for security and service. The quality of the coins produced there was very high from the time of the mint's opening through the first decade of the 20th century. Economies introduced by the Mint hierarchy in Washington brought about a visible diminishing of quality during the 1910s and '20s, but this trend had begun to reverse itself by the time of the Fifth Street mint's closing in 1937.

Farran Zerbe

In the destruction, I reason many rare coins were reduced to bullion, particularly Territorial pieces. They were not in the hands of the collectors or prized as numismatic specimens; simply keepsakes of pioneers or their families as mementoes of Early Days.

– From "A Jaunt Across the Continent" by Farran Zerbe, published in August 1906 in *The Numismatist.* Zerbe was visiting San Francisco when the earthquake struck, sparking fires that burned much of the city.

The Mint's Finest Hour

Perhaps the most dramatic moment in the history of the 1874 San Francisco Mint came on April 18, 1906. A tremendous earthquake rocked the city at dawn, and by midday fires were sweeping through the downtown area. The mint structure was seriously threatened, as every building surrounding it succumbed to the flames. Putting aside thoughts of their own safety, most of the mint's employees left their homes and reported for duty. It was only through the effective leadership of its superintendent, Frank A. Leach, and the heroic sense of duty on the part of its employees, that the San Francisco Mint was saved. As windows melted and the granite facing shattered, the employees held their ground, fighting the fire with the mint's water reserves. The mint was the only federal building in San Francisco that did not perish.

With the streets largely impassable, most mint employees were compelled to remain on-site for the next several days, and they were soon joined by a large number of refugees seeking

The San Francisco Mint withstood the city's 1906 earthquake. It was the only building for blocks that was not destroyed.

shelter in the building or on its grounds. Emergency bedding was assembled, and the mint also provided meals for all callers, as its restaurant was the only such operation surviving for miles in any direction.

Within a day or two it became evident that the mint was also the only financial structure to escape destruction. The city's banks were in ruins, their records and cash reserves untouchable until the metal vaults cooled enough to avoid instant incineration of their contents upon exposure to air. Under these circumstances, the San Francisco Mint assumed an unprecedented role as the city's sole financial institution. Banks had emergency funds transferred from the East, and used the mint's vaults to store this wealth. Checks could then be issued by the banks against credit they held with the mint, and this was how San Francisco began to clear away its debris and start the rebuilding process. So exemplary was Superintendent Leach's handling of the entire episode that Mint Director George E. Roberts wrote him on April 23, "The Bureau of the Mint is living in the light of your glory these days."

Frank A. Leach

San Francisco visited early this morning by terrible earthquake followed by fire which has burned the greater part of business district. Mint building not damaged much by shock. Every building around the mint burned to the ground. It is the only building not destroyed for blocks. I reached building before the worst of the fire came, finding a lot of our men there, stationed at points of vantage from roof to basement, and with our fire apparatus and without help from the fire departent we successfully fought the fire away, although all the windows on Mint Avenue and back side third story were burned out; fire coming in drove us back for a time. Adjusting rooms and refinery damaged some and heavy stone cornice on that side of building flaked off. The roof burned some little. ...

– Telegram from Frank A. Leach to Mint Director George E. Roberts, sent the evening of April 18, 1906

A New Mint

Leach went on to succeed Roberts as Mint director the following year, and business as usual resumed at the San Francisco Mint. The opening of the Denver Mint in 1906 gradually led to that facility taking over much of the former's role as the U.S. Mint's principal bullion depository, and the overall importance of the San Francisco Mint diminished. Eventually declared obsolete, a replacement structure was authorized in 1934, and construction of the new mint at Hermann and Duboce Streets began the following year. A dedication ceremony was held May 15, 1937, and production commenced in October. Surprisingly, the new mint building was not significantly larger than the old, an apparent oversight that would doom it to obsolescence just 20 years later.

Though highly touted as one of the most secure structures in the world, the new San Francisco Mint was nonetheless broken into the very next year. Rather than being victimized by a gang of thieves bent on looting it of gold and silver, the mint was violated by two teenage boys named Paul Francis and William Gallagher who were simply doing it for the thrill. Their slim frames, the result of Depression-era hardship, allowed them to slither through a ground-floor window before quickly being apprehended by a guard.

Embarrassed officials ordered a quick retrofitting of bars on all accessible windows, as well as the installation of floodlights, three sets of iron gates, and a five-foot-high rock wall around the grounds.

Following World War II, the U.S. Mint sought to employ the lessons learned from America's rapid retooling by instituting widespread improvements in efficiency. The most pressing need was for greater rolling mill capacity so that larger ingots could be run into much

Safeguards against holdups will be numerous and effective. Heading the list will be a network of pipes by which the place can be flooded with tear gas almost instantly. A gun tower will cover all approaches. Defense lights, set in the walls, will illuminate the exterior at night. Both front and rear entrances will have two electrically-operated steel doors, so controlled that only one of each set can be opened at a time. A self-starting power generator will automatically begin running the moment anyone tampers with the regular service and thus foil efforts to darken the building and cripple its protective devices. There will be two alarm systems, a watchmen's report system and a radio communication system. To keep Uncle Sam's gold and silver safe, the storage vault and the melting and refining vault will have reinforced concrete walls two feet thick.

– From "New Mint Strong as a Fortress," published October 1936 in *P.G.&E. Progress* (Pacific Gas & Electric)

longer strips for the blanking presses. This change required very long spaces, something the Philadelphia and Denver Mints possessed but the compact San Francisco Mint sorely lacked. While productivity at the former two steadily improved, the San Francisco Mint continued to struggle with its limited capacity. By the mid-1950s, U.S. Mint auditors determined that it was more cost-effective to produce additional coins at the Denver Mint and ship them to San Francisco than it was to actually make them in California. The San Francisco Mint thus ceased coining on March 31, 1955, though it continued to function as a federal assay office for the next several years, this title becoming official in 1962.

The Mint Makes a Comeback

The massive nationwide coin shortage of the early 1960s caught the U.S. Mint totally unprepared and prompted a number of radical emergency measures. Among these was a partial reactivation of the San Francisco mint in 1964. Though its coining presses had long since been removed, in the fall of that year it began punching blanks for shipment to the Denver Mint. A year later, with the general coin shortage now complicated further by the introduction of copper-nickel-clad coins, the San Francisco Assay Office began coining cents and dimes. To avoid any hoarding of the always-popular S-Mint coins, these lacked mintmarks and were thus indistinguishable from those made at Philadelphia.

The presses used were on loan from Denver, which had obtained them a short time earlier from the Department of Defense. These slow-action presses were originally made for stamping artillery shell cases, but had been refitted as coin presses by the Denver Mint to augment its existing production during the coin shortage.

Mint Director Mary Brooks

As the San Francisco Assay Office continued to make coins during the next several years, it eventually received conventional coin presses. The S mintmark was restored in 1968, though only cents and nickels were coined there for circulation. Hoarding of these coins led Mint Director Mary Brooks to remove the mintmark yet again in 1975. Only during 1979 to 1981 were coins bearing the letter S once more produced for circulation, these being the ill-fated Anthony dollars. Most of this facility's work since then has consisted of striking commemoratives and proof coins for collectors, though S-less cents were struck for circulation as late as 1983.

San Francisco's status as a United States mint was finally restored in 1988. Normally closed to visitors, guided tours were offered on a very infrequent basis and were invariably sold out within hours of being announced. Because of its small size, the mint has no visitors' gallery, and tours were thus of the coining floor itself, accounting for their great desirability. Security measures prompted by the 9/11 terrorist attacks imposed an indefinite suspension of tours.

The foundation of the 1937 San Francisco Mint goes deep into a hill of solid rock and was engineered to withstand earthquakes. The site has steep cliffs on three sides and sits 100 feet above traffic on the fourth.

A Historic Legacy

The San Francisco Mint building of 1854 was sold to commercial interests after 1874 and extensively rebuilt in the decades that followed. The structure that stood on that site in 1906 was swept away by the earthquake and resulting fire. Only parts of the basement remain, and these are on view from street level through a glass enclosure in the existing modern building. A plaque was mounted outside many years ago to mark this important site, and it remains in place today.

The mint building of 1874 was used by various federal agencies until being abandoned in 1968 after years of external deterioration. A plan to demolish the structure to make way for the construction of a downtown college building was vigorously opposed by local preservationists and the California State Numismatic Association. When the mint was transferred from the General Services Administration back to the United States Treasury Department, the way was cleared for its restoration and reopening as a museum of numismatics and Old West history.

The museum debuted in stages during 1973 and 1974, but poor publicity, an even poorer neighborhood, and gradually diminishing displays led to generally low attendance. Though the area was already undergoing an economic revival, the museum was hastily closed in 1993. A brief reprieve failed to prevent final closure the following year, and the building currently remains unoccupied. As this is written, however, a viable plan has been submitted for mixed educational and retail use that still awaits funding.

1908-S Indian Head cent (19 mm)

One Artist's Vision

Once daguerreotype photography became available in the United States, there was less work for portrait painters, even one as talented as James Barton Longacre. After Chief Engraver Christian Gobrecht died in 1844, Longacre was relieved to be hired as his replacement, a post he acquired through the political influence of Senator John C. Calhoun. Though he was a respected intaglio portrait engraver, he soon found himself in an uphill battle with Mint officials who were, understandably, prejudiced against him for his lack of training in coin and medal engraving.

Longacre persevered, however, and remained chief engraver until his death in 1869, his artistic vision gracing 60 years of American coins.

Though many appreciate his work, he does have his critics. In his book *Numismatic Art in America*, Cornelius Vermeule wrote, "Uniform in their dullness, lack of inspiration, and even quaintness, Longacre's contributions to patterns and regular coinages were a decided step backwards."

Longacre executed these sketches as possible designs for the "standard silver" coins. The pattern coin seen above is the obverse of a 25¢ standard silver piece. *(See page 91)*

James Longacre in a watercolor self-portrait, circa 1845. His engraving tools can be seen in the foreground.

Each of these sketches of Lady Liberty – the coronet, plumed headdress, and feather headdress designs – appeared on United States coins.

CHAPTER SIX

A New Problem–Too Many Coins

While the first 60 years of the United States as a nation were defined by chronic coin shortages, the period between 1853 and the onset of the Civil War in 1861 saw Americans inundated by an overabundance of certain coins. Beginning in 1853, the new reduced-weight, subsidiary silver coins were supplied in far greater numbers than the economy could absorb. The same was true for the new small cents introduced in 1857. How these situations arose makes for a fascinating study in the economics of supply and demand.

The Act of February 21, 1853, stipulated that the subsidiary silver coins would be issued only in exchange for gold coins. This was necessary to prevent a redundancy from developing. No longer being a standard of value, these coins carried a legal-tender limit of just $5, and there was no provision in the law for redeeming quantities in excess of that amount. Tying the amount of silver coins in circulation to the gold supply assured that the silver pieces would not become a nuisance to merchants and bankers.

This policy was clearly understood by Congress, but in 1853 the nation was starved for silver coins. The need to get the new issues into circulation was so great that it overruled both the law and common sense. To speed their distribution, Mint Director George N. Eckert offered to pay out the subsidiary silver coins in exchange for either gold or silver bullion, at the option of the seller. This risky practice was continued by his successor, James R. Snowden. Incredibly, such a blatant violation of the law received official sanction from Treasury Secretary James Guthrie on April 7, 1853.

This activity would not have been a serious economic problem if the Mint made its silver purchases at prevailing market values. Instead, in an effort to speed the distribution of silver coins, it announced a fixed price of $1.21 per

CAUTION!!

COLORED PEOPLE

OF BOSTON, ONE & ALL,

You are hereby respectfully CAUTIONED and advised, to avoid conversing with the

Watchmen and Police Officers of Boston,

For since the recent ORDER OF THE MAYOR & ALDERMEN, they are empowered to act as

KIDNAPPERS

AND

Slave Catchers,

And they have already been actually employed in KIDNAPPING, CATCHING, AND KEEPING SLAVES. Therefore, if you value your LIBERTY, and the *Welfare of the Fugitives* among you, *Shun* them in every possible manner, as so many *HOUNDS* on the track of the most unfortunate of your race.

Keep a Sharp Look Out for KIDNAPPERS, and have TOP EYE open.

APRIL 24, 1851.

Disagreement over the issue of slavery was a root cause of the Civil War. Some historians believe the war actually began in 1619, when the first slaves arrived in Jamestown, Virginia. Others blame the cotton gin, whose invention created a "cotton kingdom" in the South that relied heavily on slave labor. This 1851 broadside warns escaped slaves to avoid capture in Boston.

Legislation authorizing the new smaller-size cent had not yet been enacted, so the approximately 1,500 Flying Eagle cents struck for 1856 were not authorized Mint issues. (19 mm)

1855 pattern for the Flying Eagle cent (about 25 mm)

ounce. This figure was sufficiently high that the Mint was virtually flooded with silver whenever the market value of this metal dipped even slightly. With no option but to coin this silver into fractional pieces, the excess of these coins in circulation soon became as much of a problem as their scarcity had been just a couple of years earlier.

Belatedly recognizing the situation, Director Snowden ordered that payments for purchases of bullion would henceforth be made only three-fourths in silver, the balance to be paid out in gold coin. Still, this was not enough to stem the flood of fractional silver into circulation. Since most of the Mint's bullion purchases were of silver and only three-fourths of its payments were in that metal, the Mint soon acquired an unmanageable surplus of the subsidiary coins.

Merchants and bankers complained bitterly about the huge accumulations of silver pieces they had received in the course of normal business activity. These coins were not acceptable in payment of taxes or customs duties, since they were not defined as "lawful money" of the United States. This left holders of these hoards no option but to sell their silver coins at a discount to brokers, who then dispersed them in smaller quantities, from which new hoards soon developed. This endless cycle was a continual problem after 1853, and it was not solved until 1862, when the economic conditions imposed by the Civil War again drove silver from circulation.

Mint medal depicting Director James R. Snowden (82 mm)

In addition to problems with silver coinage, the U.S. Mint began to address the obsolescence of large copper cents and half cents. The half cents in particular were never popular and were coined in relatively small numbers throughout their 65-year history. In the words of Mint Director Snowden, "People will not take the trouble to make a cent with two pieces of money." On the other hand, the cent denomination was crucial to daily commerce, though its cumbersome size weighed against its utility.

The scarcity of silver coins during 1849 to 1853 had pushed both of these coins to the forefront and only served to highlight their shortcomings. Merchants of the time were often compelled to make change with large handfuls of coppers and subsidiary silver trimes, the cents being particularly unwelcome when delivered in quantity. In addition, the Mint was hard pressed to make enough of the coppers, and it was at risk of suffering a loss in their coining. While the cent and half cent at one time produced a small profit, in the 1850s Snowden remarked that they "barely paid expenses."

With the silver shortage relieved after 1853, a redundancy of coppers developed, the half cents being especially difficult for the Mint to distribute. Efforts to find a suitable replacement for the cent prompted a series of pattern coins beginning in 1850. A number of experiments tested the concept of a coin with a center hole. This peculiar format was derived from the desire to reduce the size and weight of the cent while retaining its intrinsic value. The use of metals such as billon (an alloy of one part silver to nine parts copper) and various blends of copper and nickel revealed that Congress still clung to the outdated notion that the cent must be worth nearly its face value in metal. Other patterns included copper coins just slightly smaller and thinner than the existing type. A number of these featured a beautiful rendition of the Peale/Gobrecht soaring eagle used for the silver dollars of 1836 to 1839. The real solution, however, lay in a much smaller coin than the current cent, whatever its composition might be.

After the usual political wrangling, a bill was signed into law on February 21,

1857, that introduced a number of important improvements to the nation's coinage. In addition to abolishing the half cent and revoking the legal-tender status applied previously to many foreign coins out of sheer necessity, the new law called for a smaller cent weighing just 72 grains and composed of .880 copper and .120 nickel. Designed by James B. Longacre, the Flying Eagle cent features on its obverse the Peale/Gobrecht soaring eagle, used previously only on coins of limited production. Around the periphery are the legend UNITED STATES OF AMERICA above and the date below. The reverse of this type bears the wreath of corn, wheat, cotton, and tobacco already used on gold dollars and $3 pieces, enclosing the value ONE CENT.

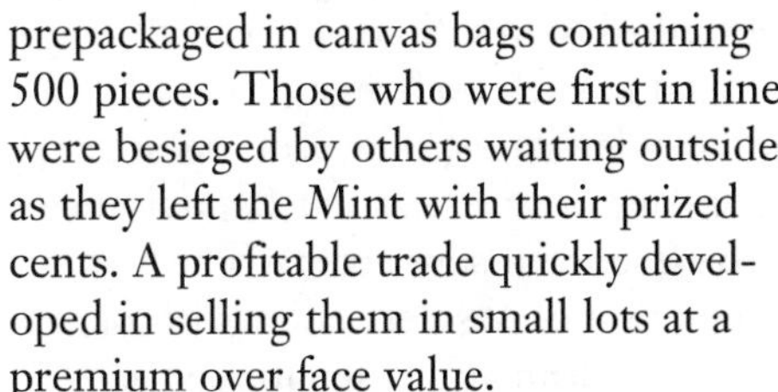

James Guthrie

To speed the withdrawal of obsolete coins, a clever and wide-ranging redemption plan was devised for the new cents. In addition to exchanging them for United States gold and silver coins, the copper-nickel cents would be traded to the public for old copper cents and half cents, as well as any Spanish-American silver coins. The latter, whatever their condition, would be exchanged for a period of two years from the date of passage at their traditional values of 25¢ for the 2-*real* piece, 12½¢ for the *real* and 6¼¢ for the *medio*, or half *real*. Since most of the Spanish coins in circulation were badly worn and subject to discounting, this led to brokers buying them up at their bullion value and then redeeming them with the Mint at their higher exchange value. While the government did not welcome such profiteering, it was considered a necessary evil if the obsolete coins were to be retired. Though the new silver coinage of 1853 had been partially successful in driving these foreign coins from the cities, by common custom they continued to circulate widely in rural areas as late as the 1870s. The law of February 21, 1857, revoked the legal status of all foreign coins, a goal of Congress since the earliest days of the U.S. Mint. In keeping with a tradition established in 1792, the new cent likewise carried no legal-tender status.

By May 25, 1857, the official release date for the small cents, the Philadelphia Mint had produced some three million pieces. Mint Director Snowden wrote to Treasury Secretary Guthrie, "Nearly all of this amount will be paid out today." A pair of booths was erected at the Mint that day to facilitate the much-heralded exchange of coins. One was labeled "cents for cents," another "cents for silver." The new coins were prepackaged in canvas bags containing 500 pieces. Those who were first in line were besieged by others waiting outside as they left the Mint with their prized cents. A profitable trade quickly developed in selling them in small lots at a premium over face value.

The *Philadelphia Bulletin* made a prescient observation in speaking of the half cents and large cents turned in that day: "... as regards the old cents there will be 'nary red' to be seen, except such as will be found in the cabinets of coin collectors." Indeed, many 19th-century numismatists later attributed their passion for collecting to the retirement of the old coppers. So successful was this redemption program that it was extended when the original two-year deadline loomed in 1859.

There was one inherent flaw, however. While the U.S. Treasury would exchange new cents for Spanish silver at an official rate of 8 *reales* to the dollar, the value of these coins to banks and all other government offices was some 10 *reales* per dollar. In other words, a coin carrying a face value of 2 *reales* had a market value of only 20¢ but an exchange value at the Mint of 25¢. Brokers were soon buying worn, foreign silver coins at a discount from people who could not travel to the

1840 Braided Hair half cent (23 mm)

1850 Braided Hair large cent (28 mm)

1859 cent (19 mm)

From 1860 to 1909, this cent reverse with a shield and arrows replaced the simple wreath and bow seen above.

Philadelphia Mint or to one of the various sub-treasury locations. Exchanging these pieces for their full redemption value, the speculator then used the new cents received to buy additional obsolete silver in a revolving racket.

This operation was sufficiently profitable that brokers actually resorted to advertising for foreign silver coins, offering to pay a premium over their market value, yet still leaving themselves enough room to profit on their redemption value when exchanged for cents. This practice actually encouraged the importation of additional foreign coins into the United States. Since the cents being paid out in such exchanges bore no legal-tender status, they soon became redundant and were as much a nuisance as the fractional silver coins. The redemption of obsolete coins with new cents was ultimately discontinued in 1860, and the onset of the Civil War shortly thereafter drove all coins from circulation, abruptly ending this embarrassment of riches.

1863 Seated Liberty half dime (15.5 mm)

With all United States coins other than the silver dollar circulating freely, the Mint was now able to concentrate on improvements in its designs. As its chief engraver since 1844, James B. Longacre gradually overcame the lack of experience in die sinking and relief engraving that characterized his early years at the Mint. While all of the silver coins and a number of the gold coins received some form of retouching between 1858 and 1860, the most obvious changes were to the cent, half dime, and dime.

The copper-nickel cent introduced in 1857 proved to be successful in concept, yet its design did not strike up well with any consistency. The inherent difficulty in working the hard, copper-nickel alloy contributed to this problem. A wide variety of pattern coins was produced in 1858, as possible alternative designs were tested. The most popular of these designs, and the one ultimately chosen for mass production beginning in 1859, was Longacre's bust of Liberty, facing left and adorned with a feathered headdress. UNITED STATES OF AMERICA is inscribed around the obverse periphery, with the date below Liberty's bust. Though the goddess clearly does not bear Native American features, these coins long ago acquired the popular title "Indian Head" cents. The reverse of this type features two laurel branches, fashioned into a wreath and tied with a bow at the bottom, enclosing the value ONE CENT. Evidently, this simple wreath was deemed undesirable, as a more elaborate oak wreath with arrows and topped by a Union shield was adopted for the cents of 1860 and subsequent years. The shield was added at the urging of Mint Director Snowden, who believed it gave the coin "more National character." One concession to the previous type was made in the placement of a small laurel sprig around the arrows. Not until 1864 did Longacre sign his work, and his initial appears thereafter as a tiny letter L on the vertical ribbon in Liberty's hair.

The silver dime and half dime were also revised in 1860. Their slim laurel wreaths were replaced with much fuller ones of corn, wheat, oak, and tobacco. This prompted removal of the legend UNITED STATES OF AMERICA to each coin's obverse, in place of the stars used previously. These revisions have been tentatively attributed to Assistant Engraver Anthony C. Paquet, whose distinctive style of tall, shadowed lettering is evident in the new legend. Dimes of this type remained in production as late as 1891, while the half dime met an early demise with the Mint Act of 1873.

Chapter Seven

Civil War and the U.S. Economy

Abraham Lincoln

The 1860s dawned under ominous clouds of discontent. While all was seemingly well with the U.S. Mint and its coinage (with the sole exception of the forlorn silver dollar), the same could not be said of the nation as a whole. In fact, the United States of America would soon cease to be whole, as the election of Abraham Lincoln as president in 1860 became the final straw for the already disgruntled Southern states. The fury of secession was in the air. Beginning with South Carolina, seven states withdrew from the United States and formed their own loose assembly known as the Confederate States of America (CSA). Four more states joined the CSA soon afterward, while President Lincoln pledged that federal troops and state volunteers would take back by force those states in rebellion. When Southerners began their siege of Fort Sumter in South Carolina's Charleston Harbor in April 1861, the war of words escalated into a war of hastily raised armies that would last four more years before the Confederacy was ultimately defeated.

Even before the fighting started, the mints at New Orleans, Charlotte, and Dahlonega were seized by their respective state governments and later turned over to the Confederacy. Small numbers of gold coins were produced from United States dies at all three facilities after their seizure, and a somewhat larger quantity of half dollars was coined at the New Orleans Mint. Within months, however, the existing supplies of bullion ran out, and the introduction of paper currency by both sides soon drove all hard money from circulation. The mint at New Orleans was recaptured by federal troops in 1862, and the other two near the end of the war, but none of them were operated by the United States during the war years. In fact, only the New Orleans Mint resumed coining, and that was not until 1879.

Because "greenbacks" were not redeemable in coin on demand, worried citizens began hoarding gold and silver coins.

War inevitably has some effect on a nation's economy, and this disruption is often mirrored in its changing coinage. Still, nearly a year passed before the first signs of trouble appeared. In order to finance the war effort, both the United States of America and the Confederate States of America issued paper money. While the CSA notes were mostly payable after the war's conclusion and

Plainly the central idea of secession is the essence of anarchy. A majority held in restraint by constitutional checks and limitations, and always changing easily with deliberate changes of popular opinions and sentiments, is the only true sovereign of a free people. Whoever rejects it does of necessity fly to anarchy or to despotism. Unanimity is impossible. The rule of a minority, as a permanent arrangement, is wholly inadmissible; so that, rejecting the majority principle, anarchy or despotism in some form is all that is left.

– From President Lincoln's inaugural speech, March 4, 1861. The Civil War began on April 12, when Confederate forces fired on Fort Sumter.

thus quickly depreciated in value, the first issue of United States notes (known as Demand Notes) was payable "on demand" and was considered more trustworthy. The Demand Notes debuted in the summer of 1861 and were initially successful, yet there appeared a growing tendency on the part of note holders to quickly redeem them for specie (gold and silver coins). This, of course, entirely defeated the purpose of the notes, which was to enable the government to acquire and reserve gold for making international payments. As their reserves of hard money were gradually depleted, in December of 1861 banks across the country declared that they would no longer pay out gold in exchange for notes. The latter then found their way to the Treasury and the various sub-treasuries in such numbers that the government had no choice but to follow the banks and suspend specie payments early in 1862.

This action quickly diminished the public's faith in the Demand Notes. Their fears were reinforced when the next issue of paper currency (known officially as United States Notes, but commonly referred to as "greenbacks") was not redeemable in coin on demand. Combined with the general sense of unease that set in as the war entered its second year with no end in sight, this development led to economic uncertainty and the widespread hoarding of first gold, then silver coins. Payment of the latter was suspended in June 1862, and by summer both metals had vanished from circulation. Even the lowly copper-nickel

Canadian Coins in American Circulation

An interesting supplement to the history of America's coinage is the cross-circulation of U.S. and Canadian coins. United States coins circulated freely in Canada and were quite commonplace during the 19th century. This was particularly true after 1862, when economic conditions in the U.S. precluded the domestic circulation of silver coins and made it profitable to ship them northward. So abundant were American fractional silver pieces that they became a national nuisance to Canadians. Since U.S. coins did not have legal-tender status in Canada, banks could legally refuse to accept them for deposit. Desperate merchants typically paid brokers to dispose of the coins, and these brokers would take them only at a steep discount. The brokers then put the foreign coins right back in circulation at face value, ensuring a profit for themselves and repeating the bothersome cycle.

When the Dominion of Canada began receiving its own coinage from London's Royal Mint in 1870, it was hoped that these pieces would finally displace the American coins. The number of Canadian coins issued initially proved inadequate, and Canada was ultimately forced to undertake costly measures to bring back the American pieces. This had been largely accomplished by the time Canada's own mint began operating at Ottawa in 1908.

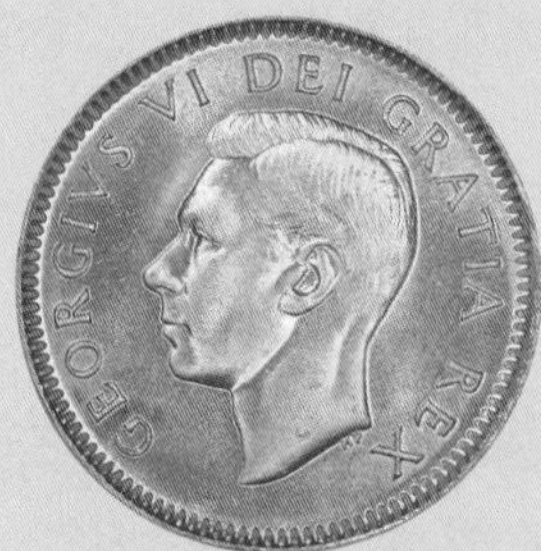

1950 Canadian 10-cent piece with a portrait of Britain's King George VI

During the 20th century, Canadian coins were commonly seen in American border states, and it is likely that U.S. issues were just as common in southern Canada. At the beginning of the 21st century, however, Canadian coins have become a rarity in this country. The disparity in value between U.S. and Canadian dollars is partly to blame, but there also exists a more conscious effort to exclude Canadian coins. When both countries used silver coinage (Canada's lasted until 1968), the pieces exhibited similar properties and would work in vending machines. But when the U.S. switched to a copper-nickel-clad composition for its coins of 10¢ and higher, and Canada to pure nickel for the same denominations, their respective issues were no longer compatible. The cross-circulation of Canadian and American coins is now greatly reduced.

cents were ultimately considered a commodity rather than a currency. While just two years earlier cents and silver coins had been viewed as an overabundant nuisance, they were now too precious to spend. With their face values linked to that of the depreciating paper dollar, coins became worth more as metal than as a medium of exchange.

The disappearance of gold coins from circulation is easily understood, since the depreciating value of paper money made gold the object of hoarding. The loss of silver, however, was also linked to a peculiar aspect of the North American economy. For some years before the war, Latin American countries and Canada had been importing United States silver coins to make up for the inadequate supply of silver fractions furnished by their own governments. In Canada, both U.S. and Canadian silver coins were accepted at par with gold, and this condition remained in effect even after the American Civil War began. As Demand Notes and United States Notes steadily lost their value through the early months of 1862, American banks and brokers began buying U.S. silver coins with paper money at par. They then shipped the coins to Canada and exchanged them at face value for gold coins. These were deposited at the U.S. Mint, payment being made to the depositor by the Treasury in paper money. Since gold was then at a premium to greenbacks, the dollar value of paper received in payment for this gold exceeded the amount originally used to purchase silver coins, this difference being the broker's profit. As soon as the paper dollar depreciated below 97¢ in gold coin, this scheme became sufficiently lucrative to cover expenses, and the United States was steadily drained of silver coins.

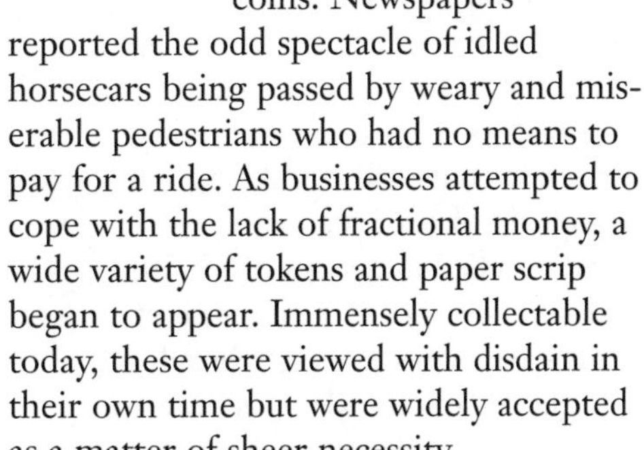

3¢ stamp in a Gault case

The withdrawal of gold and silver throughout most of the country was little noticed in the West. In a remote land where commodities and services were scarcer and more highly valued than cash, subtle variations in the relative values of gold and silver simply had no impact. In addition, paper money was largely unknown to Westerners until the early years of the 20th century, and those who attempted to introduce it were viewed with suspicion. Both silver and gold continued to circulate side-by-side throughout the 1860s and '70s, as though the West were a different country altogether.

By July 1862, the disappearance of coins was nearly complete. Businesses in cities throughout the eastern half of the nation found themselves without any means of making change of less than a dollar, which was the lowest denomination of paper money being issued. Hardest hit were transportation companies, which had long been the biggest recipients of small coins. Newspapers reported the odd spectacle of idled horsecars being passed by weary and miserable pedestrians who had no means to pay for a ride. As businesses attempted to cope with the lack of fractional money, a wide variety of tokens and paper scrip began to appear. Immensely collectable today, these were viewed with disdain in their own time but were widely accepted as a matter of sheer necessity.

United States postage stamps were soon pressed into service as a medium of exchange. Despite their tendency to wear quickly and become filthy, they at least offered the attraction of an established value. At one point Congress actually legalized this practice, since it then had no alternative plan in effect. Though given no legal-tender status, stamps were made receivable for government dues in amounts under $5 and were redeemable for greenbacks.

Perhaps the most innovative solution to the shortage of change was devised by John Gault, who encased postage stamps in round, brass frames to produce pseudo coins. So widespread was the use of

Copper "Civil War tokens" of cent size were commercially manufactured and filled the need for small change during 1863 and 1864. The pieces shown are "store cards," because they include the issuer's advertisement. (19 mm)

1863 Civil War merchant card for V. Benner & Ch. Bendinger, wine and liquor dealers

1863 merchant card for medalist Jos. H. Merriam

The 1861 copper-nickel Confederate cent was designed and minted by Robert Lovett Jr., a Philadelphia die-sinker and engraver. He struck only 12 coins. Lovett feared being branded as an enemy of the United States and decided not to deliver the coins, which, along with the dies, were hidden in his cellar. (about 19 mm)

postage as fractional currency, however, that his invention fell victim to an inadequate supply of stamps!

Congress ultimately took the concept of postage currency a step further by producing fractional notes in a variety of denominations ranging from 3¢ to 50¢; in fact, the first issue actually depicted postage stamps in its designs. There were five issues of fractional currency notes between 1862 and 1875, each one more reviled than the last. The public clearly wanted coins in place of these little "shinplasters," but the prevailing economic conditions simply prevented this. Both Congress and the Mint were acutely aware of public dissatisfaction with paper money of all kinds, but there was no general agreement on a solution. A few measures were taken to ease the situation, and some of these were to have a lasting impact on America's coinage system.

The first action by Congress affected the cent. Initially, the premium value attached to cents was based not so much on their intrinsic worth as simply on their utility. The only coins still circulating in the spring of 1862, cents were often bundled in groups of 25, 50, and 100 pieces to serve in place of coins having those respective values. But, as fractional notes began to appear the following year, cents were increas-ingly viewed as the only real money left in circulation. The public then began hoarding them for that reason alone. Despite the record numbers coined during 1862 and 1863, cents developed an even greater premium value and were afterward in continually short supply.

Observing that privately issued copper or bronze tokens of cent size circulated freely and seemed to be preferred over scrip, Congress provided for the replacement of the existing copper-nickel cent with one of "French bronze." The Act of April 22, 1864, authorized the coining of cents in an alloy consisting of .950 copper and .050 zinc and tin, which gave the coins a metallic value well below their face value. The cent's design, however, remained unchanged. A two-cent piece of the same composition as the cent and weighing exactly twice as much was also created under this law. These coins were a legal tender for up to 10¢ and 20¢, respectively, and were to be issued only in exchange for lawful money of the United States.

Although postage currency was redeemable for 5¢ or 10¢ stamps, it made a poor substitute for coins.

Chief Engraver James B. Longacre enjoyed a monopoly on designing coins for the U.S. Mint, and his two-cent piece is an especially attractive composition. A Union shield dominates the obverse. Two crossed arrows appear behind the shield, which is flanked by an inverted laurel wreath. The motto IN GOD WE TRUST is inscribed on a banner above the shield. The reverse of this coin type displays a wreath of wheat enclosing the value 2 CENTS, with the legend UNITED STATES OF AMERICA around the periphery.

Making its first appearance on a United States coin, the motto IN GOD WE TRUST was introduced in response to the heightened religious sentiment of the war years, as Americans struggled with a conflict that literally tore families apart. As early as 1861, The Reverend M.R. Watkinson of Ridleyville, Pennsylvania, had written to Treasury Secretary Salmon P. Chase advocating some reference to the Almighty on the nation's coinage. The exact wording went through several experimental stages before its final form was determined. In 1866, this motto was extended to those silver and gold coins whose size would accommodate it. Now mandated by law on all United States coins, the motto has also been a fixture on our nation's paper money since 1957.

1864 two-cent piece (23 mm)

The law of 1864 prohibited the issuance by private parties of any coin or token meant to pass as a one-cent or two-cent piece. Thus, the privately issued emergency pieces, known to collectors as Civil War Tokens, were banished from the scene. Today, they offer the numismatist a rich assortment of images and themes: some of them are patriotic or political in nature, while others are purely commercial. For the most part inexpensive, they are perhaps the items most accurately described as the true coinage of the Civil War.

Both the bronze cent and two-cent piece were initially quite successful, circulating freely once enough had been coined to make them familiar. The new cent proved particularly popular, and its descendants were coined as late as 1982, when the rising value of copper prompted a near total replacement of this metal with zinc. The two-cent piece, however, diminished rapidly in usefulness as the supply of cents grew, and it was evident by the end of the 1860s that its coinage was no longer necessary. Nevertheless it remained in production through 1872 with ever-diminishing mintages. The final coinage, dated 1873, consisted solely of Proof pieces made for collectors, and the sweeping legislation passed that year abolished the denomination.

As the Civil War drew to a close in 1865, another new coin was introduced in a move to redeem the three-cent notes. The notes had themselves been issued as a replacement for the silver trime, which, after 1862, had been issued merely to settle accounts with depositors and to satisfy occasional requests from collectors. The three-cent notes had proved to be the most disliked of all the fractional paper issues, so Congress could not afford to wait for the return of silver to circulation. Legislation enacted March 3, 1865, authorized the coining of three-cent pieces in an alloy of three parts copper to one part nickel. The new coins were to be a legal tender for amounts up to 60¢, while the legal-tender limits of the cent and two-cent piece were reduced by this law to just 4¢. Another provision of this act specifically prohibited the issuance of fractional paper valued below 5¢, a clear indication that the new coins were intended to retire such notes.

In a tacit acknowledgment of the government's desire to one day restore silver to circulation, this law contained no language discontinuing silver three-cent pieces. Just to maintain the illusion that they were still a current issue, trimes were minted in ridiculously small numbers as late as 1873, when a major reform of the nation's coinage abolished this coin.

Resourceful as always, J.B. Longacre simply revised an existing image of Liberty for the obverse of the nickel three-cent piece. The same classical profile that appears on the Indian Head cent, the gold dollar, and the $3 piece is seen fitted with a new hairstyle and a studded coronet inscribed LIBERTY. The legend UNITED STATES OF AMERICA is around the periphery, with the date below the bust. The reverse features a Roman numeral III, as on the silver edition, but it is enclosed by a

No nation can be strong except in the strength of God, or safe except in His defense. The trust of our people in God should be declared on our national coins.

You will cause a device to be prepared without unnecessary delay with a motto expressing in the fewest and tersest words possible this national recognition.

– A letter from Treasury Secretary Salmon P. Chase to James Pollock, superintendent of the Philadelphia Mint, November 20, 1861. Chase was responding to pleas from the public to include a reference to God on U.S. money.

1865 copper-nickel three-cent piece (17.9 mm)

1866 copper-nickel five-cent piece (20.5 mm)

laurel wreath instead of the other coin's ornamented letter C. Its edge is plain, typical of U.S. minor coins after 1795.

The same reasoning behind the adoption of a nickel three-cent piece in 1865 brought about a similar five-cent coin the following year. The Act of May 16, 1866, ushered in what would become one of the mainstays of the country's coinage. Issued to redeem and replace the five-cent notes, the new coins were immediately accepted by the public, though a smaller coinage of half dimes continued until eliminated by law in 1873.

Like his previous two-cent piece, Longacre's nickel, as this coin came to be known, features a Union shield on its obverse. It, too, is draped by a laurel wreath and accented by two crossed arrows, with the date appearing below. Added above the shield, however, is a cross of ancient style and uncertain origin. Despite its conceptual similarity to the charming two-cent piece, the whole effect is overly sentimental and rather unappealing. Even Joseph Wharton, the major proponent of nickel as a coining metal, disapproved, describing this ensemble as "a tombstone surmounted by a cross and overhung by weeping willows ... ." Even more controversial was the new coin's reverse. It featured a large numeral 5 surrounded by a circle of 13 stars. Rays flow from among the stars, the whole composition reminding many of the "stars and bars" motif of the recently defeated Confederacy. The rays were removed in 1867 to improve striking quality and extend die life, but not before the "tombstone nickel" had been branded by many as the "rebel nickel."

The new coin was also disproportionately large and heavy in relation to the three-cent piece of the same composition. This was ostensibly to give it an even metric weight of 5 grams, the United States having become infatuated with this system of weights and measures imported from Europe. While 4 grams would have achieved the same end and been of a more convenient size, the higher weight won out at the prompting of those owning domestic nickel mines, chiefly Joseph Wharton. Better remembered today for the school of economics bearing his name, Wharton was no stranger in the halls of Congress during the 1860s. His presence prompted a long series of pure nickel and copper-nickel pattern coins struck as late as the 1880s. At one time, the Mint was even flirting with a uniform minor coinage of nickel to have included cent, two-cent, three-cent and five-cent pieces.

Like the law authorizing the new three-cent piece, the five-cent bill provided that these coins could be purchased in "lawful currency" of the United States, excepting half cents, cents, and two-cent pieces. It also prohibited the further issuance of fractional paper valued at less than 10¢. The nickel was made a legal tender in amounts up to $1 and could be redeemed for "national currency" when presented in sums not less than $100.

This last provision was of the very greatest importance. As had been the case with fractional silver pieces from 1853 to 1861, the new minor coins introduced in 1864 to 1866 had a way of accumulating in the hands of merchants in numbers far greater than could be paid out as change. Banks usually refused to accept such coins beyond their legal-tender limit. With no other means of disposing of them, merchants were once again forced to surrender the unwanted coins to brokers, at a loss. In fact, it was this very problem that prompted the Act of March 3, 1871, which extended to all minor coins (those made of base metals) unlimited redemption value when presented to the Treasury in sums not less than $20. In a clear understanding of how these coins could become redundant, the new law also authorized the Secretary of the Treasury to reduce or discontinue their production whenever the number being redeemed indicated that a redundancy existed. This authority was behind the greatly reduced minor coinages of the 1870s, which culminated in 1877 and 1878 when the three-cent and five-cent coins were minted only as Proofs for collectors.

Chapter Eight

Restoring the Nation's Coinage

The flush times were in magnificent flower! The "city" of Virginia claimed a population of 18,000, and all day long half of this little army swarmed the streets like bees and the other half swarmed along the drifts and tunnels of the Comstock hundreds of feet down in the earth directly under those same streets. Often we felt the jar, and heard the faint boom of a blast down in the bowels of the earth under the office.

– Mark Twain writing about his days as a young reporter at the Virginia City *Territorial Enterprise*

Successful as the new minor coins were, they were still no substitute for silver, at least with respect to values above five cents. While there was some discussion in Congress about replicating the quarter dollar and half dollar in base metals, this notion was always met with howls of outrage at the thought of such debasement. A compromise of some sort seemed to be the solution, though there was no general agreement on how it could be achieved.

One scheme that resulted in a rich array of pattern coins during the years 1869 to 1871 was a proposal to reduce the weight of the silver coins while maintaining their existing fineness of nine parts silver to one part copper. Such patterns bore the inscription STANDARD SILVER or simply STANDARD. It was hoped, of course, that these coins would be issued only as a temporary measure until the depre-ciated paper money rose sufficiently in value against gold that silver coins of the 1853 standard would no longer be worth more as bullion than as money. If this seems complicated to you, the reader, then you are no different from the typical member of Congress at that time. In fact, the debate over what to do about restoring silver coins to circulation actually took so long that the problem finally solved itself, as the value of that metal began to fall rapidly after 1873.

◀ *Virginia City during its boom town days in the mid-1870s, the peak years for mining Nevada's silver. A United States branch mint was located at nearby Carson City. (From* Frank Leslie's Illustrated Newspaper, *March 2, 1878)*

As noted earlier, precious-metal coins circulated freely in the far West throughout this period of debate in Washington. In a nation only recently divided into North and South over the issues of states' rights and slavery, an economic division continued to exist between East and West. In the Western states and territories, both silver and gold went on circulating with nary a greenback to be seen.

The peculiar aspects of an inflated price scale in the commodity-poor West made this ironic situation sustainable even while the East was overwhelmed with paper money. Combined with rich discoveries of silver in Nevada beginning in 1859, the uninterrupted circulation of hard money in the West prompted the establishment of a new mint in 1866 at Carson City, Nevada. The first coins from this facility were struck in 1870, and all denominations of silver and gold were ultimately produced there with the exceptions of the silver trime and half dime, and the gold dollar, quarter eagle, and $3 piece.

The initial reluctance of Congress to authorize yet another branch mint ultimately proved to be correct. Through economic conditions peculiar to this region, miners and bankers sometimes found it more profitable to send their

In this January 19, 1878, cartoon, Thomas Nast showed his disdain for the Greenback Party, which sought to repeal the Specie Resumption Act of 1875. The party wanted to keep the old greenbacks in circulation and urged that more be printed. They also supported the unlimited coinage of silver. Nast believed these "soft soap" money schemes were immoral and would ruin America's credit abroad. (*From* Harper's Weekly)

bullion over the mountains to San Francisco for refining and minting. While Carson City did take in a fair amount of bullion, at the request of the depositors it was typically returned in the form of refined or unrefined bars for shipment east. Thus, the Carson City Mint (whose issues bore a CC mintmark) never produced coins in any great quantity except for a brief flurry of activity in 1876 and 1877, and minting ceased there after 1893.

While Congress debated the proposed reduction in the weight of silver coins, the value of greenbacks began to slowly rise to the point at which the market value of a paper dollar nearly achieved parity with an equivalent face value in silver coins. In theory at least, this enabled the Mint to resume paying out silver coins at par in exchange for paper money. Existing laws, however, precluded such exchanges. Desperate to return silver to circulation and speed redemption of the hated fractional notes, in 1873 Mint Director Henry Linderman devised a way to seemingly comply with the letter of the law while simultaneously sidestepping its intent – he simply directed all federal offices to make change with silver coins instead of the familiar fractional notes. This got the coins into circulation well enough, but the bubble burst after only two months when the value of the greenback suffered a slight reversal as measured against gold. When it appeared that the newly released silver coins might be withdrawn by speculators, the effort to redeem the fractional notes was temporarily postponed.

Nevertheless, Congress confidently passed the Specie Resumption Act of January 14, 1875. To some extent this law merely legitimized Linderman's policy of issuing silver coins as change. But in addition to authorizing the redemption of all fractional currency notes with fractional silver coins, this law specified that after January 1, 1879, the U.S. Treasury would be required to redeem greenbacks in "coin," meaning gold. This offered the prospect of a return to circulating gold coinage.

It was critical to the nation's international credit that the United States be able to redeem its bonds and other fiscal obligations in gold coin. The war had been largely financed through the sale of bonds redeemable in gold, and America's creditors, primarily Great Britain, were watching developments very carefully. In fact, since 1868 British creditors had largely rejected payment in silver bullion. The domestic surplus of this metal that resulted had caused a sharp rise in the production of silver dollars that same year and for the next several years. When the silver dollar was rendered obsolete by the Mint Act of 1873, the nation's silver producers were left with an insufficient market for their metal, and its value fell. Adding to silver's woes was the adoption by several European nations, most notably the newly unified Germany, of gold as their sole standard of value. Though still prized by Asians, in the West silver was a pariah.

It was around this same time that full-scale minting of fractional silver pieces resumed. Though the price of silver was still perilously close to the point at which the newly issued coins would be subject to hoarding, the steadily declining value of this metal, combined with the rising value of paper money against gold, meant that the economic cloud was finally lifting. Beginning in the late spring of 1873, silver coins once again appeared after a drought of more than 10 years. Still, only time would tell whether the Treasury would be able to meet its deadline to reissue gold coins in 1879.

Fractional silver coins were minted in enormous quantities during the years 1875 to 1877, as a torrent of paper money was cashed in and consigned to oblivion. Aiding in the production of these coins was the new San Francisco Mint, which opened in 1874. A massive Greek Revival structure, it replaced the cramped and inefficient building that had been used since 1854. At the time of its opening, the new mint was the largest and most efficient facility of its type in the world. It was thus no coincidence that contracts to produce coins for other nations were first accepted around this time; the vast capacity of the new mint made such additional production possible.

The various emergency measures taken to address the nation's coinage needs during the 1850s and '60s had left a number of redundant and obsolete provisions. Among other problems, the newly authorized coin types were being issued alongside non-circulating coins of the same denominations. As it had in 1837, the United States Mint sought a general revision of the existing, often conflicting, statutes. In his 1869 annual report, Treasury Secretary George S. Boutwell expressed concern over the growing complexities of the Mint's operations and multiple facilities, which included not only the various branch mints, but the federal assay offices as well. He recommended that the Mint be established as a bureau of the Treasury Department, with its overall administration moved from Philadelphia to Washington, D.C.

The work of drafting a new and comprehensive coinage law was assigned to John Jay Knox, the deputy comptroller of the currency. Assisting him in this project was former Mint director Henry R. Linderman.

Knox and Linderman had their work cut out for them. Given the confused state of the nation's coinage in the early 1870s, many elected representatives feared that additional changes would simply make things worse. As a result of this uncertainty, some three years of drafting, debating, and revising the Mint bill occurred before Congress finally passed it on February 12, 1873. This act contained dozens of clauses completely restructuring the United States Mint and redefining its operations and personnel, but these make for very dry reading and will be overlooked in this study. The most significant administrative change was the establishment of the Mint as a bureau within the Treasury Department. This elevated the Mint director to an office in Washington from which he gave instructions to the superintendents of the various mints and assay offices across the country. Though it still enjoyed a monopoly on designing coins and preparing dies, the Philadelphia Mint was otherwise rendered on a par with the other mints, and its chief officer was now a superintendent answerable to the director in Washington. In addition, the other facilities were no longer referred to as simply branches of the United States Mint, but rather were U.S. Mints in their own right.

The new law of 1873 also eliminated several coins that were considered obsolete. These included the two-cent piece, silver three-cent piece, half dime, and silver dollar. Added to the roster of United

Medal honoring Mint Director Linderman (76 mm)

After consulting with some of the most prominent and intelligent Chinese merchants as to its probable success, I do not hesitate to recommend, in lieu of our old dollar, a new coin or disk, which shall be slightly more valuable than the Mexican dollar, to be made only upon request of the owner of the bullion, and to be paid for by him. ... It will not be a coin of circulation, or legal-tender in payment of debts, but simply an agent in our commerce with foreign countries.

– From a report by Mint Director Henry Linderman supporting production of a silver trade coin

You must know that the "Eagle Trade Dollar" that has lately come to Hong Kong has been jointly assayed by officers specially appointed for the purpose, and it can be taken in payment of duties, and come into general circulation. ***You must not look upon it with suspicion.*** *At the same time, rogues, sharpers, and the like, are hereby strictly forbidden to fabricate spurious imitations of this new Eagle Dollar, with a view to their own profit.*

And should they dare to set this prohibition at defiance, and fabricate false coins, they shall, upon discovery, most assuredly be arrested and punished. Let every one obey with trembling! Let there be no disobedience!

– From *Bankers Magazine*, November 1877, quoting a proclamation issued in China in October 1873

States coins was the Trade dollar, a coin similar in dimensions to the old standard silver dollar, but slightly higher in silver content. This coin was intended exclusively for sale at its bullion value to Americans doing business in East Asia, where Mexican dollars remained the preferred medium of exchange. Since the great demand for Mexican dollars enabled bullion brokers to charge a premium for them, a competing U.S. coin of equal bullion value had been desired for some years. Though the Trade dollar was not intended for domestic circulation, Congress unwisely felt the need to set its legal-tender ceiling at $5, an action that would come back to haunt its members just three years later.

1874 silver Trade dollar (38.1 mm)

While all U.S. silver coins of the time carried the same image of Liberty seated, the Trade dollar was similar in concept but noticeably different in execution. William Barber succeeded James B. Longacre as the Mint's chief engraver in 1869, and he created a distinctive figure of Liberty for the new coin. She sits by the sea on a bale of cotton, behind which appears a sheaf of wheat. Liberty holds in her left hand a banner inscribed with her name, while her right hand is lifted up and grasps an olive branch. Beneath the cotton bale is another banner reading IN GOD WE TRUST, while 13 stars are arranged in an arc around the periphery.

The reverse of the Trade dollar features a standing and facing eagle, this time without the traditional shield on its breast. It clutches three arrows in its right claw and an olive branch in its left, a reversal of the positions seen on other coins of the time.

Above our national bird is yet another banner with the legend E PURIBUS UNUM. The legend UNITED STATES OF AMERICA appears around the upper periphery, with the declaration TRADE DOLLAR around the lower part. The inscription 420 GRAINS, 900 FINE is immediately beneath the eagle, reinforcing the intent that this coin was to trade primarily at its bullion value.

One of the least significant actions of the 1873 law was that it raised the weights of the dime, quarter dollar, and half dollar a very slight amount. This was done to make their weights more easily expressed in metric terms at a time when the United States was flirting with the metric system. Curiously, a similar movement to adopt this system of weights and measures arose just about a century later, though it likewise resulted in only partial success. Americans still buy their potatoes by the pound rather than the kilogram.

The increase in weight made almost no difference. For example, the half dollar was increased from 12.44 grams to just 12.50 grams, while the other two coins were altered in proportion. This weight change was so slight that the pre-1873 coins actually fell within the legal tolerance for coins of the new issue! Even so, the various mints were ordered to destroy any existing stocks of the old silver coins, creating several numismatic rarities in the process. To denote the change in weight, the Mint added arrowheads on either side of the date for each denomination, just as it had done in 1853. The arrowheads were continued through 1874 and then dropped, though the new weight standard remained in effect until 1965.

The U.S. Mint at Carson City

In 1965 the retired mint at Carson City, Nevada, was brought to life once again, albeit indirectly. A nationwide coin shortage, which had been building since the early 1960s, reached its peak in 1964 and 1965, and every available resource of the United States Mint and its auxiliaries was called into service. The San Francisco Assay Office, which had not functioned as a mint since 1955, was set to work punching blanks for shipment to the Denver Mint. When this still proved insufficient to meet the demand for fresh money, San Francisco was authorized to begin striking coins again. With its presses having been shipped to other facilities years earlier, this created a general shortage of coin presses. To the rescue came the old Carson City Mint. Though long since deactivated and serving now as the Nevada State Museum, one of its prize exhibits was an old flywheel coin press from the 1870s. In sheer desperation, this antique was shipped to the Denver Mint and put into service.

This is just one of the many fascinating tales associated with the United States Mint at Carson City. Though it coined gold and silver only, from 1870 to 1893, it has left American numismatics with a rich legacy. Most of its coins are scarce to rare, some of them being tremendous rarities. Others, such as the silver dollars of 1882 to 1884, have survived in vast numbers for reasons that have nothing to do with their original mintage figures. All of these coins, whatever their rarity or market value, carry romantic associations with the Old West and the great bonanza years of the late 19th century. The tiny letters CC, the only dual-character mintmark among United States issues, never fail to stir visions of grizzled prospectors, callous gunslingers, and instant millionaires. The era in which the Carson City Mint produced coins is perhaps the most fabled in American history.

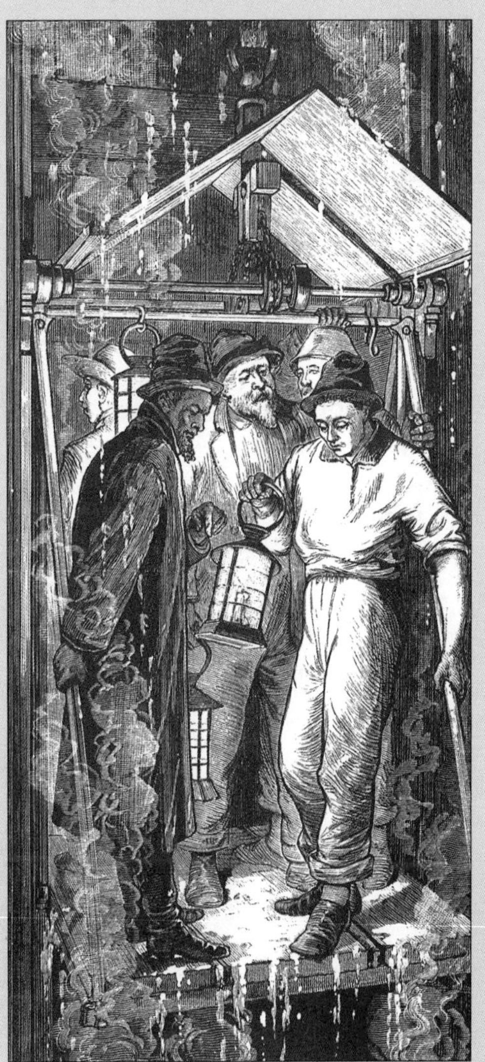

◀ *Elevators at the Consolidated Virginia Mine in Virginia City were topped with metal roofs to deflect falling rock. Candle lanterns lit the 1,550-foot ride down the shaft, which took 40 seconds. According to* Frank Leslie's Illustrated Newspaper, *providing light for miners working the Consolidated Virginia required approximately 5,000 candles a day. (From* Frank Leslie's Illustrated Newspaper, *March 9, 1878)*

If the rock was moderately promising, we followed the custom of the country and used strong adjectives, and frothed at the mouth as if a very marvel in silver discoveries had transpired. If the mine was a "developed" one, we would squander half a column of adulation on a shaft, or a new wire rope, or a dressed-pine windlass, or a fascinating force pump.

– Part of Mark Twain's reporting job at the *Enterprise* was shameless promotion of Virginia City and the mines.

The first permanent settlement was established in the spring of 1851 by Colonel John Reese, a Mormon, who planned to open a trading post on the overland trail. He was a partner with his brother Enoch in the J.&E. Reese Mercantile firm at Salt Lake City. The party arrived in Carson Valley with 13 wagons loaded with eggs, bacon, flour, seed grain and other kinds of seeds. ... On November 12, 1851, the settlers formed and organized a settler's or squatter's government. ... The settlers adopted rules for taking up land and elected John Reese recorder and treasurer. Reese recorded the first claim for himself in December of 1852 in the new Utah Territory settlement he named Mormon Station (Genoa).

– From *The History of Genoa* by Billie J. Rightmire

A Frontier Land

Though it is the state capital of Nevada, Carson City is not a large town, nor has it ever been. In fact, the entire area that now comprises the State of Nevada was sparsely populated during the 1860s, and the territory seemed an unlikely candidate for statehood. That Nevada was made a state in 1864, before achieving the requisite minimum pop-ulation, is simply a reflection of the times. With the Civil War raging it would have been unwise for the Union to neglect Nevada Territory, which had vast mineral wealth. Congress hastened its admission to the Union simply to cement its residents' loyalty to the United States and prevent the spread of sympathy toward the Southern cause.

This was all some years away when settlers arrived in Carson Valley (later Eagle Valley) in 1851. Taking advantage of the great migration to California, they established a trading post that thrived for just a few years. The future State of Nevada was then known as Carson County, part of the Utah Territory. As the Gold Rush subsided the opportunists left, and only a handful of Mormon settlers remained. When Mormon Church leader Brigham Young ran afoul of federal authorities over the issue of polygamy, his followers were recalled to Salt Lake City, where they could better protect themselves. The land in Eagle Valley was considered almost valueless, and it was purchased for a very reasonable price by a mountaineer named John Mankin.

Temperatures hundreds of feet below the Earth's surface often exceeded 120 degrees, so workers in the Consolidated Virginia Mine wore as little clothing as possible. (From Frank Leslie's Illustrated Newspaper, *March 9, 1878)*

A few years later, New Yorker Abraham Curry, disappointed to discover that land in California was so expensive, retraced his steps eastward across the Sierra Nevada Mountains. In the company of B.F. Green, J.J. Musser, Frank M. Proctor, and their families, Curry rode out from the established community of Mormon Station (today called Genoa) to find even cheaper land farther north in Eagle Valley. Curry and his associates purchased John Mankin's entire Eagle Valley holdings for $500 and a few horses.

As unpromising as the land seemed, the group set about to establish a trading post that would rival that of Mormon Station. Curry had

Laborers in a Virginia City retort house removed mercury from silver amalgam so it could be used again. The silver was then cast into bars at an assay office. (From Frank Leslie's Illustrated Newspaper, *April 20, 1878)*

bigger plans, however, and he sought to create a full-fledged city. The scheme seemed improbable, yet it was here in 1858 that Curry founded Carson City, named for the famed mountaineer and trailblazer Kit Carson. It was about this time that the western portion of Utah Territory was designated the Territory of Nevada, and Curry's scheme no longer seemed so foolish. After the 1859 discovery of the comstock Lode, one of the richest deposits of silver ore ever found, the success of Carson City was assured. It soon became the territorial capital and grew rapidly over the next few years. When Nevada became a state in 1864, Carson City was, naturally, named its capital. As the town's biggest real estate holder, Abraham Curry prospered accordingly.

A New Mint?

Most of the rich silver ore (and lesser amounts of gold) was shipped over the Sierra Nevada Mountains to the United States Mint at San Francisco. This was costly and involved some risk. Though Indians were no longer a factor in Nevada and California, bandits were. The mine owners petitioned Congress for a branch mint in Nevada, and this question was put to Treasury Secretary Salmon P. Chase on June 2, 1862. Chase deferred to Mint Director James Pollock who, as an opponent of all branch mints, naturally spoke against it. Pollock's view was largely ignored, and the House Ways and Means Committee reported favorably on the establishment of a mint in Nevada Territory.

In addition to the arguments in favor of a new mint already cited, the

The south side and east façade of the Carson City Mint, circa 1879

committee pointed out that much of the refined metal emanating from the San Francisco Mint, whether in the form of coins or ingots, was shipped overseas and lost to the domestic economy. It was declared that a mint farther inland was likely to keep its product within the U.S., thus, somehow, saving the Treasury $500,000 annually. The exact cause-and-effect relationship of this savings was not explained, but its appeal was sufficient to get the Nevada mint bill passed by both the House and the Senate in a single day – March 3, 1863.

The legislation did not specify an exact site for the new mint, other than that it was to be in the Territory of Nevada. Treasury Secretary Chase dispatched Colorado Congressman Hiram Pitt Bennet to Nevada to investigate suitable locations. As the territory's most enthusiastic booster, Abe Curry proceeded to sell Bennet on Carson City as the site for the mint. In addition to being centrally located to all the mines, Curry noted, it was within a promising agricultural region. This latter claim proved to be highly optimistic, but Carson City was ultimately chosen to host the new federal mint based on its proximity to the mining regions.

Delays imposed by the ongoing Civil War held up the mint's progress, though a lot was purchased in February 1865. Chosen on Bennet's recommendation, it was acquired from James L. Riddle and Moses and Margaret Job. A commission to oversee mint construction was appointed by Secretary of the Treasury Hugh McCulloch on December 27, and included Abraham Curry, Henry F. Rice, and John H. Mills.

When it seemed that there would be no further delays, a movement developed in Congress to replace the proposed mint with a federal assay office which, of course, would not actually mint coins. Nevada Senators James Nye and William Stewart stepped in to thwart this action by renewing the original authorizing legislation, which their opponents were claiming had lapsed due to inactivity. Nye and Stewart managed to revive the mint and extract an authorization of $150,000 for its construction.

There remained some lingering opposition within the Treasury Department itself, and it was not until July 17, 1866, that the promised plans and authorizing documents finally arrived in Carson City amid much public celebration. By this time Curry had managed to have himself named as contractor, a decision he would ultimately come to regret. This was all in the future, of course, and the groundbreaking was undertaken the very next day with great gusto. The cornerstone was laid September 24, once again with considerable fanfare.

To find a petrified man, or break a stranger's leg, or cave an imaginary mine, or discover some dead Indians in a Gold Hill tunnel, or massacre a family at Dutch Nick's, were feats and calamities that we never hesitated about devising when the public needed matters of thrilling interest for breakfast. The seemingly tranquil ENTERPRISE *office was a ghastly factory of slaughter, mutilation and general destruction in those days.*

– Mark Twain reminiscing about his days as a reporter at the *Territorial Enterprise* in Nevada, from *Letters from Washington, IX*

Construction Woes

Problems soon arose when it became evident that the $150,000 appropriation, deemed sufficient to erect such a structure in the East, did not allow for the inflated economy of the West. Labor was expensive, materials in short supply, and transportation of anything from the eastern states was a major undertaking.

To stretch his dollars as far as possible, Curry hired a number of Chinese laborers, which led to widespread protests from the townspeople. Concerned, Mint Director William Millward visited the construction site that same year. Despite the misgivings of J.M. Eckfeldt of the San Francisco Mint, who accompanied Millward, the director gave the proceedings a favorable assessment in his annual report.

Chinese laborers, who performed the most menial of tasks, were frequent victims of discrimination. (From Harper's Weekly, *September 26, 1885)*

When work was actually being done on the mint, things went quite well, but Curry's increasing financial strains, due to inflated costs and aggravated by frequent labor disputes, threatened the entire project. The shell of the structure was already in place when, on December 5, 1867, Abraham Curry journeyed to Washington to plead his case for more funds. He spent the greater part of 1868 making the rounds of both Washington and Philadelphia in his attempts to procure more money, while all the time work continued on finishing the structure and installing its boilers and plumbing. Curry returned to Carson City a hero on September 11, though another few weeks would pass before he actually received enough money to complete the building.

The mint's machinery, consisting of coin presses, blanking presses, rolling mills, and a variety of other implements, had to come by sea "around the Horn," and the greater bulk of it did not arrive until November 23, 1868. At that point it seemed certain that the

Carson City Mint would begin striking coins the following year, but numerous additional delays prevented this. One of these was prompted by the lack of bricks in Nevada, which kept workmen from completing the chimney. When they did finally arrive, it was too late in the season. Work had to be discontinued during the long and harsh winter, as it had been each year since the project began.

While Curry and his workmen waited out the winter, a bill appeared in Congress that would prohibit the refining and assaying of metals at the branch mints, effectively rendering them useless. After protracted debate, this ridiculous legislation ultimately died, but it did nothing to bolster confidence in Carson City. Another problem arose when it became evident that the skimpy salaries authorized by the Treasury Department, figures deemed sufficient by Eastern standards, would not be enough to procure skilled individuals to fill the role of assayer and that of melter and refiner. Once again, the inflated Western economy had not been taken into account by those in Washington.

These problems were ultimately overcome and Curry, who was now the mint superintendent, waited impatiently for the arrival of dies from Philadelphia. The machinery was tested at various times during 1869, and everything was deemed to be in readiness. By December, dies still had not arrived, and Curry hastened to point out that dies dated 1869 would no longer be of any value at that point and that they should be dated 1870. In due course these did in fact arrive by Wells Fargo Express, but not until January 10, 1870.

Welcome as it was, this long-awaited development nearly seemed an anticlimax after the events of two weeks previous. On December 28, 1869, at 6 o'clock in the evening, the entire Carson City area was rocked by a tremendous earthquake, the greatest anyone present could recall. Though there were a number of damaged buildings in town, the mint was not among them. Just a couple of weeks earlier, supervising architect A.B. Mullet had pronounced the mint to have been built in accordance with the plans, despite the severity of its budget. Evidently it was built well, too, since it survived the earthquake without any signs of damage.

Assay office workers at a Comstock mill making bars out of melted bullion. To prevent thievery, molten metal was sometimes made into bars so large that a man could not carry one by himself. (From Frank Leslie's Illustrated Newspaper, *April 20, 1878)*

Coining Finally Begins

When the dies arrived, the first denomination struck was the silver dollar, the very symbol of Nevada's majesty. These were of the Liberty Seated type, and each bore on its reverse a pair of letters C. The first bullion depositor to receive payment in coin was a Mr. A. Wright, who was paid 2,303 silver dollars bearing the CC mintmark on February 11, 1870.

The coining of gold followed three days later, when eagles were minted. These bore Christian Gobrecht's bust of Liberty wearing a coronet on the obverse and a heraldic eagle with shielded breast on the reverse. Unlike the silver coins, which depicted the eagle with wings folded and just slightly open, the gold coins showed the eagle's wings upraised. These coins, too, carried a small CC mintmark beneath the eagle.

Corresponding designs were used on the coins that followed over the next few months. Half eagles were first minted on March 1, while the first double eagles were struck March 10. Silver coinage continued with the half dollar on April 9 and the quarter dollar on the 20th. No dimes were coined at Carson City until 1871, and no half dimes would ever be minted there, that denomination being shunned by Westerners as too little money to bother with. The CC Mint also declined to produce gold dollars, quarter eagles and $3 gold pieces, though these denominations were current during most of the mint's period of operation. For two years only – 1875 and 1876 – Carson City coined the short-lived 20-cent piece.

Abe Curry opted to resign as superintendent in September 1870 to pursue what proved to be an unsuccessful campaign for lieutenant governor. He was replaced in office by H.F. Rice, and business continued as usual.

1889-CC Morgan dollar (38.1 mm)

Troubled Times

During its first few years of operation, the Carson City Mint failed to produce significant numbers of coins. The sole exception, perhaps, was the new Trade dollar authorized in 1873 as a coin intended almost exclusively for export; these were struck in quantity during 1873 and 1874. For the most part, however, it was not until 1875, when all of the U.S. mints were set to work making coins to replace the now-obsolete fractional paper currency, that pieces bearing the CC mintmark were struck in large numbers.

The small mintages of its early years were not the fault of the Carson City Mint. Though it seemed logical that Nevada miners would deposit their gold and silver ore at the mint for processing into coins, this was more often the exception than the rule. Many found that it was still more economical to have their bullion refined at the San Francisco Mint while, of those selecting the Nevada facility, many opted to receive payment in ingot form rather than coin. Indeed, the processing of ore into bars far outweighed the coining operations. Were it not for the millions of silver

1890-CC half eagle (21.6 mm)

A campaign ribbon supporting Grover Cleveland's run for the presidency

dollars mandated by the Bland-Allison Act of 1878, there would have been precious little activity at the mint during the 1880s.

Those sympathetic to the Carson City Mint argued that the facility was inadequate to the demands being placed on it, and they petitioned Congress for money with which to expand. Additional money was needed, too, for officers' and workmen's salaries. The cost of running a mint in distant Nevada had been underestimated at every stage of the project's development, and this shortfall actually prompted a pay cut of 15% for non-salaried workers in 1876. The effect of such action on employee morale can easily be imagined.

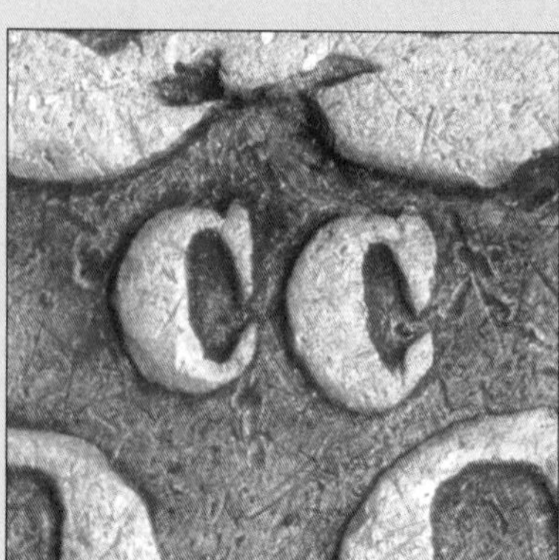

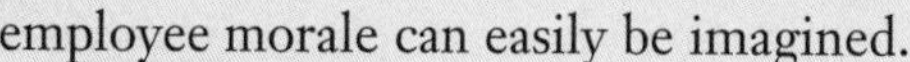
For collectors, the CC mintmark holds the cachet of the Old West.

Also damaging to everyone's spirits were the frequent and virulent attacks on the mint's integrity from those inclined to favor the San Francisco Mint. The San Francisco newspapers abetted this activity by printing any negative reports that came their way. A frequent victim of politics, the Carson City Mint was subject to periodic budget cuts and threats of closure. It also seemed that every congressman wanted a mint in his own district, and the high cost of minting coins in Nevada was cited as grounds for closing it and opening a new mint closer to some population center.

The CC Mint was dealt a serious blow when Grover Cleveland was elected president in November 1884. The first Democrat to hold this office during the mint's years of operation, his election was correctly seen as a threat to the livelihoods of the mint's officers, all of whom were faithful members of the Republican Party. The mint was closed on September 11, 1885, and its employees let go.

The mint did not reopen for more than a year, and then only as an assay office. When the election of 1888 sent Republican Benjamin Harrison to the White House, the Carson City Mint's staff of Democratic political appointees was dispatched and replaced with victorious Republicans. When the new fiscal year began on July 1, 1889, the mint received the funding necessary to resume coining operations. Due to years of idleness, however, the machinery was not ready for a couple of months, and coin production did not begin until September 9.

Minting continued more or less steadily until the spring of 1893. All this time, however, the production of the Nevada mines was falling off, and the price of silver bullion continued to experience a serious decline. The Sherman Silver Purchase Act of 1890 had led to a run on the Treasury's gold supply, and the federal government was growing increasingly frightened by the overall economic situation. The Carson City Mint, which had been plagued by reports of both incompetence and corruption – some fanciful and others valid – was now viewed as an expensive and disposable frill. On June 1, 1893, Acting Mint Director Robert E. Preston ordered coining operations to cease, though the mint would continue to function as a federal assay office.

Remembering the closure of 1885, Nevadans assumed that this action, too, would ultimately be reversed. Unfortunately, there was almost no chance that coining would resume after it was proved beyond any doubt in 1895 that several employees, in conjunction with a number of prominent community figures, were systematically pilfering bullion from the mint. The facility was closed on April 18, and Superintendent Jewett W. Adams was forced to suffer the humiliation of opening an "Embezzlement Account" to replace the losses.

Amazingly, the mint did reopen in June 1896. Once again, its activities were limited to refining bullion into ingots. The community's continued hopes that it would once again coin money were dashed with finality in 1899 when Congress passed a bill officially declaring the facility a federal assay office. Thus, no coins would ever again be minted at Carson City. In August some 22 tons of remaining CC silver dollars were taken away by train, and all the coining equipment was disassembled and shipped to other facilities. Several reverse dies for the silver dollar were repunched with the New Orleans Mint's letter O, creating the popular 1900-O/CC varieties.

The Carson City Mint produced most of the silver and gold denominations authorized by law during the years of its coining operations, 1870 to 1893. So many of the coins minted at Carson City are rare that it is simpler to list the exceptions. Among the more readily available issues are the silver dollars dated 1878 and 1880 to 1885. Along with a few less common dates, these survived in Treasury Department hoards until the 1970s, when they were auctioned to collectors by the General Services Administration. As a result, thousands of Mint State pieces are available today.

The people of the United States are entitled to a sound and stable currency and to money recognized as such on every exchange and in every market of the world. Their Government has no right to injure them by financial experiments opposed to the policy and practice of other civilized states … .

– President Grover Cleveland calling for the repeal of the Sherman Silver Purchase Act of 1890, August 8, 1893

Decline and Rebirth

The story of the Carson City Mint did not end in 1899 with its reduction to assay office status. It continued to refine raw gold and silver ore recovered from the mines of Nevada and neighboring states until 1933. In that worst year of the Great Depression, the U.S. Mint's employee roster reached an historic low for modern times. One of the victims of this severe cutback was the federal assay office at Carson City. It failed to receive an appropriation for the new fiscal year, and its doors were closed, seemingly forever.

In 1941 the old structure became the new home of the Nevada State Museum, a role in which it continues to the present day. Struck by another earthquake in 1989, the building was closed for seismic retrofitting between early July 1990 and May 22, 1992. The museum's reopening was scheduled for 8:30 a.m. – the same hour at which the old mint had opened its doors to the public.

1876-CC 20-cent piece (22 mm)

Among the museum's exhibits is a collection of coins minted there between 1870 and 1893. Though it lacks the famed 1876-CC 20-cent piece – one of the great American rarities – as well as the rare 1873-CC dime and quarter dollar without arrows, this assemblage is otherwise complete by date and denomination. It also includes vintage dies used by the mint. One of the facility's most popular exhibits is a recreation of a Nevada mine, the very lifeblood of this region during its most fabled days.

For numismatists, however, the real story of the Carson City Mint survives in the coins produced there during the days of the Old West. The fascination that collectors find in holding a silver dollar or gold piece bearing the tiny letters CC is an endless one, a fascination that is renewed with each successive generation of coin enthusiasts.

A Mint at The Dalles, Oregon

The U.S. branch mint at The Dalles, seen here during construction in 1869, was later used as part of Ralph's Moving and Storage.

The mint's basement arches, made of brick and stone, were completed before construction ceased.

During the California Gold Rush, men from Oregon, suffering from gold fever, flew southward to try their luck. They came home with a significant amount of gold dust, and over time even more gold flowed into Oregon as payment for lumber and food crops shipped southward to support the miners.

Because the value of un-assayed gold dust was difficult to establish, its value in the marketplace was less than that of gold coins of known worth. What Oregon Territory needed was a mint, but both territorial and federal governments refused. A private firm came to the rescue, minting $5 and $10 pieces, but it operated for less than a year.

In 1866, Congress finally appropriated $100,000 for construction of a branch mint at The Dalles to coin gold from regional mines and California. Unfortunately, by 1869 when construction began, the gold supply had begun to dwindle. Though sandstone walls were already in place, the project was suspended.

When it appeared there would be no United States mint, the Oregon Exchange Company struck $5 (above) and $10 "beaver money" gold coins dated 1849. (22 mm)

Chapter Nine

The Battle over Silver Versus Gold

United States notes issued since 1862 served as a circulating currency, but they were understood by the government to be little more than a loan made to itself as a means of financing the war. The notes remained on the books as an outstanding national debt, and the Specie Resumption Act of 1875 called for the redemption of most of them so the United States could re-establish its credit both at home and in world markets. This law stated that after January 1, 1879, the notes would be redeemed "in coin." While gold was not specifically mentioned, it was understood that only by paying for the notes in gold could the United States square its debts to everyone's satisfaction. It was close, but by December 1878, the value of greenbacks finally achieved parity with gold, and the redemption began. Gold, which had already been made the dollar's single standard of value by the laws of 1853 and 1873, was now more visibly its standard, and gold coins were free to circulate side-by-side with silver coins and paper money.

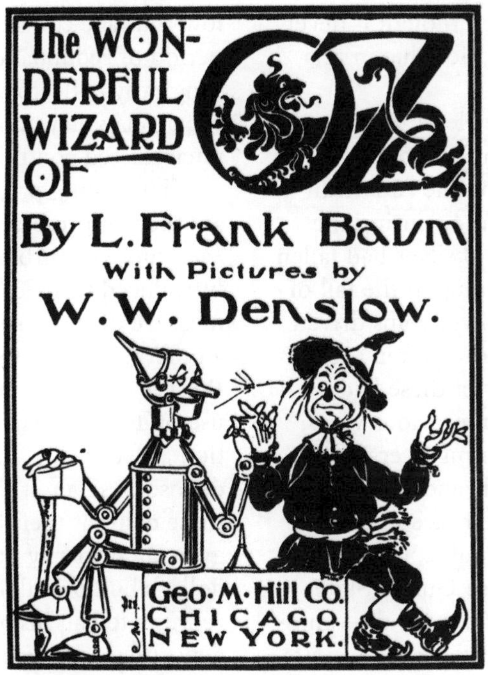

A curious change was evident, however, in that most Americans had become so accustomed to the convenience of paper money that they now preferred to carry it in place of gold. The fact that gold coins were available when desired was enough to finally establish faith in the value of federal paper money, and most people did not feel compelled to put this redemption to the test. Only in the far West, where gold and silver had never ceased circulating, did coins still prevail. In fact, it was not until the United States entered World War I in 1917, at which time gold coinage was suspended, that Westerners finally became familiar with low-denomination paper money and accepted it on faith. The sight of gold coins passing from hand to hand became a rarity there after 1917, as it had been in the rest of the nation since 1862.

Though the restoration of gold pleased the financial community both at home and abroad, it did nothing to relieve the anxiety of silver producers. Several factors influenced the declining value of this metal during the 1870s. Never mined domestically in any great quantity before 1859, since that time

Few who enjoy L. Frank Baum's The Wizard of Oz *realize that the forces of good and evil in the book (and movie) represent opposing factions in the Free Silver debate. Baum, who supported the Silverites, wrote his book to illustrate the dangers of the gold standard.*

The honest and good-hearted ***Dorothy,*** *a symbol of solid middle America, is uprooted by a tornado and finds herself traveling the yellow brick road of* ***Oz,*** *which represents an ounce of gold. She is joined by the* ***Scarecrow,*** *who symbolizes the downtrodden Western farmer; the* ***Tin Woodsman,*** *who stands for the Eastern worker left rusty and heartless by his grinding toil; and the* ***Cowardly Lion,*** *who depicts the failed Silverite William Jennings Bryan.*

The foursome arrives in the ***Emerald City*** *(Washington, D.C.), puts on green-tinted glasses (the color of money), and enters the* ***Emerald Palace*** *(the White House). They struggle with the* ***Wizard*** *and the* ***Wicked Witches,*** *who represent pro-gold politicians, and ultimately unmask the Wizard as an impostor. Dorothy clicks the heels of her silver (not ruby) slippers and returns to the safety of her Kansas home.*

1876-S Trade dollar with chopmarks (38.1 mm)

silver had seemingly been discovered everywhere in the West. The biggest bonanza came in 1873, making instant millionaires of individuals such as James Fair and John Mackay. This abundance of silver was bound to depress its value under any circumstances, but these discoveries came at an especially bad time. Several European nations had recently rejected silver as a standard of value, adopting gold as the single standard for their coinage. Most notably, the newly united German Empire went off the dual standard in 1871. In the massive recoinage that followed, Germany dumped vast amounts of silver into the international market. The decline in the value of silver that had begun during the 1860s accelerated throughout the decades that followed. It was not until early in the 20th century that the price of silver finally began to recover, though it never again achieved its historic value in relation to gold.

While this decline clearly represented a problem to the world's silver producers, its impact on the American economy was driven home during the mid-1870s. The value of silver had fallen sufficiently that, beginning in the fall of 1877, the millions of silver coins driven out of domestic circulation after 1862 began to return. Many of these had simply been hoarded in previous years, but others were circulating overseas, most notably in Canada and Latin America. Now that their face value exceeded their bullion value, it was profitable to repatriate these United States coins. Vast quantities returned to domestic circulation at the very time the mints were turning out millions of new pieces. Even the pre-1853 silver coins, which the Treasury Department assumed had been lost forever to the melting pot, were included among the huge numbers reappearing in circulation.

Initially, this abundance had the desired effect of retiring the last of the fractional paper currency, and Congress then extended the redemption clause to include greenbacks. But it was not long before the absence of silver coins during the years 1862 to 1875 turned into a troublesome redundancy. Fractional silver accumulated in the hands of merchants, who received them in the normal course of business but who were unable to deposit them at banks in amounts over their legal-tender limit of $5. Once again, the bullion brokers and speculators stepped in to take them off their hands – at a profit, of course.

In 1876, Congress placed a cap of $50 million on the volume of subsidiary silver coins in circulation. Any coins over that had to be withdrawn by the Treasury. By 1878, it was evident that enough silver coins were in circulation or in Treasury vaults to meet the needs of commerce for years to come, and their production was nearly halted. Quarters and halves were made in very small numbers until 1891, though the normal minting of dimes resumed by 1882. The low-mintage coins dating from this period of redundancy were eagerly sought by collectors in their own time, so even today they are not especially rare in uncirculated condition.

The falling price of silver had yet another unforeseen effect, one that was even more disturbing. The Trade dollar, introduced in 1873, enjoyed a reasonable measure of success in its intended role as a bullion coin for the East Asian market. But the decline of silver prices led to the use of Trade dollars in domestic circulation at face value. Since those who deposited silver at the Mint were paid in these coins at their bullion value, the growing disparity between the Trade dollar's bullion value and its face value represented an instant profit to the depositor. As long as the Trade dollar retained its legal-tender value, there was nothing merchants could do but continue to stockpile these coins that banks would not accept in amounts over $5. With no perfect solution in sight, Congress was torn between raising the legal-tender limit on the Trade dollar and eliminating its legal status altogether. On July 22, 1876, it chose the latter action; the legal-tender status of the Trade dollar was revoked and its coinage restricted exclusively to overseas demand.

But the coins did not just go away. Far from eliminating their domestic circulation, this action simply meant that banks could now refuse Trade dollars in any amount. Predictably, brokers stepped in who were willing to take them off the hands of frustrated merchants, albeit at a slight discount. There was a new twist, however, one unique to the Trade dollar. These coins were being sold by the brokers to employers, who passed them off on unsuspecting workers each payday. This insidious practice was particularly widespread in the industrial cities of the Northeast, where large numbers of poor immigrants were employed in mining and manufacturing. While they had been paid in Trade dollars at face value, the workers found that many stores would take the coins only at their bullion value, which was below $1. Refusal to accept Trade dollars in one's pay envelope could lead to dismissal, and the poor were repeatedly victimized by this unfair exchange. The merchants were likewise at a disadvantage, as their refusal to accept Trade dollars at face value discouraged business.

The slide in the value of silver was so pronounced after 1876 that it soon became evident to Mint administrators and others in government and financial circles that most of the newly minted Trade dollars were being ordered specifically for domestic circulation. Despite the modest inroads achieved by these coins in Asian markets, on February 22, 1878, Treasury Secretary John Sherman ordered that their production be halted. Thereafter, Trade dollars were coined only as Proofs for sale to collectors. Selling Proofs was likewise discontinued after 1883, yet a small number of pieces dated 1884 and 1885 were struck unofficially and are among the great rarities of American numismatics.

Though demonetized and not minted since 1878, the Trade dollar remained a nuisance for another decade. By 1883, businesses were refusing to accept them in payment or would receive them only at a sharp discount. Millions of pieces already issued remained in circulation, since there was no means of redeeming them except at their bullion value, which steadily eroded during the 1870s and '80s. Those who held Trade dollars were reluctant to take such a loss, and the government would not relieve their burden by buying the coins back at face value. The unpleasantness of this situation was summed up by Treasury Secretary Charles J. Folger in his annual report for 1883:

> The reading of the laws taught the people that the trade dollar was a coin of their sovereignty, and for the redemption of which, at an unabated value, their Government was bound ... . It is plain that a busy people, finding this coin afloat in the channels of business, styled a coin of the United States, would readily believe that it was an authentic issue of the Government and to be redeemed by the Government, the same as other money put out by it ... . It is best, once and for all, to call it in and put it out of possible use.

Several bills were floated for the redemption of Trade dollars, but these typically fell victim to conflicting political interests. While the debate raged in Congress, speculators began buying up all the Trade dollars they could get at their bullion value. Thus, by the time a redemption bill was passed in February 1887, most of the coins were no longer in active circulation. The speculators realized their profit when the government agreed to buy back at full face value all Trade dollars that had not been "defaced, mutilated, or stamped." This amnesty for the Trade dollar was to last for a period of just six months, during which time they would be received by the Treasury in exchange for fractional silver coins or standard silver dollars (coinage of which had resumed in 1878). The silver recovered from the melted Trade dollars was later recoined into additional fractional silver pieces.

The redemption law's exclusion of mutilated or stamped coins is a reference to the Asian practice of "chopping" silver

The following unctuous fondness for silver was put forth by Senator [Timothy O.] Howe, afterward a delegate to the Monetary Conference of 1878:

"But we are told the cheaper metal will drive out the dearer, and gold will be banished from our circulation. Silver will not drive out anything. Silver is not aggressive; it is so much like the apostle's description of wisdom that it is "pure, then peaceable, gentle." ... Put a silver and a gold dollar into the same purse and they will lie quietly together."

– J. Laurence Laughlin, in his *History of Bimetallism in the United States*, 1898. Howe's saccharine comment came during a debate over whether to legislate the minting of great amounts of silver coinage, which was the goal of those seeking outlets for their depreciated metal.

dollars. Chopmarks are characters in Chinese or Malay script that were applied with punches to silver coins to indicate that they had passed inspection by a particular merchant or coin broker. A chop was his personal guarantee that the coin was of good silver. This device served to facilitate a coin's acceptance in circulation while also serving as an inexpensive form of advertising. Some Trade dollars were so frequently chopped that their design is scarcely recognizable, and the coins are actually bent. The fact that chopmarked Trade dollars were not redeemable led to thousands of them surviving to the present day, and these customized coins are fascinating relics of a romantic period in history. Fortunately, for those wishing to admire the beauty of the Trade dollar's intricate design, quite a number of unmarked examples also have survived.

The discontinuance of the half dime in 1873 prompted a brief coinage of 20-cent pieces under the Act of March 3, 1875. It was argued that because nickels did not circulate in the West, customers were being shortchanged when making 10¢ purchases with a quarter dollar. Only a dime could be returned in such transactions, and this became known as the "short bit," a reference to the popular name for the Spanish 1-*real* coin valued at 12½ cents. It evidently never occurred to anyone that by simply distributing nickels out West the problem would solve itself. Perhaps the western prejudice against coins not made of silver or gold precluded this action. Whatever the reason, nickels were finally shipped to the western states around the turn of the century, and the San Francisco Mint began producing them in 1912.

The real impetus for creating another silver coin had little to do with practical need. It was simply another outlet for domestically mined silver, which was being produced in greater amounts than the market could absorb. The 20-cent piece was essentially a subsidy to the silver mining industry, rather than a coin of any great utility.

Chief Engraver William Barber prepared a number of distinctive patterns dated 1874 and 1875 before the final models were selected. Though its eagle reverse was borrowed from the Trade dollar, the new coin was otherwise quite

The overwhelming supply of unwanted silver dollars struck under the Bland-Allison Act forced the Philadelphia Mint to add a steel vault for storage. (From Illustrated History of the United States Mint *by George G. Evans, 1893)*

similar in size and design to the quarter dollar. As a consequence, the two were easily confused, even though the quarter had a reeded edge and the 20-cent piece a plain one. After just two years of production for general circulation (1875 and 1876) the 20-cent piece was discontinued. It survived in the Mint's annual proof sets for collectors as late as 1878, when its coinage was terminated by law on May 2.

This ill-fated coin was just another round in a campaign of advocacy being staged by congressmen representing the silver mining interests of western states. The silver dollar had been legislated out of existence in 1873, a belated recognition that this coin had never really circulated in significant numbers. But the steadily falling price of silver prompted calls for renewal of the standard silver dollar from those seeking additional outlets for their metal. The elimination of the silver dollar was now being branded as the "Crime of '73," and this rallying cry was carelessly thrown about by parties having little real knowledge of monetary matters.

In what would become perhaps the most heated political and economic issue of the late 19th and early 20th centuries, the debate over whether to coin silver dollars began with a victory for the silver interests. The Bland-Allison Act of February 28, 1878, reinstated the standard silver dollar (as opposed to the Trade dollar) at the same standards for weight and fineness adopted in 1837 (412.5 grains, .900 fine), even though such a coin was now worth less than a gold dollar.

The new law, passed despite the veto of President Rutherford B. Hayes, required that the Treasury purchase silver bullion worth between $2 million and $4 million at the prevailing market rate each and every month, and that this bullion be coined into silver dollars of the 1837 standard. These coins backed, dollar-for-dollar, a new type of paper money known as Silver Certificates, and in actual practice the notes circulated rather than the coins. The silver dollars simply piled up in vaults in the mints and the Treasury Building until there was no space left to hang one's hat. The urgency to both coin and store silver dollars was so great that the old New Orleans Mint resumed production in 1879 after an 18-year suspension. This facility would assume much of the silver dollar production over the next few years, freeing the other mints to coin more useful denominations.

The sole virtue of the new silver dollar coinage was that it provided numismatists with a very beautiful entry in the federal series. U.S. Mint Chief Engraver William Barber was in competition with his recently hired assistant engraver, George T. Morgan. Barber and Morgan were both Englishmen by birth, but this did little to ease the rivalry. Instead, it simply raised the stakes and made both artists perform at their very best. Morgan ultimately won the contest for the new dollar with a design he had originally prepared for a proposed series of fractional silver coins. Hastily adapted to the dollar, Morgan's splendid bust of Liberty became an American classic, and this type is, accordingly, known as the "Morgan dollar."

Liberty faces left wearing the Liberty Cap and a headband inscribed with her name. Her hair is adorned with cotton bolls, tobacco leaves, and a sheaf of wheat, all of them plants reflective of American agriculture. Around the periphery are 13 stars and the legend E PLURIBUS UNUM, while the date is below Liberty's bust. The reverse of this handsome coin is dominated by an American eagle with its wings upraised. The eagle, partially encircled by a laurel wreath, clutches the traditional olive branch in its right claw and three arrows in its left. The motto IN GOD WE TRUST is directly above the eagle, while UNITED STATES OF AMERICA is inscribed around the periphery, with the value ONE DOLLAR below. Pleased with his work, Morgan placed his initial M on it twice – at the truncation of Liberty's neck and on the bow securing the wreath.

Morgan used as his model for the portrait of Liberty a Philadelphia school-

1878 20-cent piece (22 mm)

1878-S Morgan dollar (38.1 mm)

Thomas Nast's February 16, 1878, cartoon shows Uncle Sam stuck in a trap that resembles Senator Stanley Matthews of Ohio. Matthews had offered a resolution making silver legal tender for the payment of government bonds. (*From* Harper's Weekly)

teacher named Anna Williams, who was then 18 years old. As an art student, she had become acquainted with painter Thomas Eakins, through whom she was introduced to Morgan. It was at Eakins' home that Anna Williams sat for Morgan on five occasions during November 1876. Examples of her lovely portrait have survived in great numbers, due to a fortunate circumstance peculiar to silver dollars of this type. It is typical for U.S. coins of the late 19th century to be found heavily worn, their features obscured. This, however, was not to be the fate of Morgan's dollar. Because these coins did not circulate to any great extent, millions have survived in uncirculated condition, making them a favorite with today's coin collectors and preserving the profile of Anna Williams for posterity.

While it seemed that no one wanted silver dollars, the law demanded their coinage. As the value of silver continued to decline during the 1880s, the battle between those advocating a single gold standard and those promoting "bimetallism" stretched across every stratum of society. The cry of "Free Silver" (a policy of taking all offered deposits of silver bullion and paying for them in silver coin at face value) was used as a campaign motto by those who stood to benefit most from the inflationary pressures it caused. These included farmers and laborers, who were frequently mired in debt and who would be able to repay these debts in less-valuable dollars.

As though the terms of the 1878 law were not generous enough to the silver mining industry, another bill known as the Sherman Silver Purchase Act was passed July 14, 1890. This repealed the earlier Bland-Allison Act and provided for even greater government purchases of silver. The Treasury was required to buy as much silver as was offered, up to a monthly average of 4.5 million ounces. Of this, 2 million ounces were to be coined each month into silver dollars until July 1, 1891, after which the mints would coin only as much as was needed to redeem the new issue of Treasury Notes provided for in this same law.

In addition to inundating the Treasury Department with unneeded and unwanted silver dollars, this law carried with it a disastrous provision regarding the Treasury Notes: they were redeemable "in coin," either gold or silver, at the discretion of the Treasury Secretary. Since the price of silver was continuing to fall, Secretary William Windom knew that the only means of maintaining the value of the notes at a par with gold was to redeem them in that metal. This was so ordered, and the great gold rush began. Owners of silver bullion sold their metal to the government, receiving

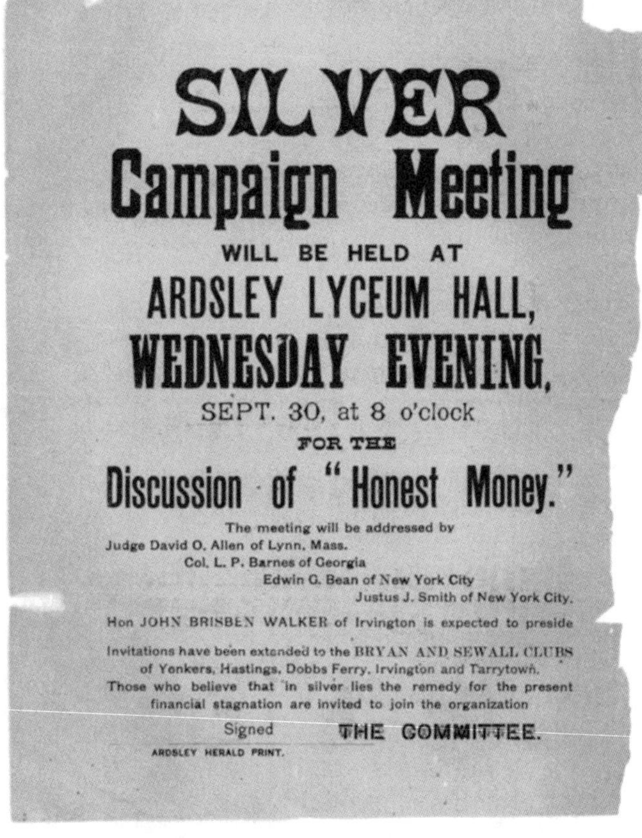
SILVER
Campaign Meeting
WILL BE HELD AT
ARDSLEY LYCEUM HALL,
WEDNESDAY EVENING,
SEPT. 30, at 8 o'clock
FOR THE
Discussion of "Honest Money."
The meeting will be addressed by
Judge David O. Allen of Lynn, Mass.
Col. L. P. Barnes of Georgia
Edwin G. Bean of New York City
Justus J. Smith of New York City.
Hon JOHN BRISBEN WALKER of Irvington is expected to preside
Invitations have been extended to the BRYAN AND SEWALL CLUBS of Yonkers, Hastings, Dobbs Ferry, Irvington and Tarrytown.
Those who believe that in silver lies the remedy for the present financial stagnation are invited to join the organization
Signed THE COMMITTEE.
ARDSLEY HERALD PRINT.

Announcement for a gathering at Ardsley, New York, in 1896

The reverse of the first Morgan dollars struck for circulation displayed an eagle with eight tailfeathers (above), one more than the traditional seven. Although a new master hub was quickly created to correct the mistake, some existing eight-feather dies were simply reworked to show just seven. On some of these dies the alteration is evident, resulting in coins that show two sets of feathers.

Having behind us the producing masses of this nation and the world, supported by the laboring interests and the toilers everywhere, we will answer their demand for a gold standard by saying to them: You shall not press down upon the brow of labor this crown of thorns; you shall not crucify mankind on a cross of gold.

– From William Jennings Bryan's three-hour "Cross of Gold" speech at the 1896 Democratic presidential convention

Treasury Notes in payment. These were then returned to the Treasury in exchange for gold coins, the difference between the intrinsic values of the silver and the gold dollar representing pure profit. Investors from England and France were particularly quick to withdraw their funds in gold, since the recklessness of the Sherman Act made them very uneasy. The redeemed notes were soon reissued along with new ones, and the Government was nearly stripped of its gold reserves in this seemingly endless cycle.

The specter of the United States being unable to back its currency with gold was so frightening that Congress ultimately repealed the Sherman Act, effective November 2, 1893. Even so, the amount of silver already purchased up to that time was so great that the mints did not use it up until 1904, at which time the production of silver dollars ceased. When the Sherman Act was finally repealed, the drain on Treasury gold had already prompted a painful deflation, causing the dollar to rise in value and both wages and prices to fall. This led to several years of economic depression and labor strife, further fueling the demand for inflationary bimetallism and the free coinage of silver. These issues reached their climax in the presidential elections of 1896 and 1900, when the Free Silver Democrat William Jennings Bryan ran against the Gold Standard Republican William McKinley. Bryan's peak of popularity came with his impassioned plea that man not be crucified upon a "Cross of Gold." But the gold advocates prevailed in both elections, and yet another law was passed in 1900 reaffirming the gold standard already in place.

Though gold was now the law of the land, two of its coin denominations were quietly retired. The gold dollar and $3 pieces had ceased to be used in everyday commerce after 1862. Even when paper money achieved parity with gold in 1879 and the government resumed specie payments, these two denominations were effectively obsolete. To a lesser extent, this was true also of the quarter eagle. All three coins continued to be produced after 1879 primarily for the benefit of those wishing to present them as gifts or fashion them into items of jewelry. So popular did coin jewelry become during the 1880s that the small-mintage issues from those years were quickly targeted by speculators, who preserved many of them in uncirculated condition. While this has proved a delight to modern-day numismatists, such activity was perceived as a racket by Mint officials, and the discontinuance of both the gold dollar and $3 coins was urged repeatedly. This finally came to pass with the Act of

The day after his speech Bryan was nominated as the Democratic Party's presidential candidate. He was also nominated by the Populist Party and the National Silver Party, and gained the support of pro-silver factions in the Republican Party. Ultimately, however, Bryan lost to William McKinley. This poster from his 1900 campaign shows Lady Liberty battling an octopus that has wrapped its tenticles around American industry.

September 26, 1890, which also abolished the copper-nickel three-cent piece.

As America entered the 1890s, its roster of coins was trimmed to just 10 issues. These included the bronze cent; the copper-nickel five-cent piece; the silver dime, quarter dollar, half dollar, and dollar; and the gold quarter eagle, half eagle, eagle, and double eagle. The cent through dollar are still with us today, though most have undergone one or more changes of composition. Only the five-cent piece of 75% copper and 25% nickel remains as it was a century ago.

The humble nickel has instead experienced a number of design changes. The original Shield design of 1866 was declared unsuitable almost from the very outset. Coins of this type did not strike up well, and for that reason the rays were removed from its reverse in 1867. This was only partly successful in improving its technical qualities. Unfortunately, this move also prompted widespread rumors that the coins without rays were counterfeit! The Mint contemplated scrapping the design altogether as early as 1867, and several pattern nickels bearing that date are known with far superior designs. Even with all its problems, the Shield nickel somehow managed to remain in production for more than 15 years before it was finally replaced.

When Charles Barber succeeded his late father as chief engraver in 1880, one of his first tasks was a general redesign of the nation's minor coins. He prepared patterns for a set of one-cent, three-cent, and five-cent pieces of matching designs that were to be coined in either copper-nickel or pure nickel. While the two smaller coins ultimately remained as they were, his design was applied to the circulating copper-nickel 5-cent piece midway through 1883. It features on its obverse a classical bust of Liberty facing left. Her hair is tied back, and she wears a coronet inscribed with her name, as, well as a garland of wheat, cotton bolls, and tobacco leaves. The bust is surrounded by 13 stars, with the date below. The reverse of this coin displays a large Roman numeral V (indicating 5) in a wreath of corn, wheat, cotton, and tobacco. Around the border are the legends UNITED STATES OF AMERICA and E PLURIBUS UNUM.

The new nickel was superior to the previous edition in all respects but one. This coin is unique among the works of Charles Barber in that it does not bear his initial "B" anywhere in its design, yet it was another element that Barber did not include that caused the Mint so much grief. Though the value CENTS appears on a number of the patterns for this type dated 1882, the version that went into circulation the following year did not include any statement of value, aside from the Roman V. This, of course, was in keeping with the original goal of producing a uniform minor coinage of copper-nickel in which the values were expressed simply with Roman numerals, as on the existing three-cent piece. Taking advantage of this coin's similarity in size to the gold half eagle, con artists quickly gold-plated the new pieces and passed them as $5. This scam was even more convincing when a reeded edge was applied to the plain-edge nickel before plating it.

One of the most amusing accounts of these so-called "racketeer" nickels allegedly involved a deaf-mute named Josh Tatum. Arrested for making a small purchase and accepting change for $5, Tatum's defense was that he never said the coin was worth $5 – the merchant merely assumed it was. As the story goes, the court found in Tatum's favor, but with a warning to pass no more of the gold-plated nickels.

Whether this particular episode is true or not, the Mint was embarrassed by its omission of a clearly stated value, and the new nickel's reverse was immediately modified to include the word CENTS. This was placed at the bottom, while E PLURIBUS UNUM was relocated in small letters above the wreath. In this form, the Liberty Head nickel remained in production for 30 years until being superseded by a new design in 1913.

1883 No CENTS Liberty Head nickel (21.1 mm)

Liberty Head nickel reverse with CENTS

Specialty Strikes

Commemorative U.S. Coins

On September 9, 1861, the first year of the Civil War, Mint officers and workers took an oath of allegiance to the United States Constitution, which was commemorated on this medal designed by Anthony C. Paquet. (31 mm)

Coins honoring individuals, events, and achievements are nearly as old as the concept of coinage. While the Ancient Greeks typically depicted the creatures of their world – both real and imagined – as well as mythical gods, it was the Romans with their realistic portraiture who defined the modern notion of commemorative coins. The privileged figures of the Republican period issued coins with their own image and name, and these vanity productions clearly may be considered commemorative in nature. Military victories and other signal events of Roman history, particularly during the first few centuries of the Imperial period, were routinely announced throughout the empire via its coinage.

The tradition of issuing commemorative coins sharply declined along with the rest of Western civilization during the Middle Ages but was revived during the early years of the Renaissance. The production of larger coins that offered the engraver a roomier canvas, along with the revival of accurate portraiture under the great Italian medallists of the 16th century, led to a general resurgence of coins as art. The propaganda value of coins in guiding popular opinion in largely illiterate populations, a quality so well understood by the Romans, was not lost on the rulers of emerging European nations.

Columbian Exposition half dollar (30.6 mm)

While many commemoratives in the modern period of coinage have been circulating issues, the trend in the past century has been toward limited editions intended for sale or presentation. This clearly has been the concept behind the United States Mint's commemorative coin series. Though officially dating only from 1892, when the first U.S. coins having a specialized design were issued, the establishment of United States commemorative coins has been said by many to date back to 1848, when a small number of quarter eagles were struck from California gold and counterstamped CAL. at the Philadelphia Mint while still in the die. Serving as an acknowledgment of the metal's source, this simple marking did indeed make this limited issue commemorative in nature, despite the conventional design of the host coin.

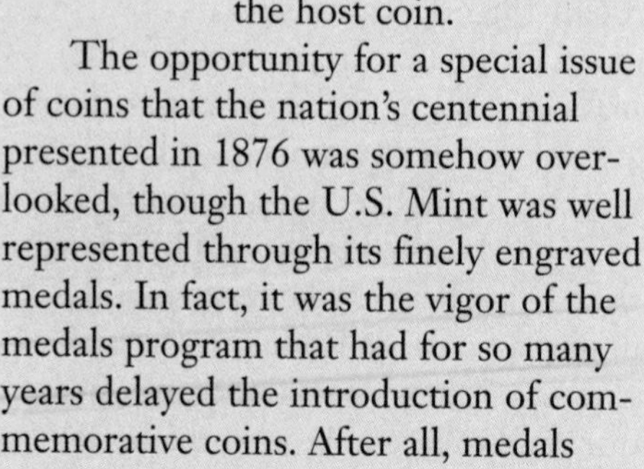

The opportunity for a special issue of coins that the nation's centennial presented in 1876 was somehow overlooked, though the U.S. Mint was well represented through its finely engraved medals. In fact, it was the vigor of the medals program that had for so many years delayed the introduction of commemorative coins. After all, medals typically presented a larger die face on which the engraver could create his art. Furthermore, medals were not bound by the restriction that they be struck just once. Limited editions by nature, medals could be produced as slowly as the relief of their designs required, each piece being sent back to the oven for annealing between successive blows of the press. Finally, issuing medals was much more agreeable to Congress than was any tinkering with the nation's coinage. It was this objection that had to be overcome before the U.S. Mint could produce strictly commemorative coins. In time this hurdle was jumped, but both Congress and the Mint eventually came to regret that the door to commemorative coinage had ever been opened.

The complete series of United States commemorative coins is a long and extensive one; it is beyond the scope of this study and deserving of a volume of its own. Presented here will be simply an historic overview of this class of coinage and how it has evolved.

The First of Their Kind

The first commemorative coin authorized by Congress was a half dollar honoring the World's Columbian Exposition, held at Chicago in 1893. This coin was designed and modeled by U.S. Mint engravers Charles Barber (obverse) and George Morgan (reverse). Unprecedented in its scale, the Columbian Exposition was intended to mark the 400th anniversary of Columbus' landing in the New World, and thus the first emission of half dollars for this event was dated 1892. When the fair was not opened until the following year, a second issue was struck with the date 1893. This misfire was a harbinger of worse things to come in succeeding commemorative programs.

The coin's purpose was not only to provide an expression of cultural pride but also to furnish a means of financing the exposition, another feature typical of United States commemorative programs. The Philadelphia Mint provided the coins to the fair's management at face value plus the cost of the dies. Sold at the fair and through the mail at $1 apiece, these coins generated profit that was used to offset the cost of staging the Columbian Exposition.

The interior of the Transportation Building at the 1893 World's Columbian Exposition

The 1900 Lafayette commemorative silver dollar (38.1 mm)

The authorizing law of August 5, 1892, provided for the coining of not more than five million Columbian half dollars, as the coins came to be known. Since there was no precedent for selling commemorative coins, it was expected that this was a reasonable figure. Despite the novelty of this uniquely designed coin, sales fell far short of the sponsors' projections. While all of the 950,000 1892 halves were distributed, more than half of the 4 million or so 1893 half dollars were returned to the Mint for melting after the exposition closed. Of those that remained, many were being held by banks as collateral against loans made to the exposition. When the fair proved a financial failure, some of these loans went unpaid. Desperate to recover some of their investment, the banks released their Columbian half dollars into general circulation at face value, accounting for the great many worn examples of both dates seen today.

The quarter dollar issued in 1893 for this same celebration fared no better, only 24,000 of the 40,000 pieces minted having been sold at $1 apiece before the balance were returned for melting. With large quantities held by speculators, both coins performed poorly in the aftermarket for many years before finally regaining their issue prices. Though the Columbian coins are now worth many times their original cost, particularly when in choice condition, they were a drug on the market in their own time and should have served as an example to sponsors of later commemorative programs. Instead, each new such enterprise was entered into with the sanguine expectation that it would be a sellout.

The next issue did not appear until 1900, when a silver dollar was authorized to commemorate America's participation in the Paris Exposition of that year and help pay for the erection of a statue in that city honoring General Lafayette.

Though dated 1900, the Lafayette dollars were actually minted on December 14, 1899, to mark the centennial of George Washington's death.

Once again, the coins were furnished to the sponsoring commission at face value plus the cost of the dies. The commission sold as many coins as it could at $2 apiece. Since few Americans could afford to attend the exposition and thus never knew of the coins, most of the sales were to established coin collectors. The latter, however, were wary of such pieces, since the Columbian quarters and halves were still retailing at less than their issue price. Of the 50,000 struck, only about 36,000 were sold. The balance was returned to the Philadelphia Mint by the commission, and the coins remained in its vaults until finally being melted in 1945!

The Series Matures

Though these first two commemorative programs had included no less than three different denominations, subsequent silver issues were restricted to the half dollar for the next 50 years, when Congress implemented a de facto ban on further commemorative coins. While there appears to exist no written explanation as to why only half dollars were used, this choice does make sense. After 1904, the silver dollar was considered an obsolete denomination, since no further provision for its coinage was expected from Congress. Thus, among the silver issues the half dollar was the largest remaining coin and provided the most room for expression of the commemorative theme. As the pace of commemorative programs accelerated

Numismatist Farran Zerbe's "Money of the World" exhibit at the Panama-Pacific Exposition

after World War I, the half dollar came to be understood as the traditional vehicle for such coins. Though silver dollar coinage was revived in 1921, sponsoring organizations opted to continue with the tried-and-true half dollar as a sales tool. There was no serious consideration of coining commemorative silver dollars at that time, and the suspension of both silver dollar and gold coinage after the mid-1930s further restricted such special programs to the half dollar denomination.

Gold coins were periodically represented in the commemorative series, though their higher face values naturally prompted higher issue prices. Predictably, this resulted in sluggish sales, despite such gimmicks as offering multiple dates and designs for the same event. After a series of commemorative gold dollars in 1903 to 1905, there was a 10-year absence of commemorative coins, Congress rejecting most proposals in favor of U.S. Mint medals.

It was not until 1915 that commemorative coinage came back with a vengeance, Congress approving an unprecedented five-coin program for the Panama-Pacific International Exposition in San Francisco. This event honored the 1914 opening of the Panama Canal, a cause worthy of celebration. Included in the program were a silver half dollar, a gold dollar and quarter eagle, and two massive $50 gold pieces. Sales of the latter two were understandably quite small, as each coin cost $100.

Though a few additional offerings of gold dollars and quarter eagles were made as late as 1926, far more common were silver commemorative half dollars. These included a rich variety of themes, though the majority honored anniversaries and events of primarily local or regional interest. Therein lay the greatest criticism of United States commemoratives, for their value as numismatic art was often quite excellent, irrespective of theme. Some of America's finest sculptors provided the models for these coins, among them James Earle Fraser and his wife Laura Gardin Fraser, Robert Aitken, Chester Beach, Charles Keck, and Jo Mora.

1915-S Panama-Pacific octagonal $50 gold piece (42 mm)

Boom and Bust

1938-S Oregon Trail silver half dollar (30.6 mm). The obverse, designed by Laura Gardin Fraser, shows an American Indian appearing to warn, "So far and no farther!" The reverse, by James Earle Fraser, displays a Conestoga wagon and a pioneer family headed westward.

The pace of commemorative issues accelerated during the early 1920s and remained fairly high through much of that decade. President Herbert Hoover's 1929 to 1933 administration routinely vetoed all proposals for commemoratives, and no more were authorized until 1933. A flurry of new issues then appeared, with more than a dozen new types in 1936 alone. Much of this activity was prompted by a speculative market in the trading of these coins that developed around the same time, and an increasing number of abuses caused Congress to question the validity of such coinage.

Laura Gardin Fraser was best known for her medallic work, but also executed huge sculptures.

Already cited is the purely local or regional nature of some of these coins. A typical example is the 1935 half dollar honoring the City of Hudson, New York, on the 150th anniversary of its founding. While that may have been a big event to the citizens of Hudson, it clearly was not worthy of a United States coin or even, for that matter, a U.S. Mint medal. Other programs seemed to have no validity at all, but were initiated simply to provide a source of personal profit for the sponsor. An example is the 1935 coin supposedly marking the 400th anniversary of the Old Spanish Trail. Research reveals that the year 1535 was of no particular significance with respect to the trail, the route of which is depicted quite inaccurately on the coin in any case. It seems that the date 1935 was selected solely as the year in which the promoter wanted to sell a lot of half dollars to eager collectors.

As the speculative market in commemorative halves took off during 1935 and 1936, the most exploitative practice associated with these coins became pervasive and was to remain so for the next sev-eral years. Many of the coin bills had not placed any restriction on the year and mint of coining – only the overall total had been specified. Since this figure was typically far higher than the number of coins that could be sold in a year, it opened the door for annual emissions of the same coin types at all three mints. Thus, instead of needing just one coin for each type, collectors found themselves having to buy three-piece sets, year after year, of coins that had been created for celebrations long since past. Issue prices also rose each year, as the sponsoring commissions and their retail distributors now had a captive audience. In addition, it was not unusual for the sponsors to announce a sellout almost immediately, when in fact the entire mintage of a particular issue had been sold to a cartel of insiders. These buyers were now the only source of the desired coins, and their selling prices were much higher than the announced issue price.

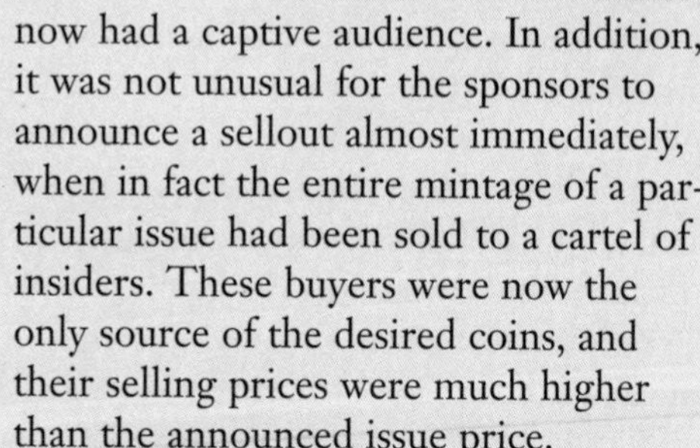

Through much of 1936, collectors rode the speculative bubble, griping all the time about such abuses but not wanting to miss out on the excitement. But with so many new coin types appearing that year, interest in commemoratives waned, and the speculative market collapsed. Subsequent issues offered in 1937 and 1938 were poor sellers, and the prices of all previous issues fell.

Far from being a total loss, the commemorative boom and bust of the 1930s did have a positive overall effect on the coin hobby. As with any such speculation, many new players jumped on the bandwagon and then just as quickly disappeared when the party was over, but the number of enthusiastic collectors was distinctly higher at the end of the cycle than before. Combined with the concurrent introduction of inexpensive coin boards and albums, the commemorative mania greatly increased the ranks of numismatic hobbyists.

By 1939 Congress had seen enough of commemoratives, and a law was passed on August 5 that terminated all programs authorized prior to March 1, 1939. Though there existed no prohibition on new programs, the atmosphere in the White House and on Capitol Hill was clearly against any such coins, regardless of merit. The onset of World War II, with its greatly increased demand for circulating coins, would have precluded the issuance of commemoratives in any case.

1951 Washington-Carver half dollar (30.6 mm)

An Uncertain Revival

With the war over, in 1946 Congress reluctantly approved two new issues of commemorative half dollars that were expected to be free of the abuses associated with earlier programs. The Iowa Centennial half dollar was, in fact, a model of how an honest and dedicated commission could handle sales to everyone's satisfaction. The other coin authorized that year, however, was to prove a repeat of the worst of the prewar programs.

The subject was worthy of commemoration. Booker T. Washington, the great black educator and founder of Tuskegee Institute, was featured in a fine portrait by sculptor Isaac Scott Hathaway. Washington's birthplace cabin was depicted on the reverse, along with the Hall of Fame of Great Americans, in which Washington is enshrined. Profits from the sale of these coins were designated for the perpetuation of Booker T. Washington's teachings and for the erection and maintenance of memorials to the great man.

The sole flaw in this bill was, once again, in its language. Failing to recall the lessons of earlier commemorative coin programs, Congress neglected to specify a single date and mint of coining. Since sales of the first issue dated 1946 were disappointing, the sponsor ordered additional coins annually from all three mints, expecting that a certain number of collectors could be counted on to buy every offering for the sake of completeness or simple speculation. Promoter S.J. Phillips then took this a step further in 1951, when he requested that the remaining authorized total be coined with a modified design featuring conjoined busts of Booker T. Washington and scientist George Washington Carver. Congress relented only because the bill included a stipulation that money raised from the sales of these coins would be used "to oppose the spread of communism among

George Washington Carver (left) and Booker T. Washington (below)

1982-S Proof George Washington half dollar (30.6 mm)

Negroes in the interest of national defense." That such an argument was successful is indicative of America's political climate at that time.

The folly of producing these coins year after year became obvious when none of Phillips' plans to memorialize Washington and Carver bore any fruit. An exhausted Congress ordered a halt to further production of Washington/Carver halves after 1954, and most people in political circles understood that there would be no further authorizations of commemorative coins. Numerous bills were introduced over the next 27 years without success, and collectors pretty much accepted that this chapter in United States coinage had closed.

Commemoratives Stage a Comeback

Given the general disregard in Congress for commemorative coins, it was with a sense of amazement and delight that collectors learned of the coin to be minted in 1982 for the 250th anniversary of George Washington's birth. The bill was not passed until December 23, 1981, so the Mint had to work fast.

Fortunately, it had as its chief engraver the very talented Elizabeth Jones. She modeled an equestrian figure of Washington for the coin's obverse and designed the reverse, which was sculpted by fellow Mint engraver Matthew Peloso. The result was an extremely attractive production fully equal to the best of the vintage issues.

1987-P United States Constitution silver dollar (38.1 mm)

Due to its novelty and the lack of a fixed cutoff date for orders, the Washington half dollar was sold in huge quantities by commemorative coin standards. While this caused its value to plummet in the aftermarket, at least the money raised from its sale was used honorably. Rather than funding the scheme of some private commission, all profits were directed toward reduction of the national debt. Sadly, this was to be the first and last time that a modern commemorative program was so free from charges of favoritism or malfeasance. Each subsequent program was designed as a fund-raising vehicle for some organization or institution, the same flaw that had led to the demise of the first commemorative series.

The success of the Washington half dollar program led to an ever-accelerating series of coin issues during the remainder of the 1980s and through much of the '90s. Most issues marked anniversaries of one sort or another. A typical example was the three-denomination set coined in 1992 for the quincentenary of Columbus' discovery of the New World, a program that brought the commemorative series full circle to its 1892 origin. More puzzling was the silver dollar issued in 1991 for the 38th anniversary of the end of the Korean War. Asked whether this odd increment represented the historic 38th latitudinal parallel, the coin's sponsors unwisely answered "no," leaving collectors to wonder what other significance could be found in the date of issue.

Commemorative coins marking the Olympic games have become commonplace, too. While the first issue in 1983 to 1984 was legitimized by the fact that an American city (Los Angeles) was hosting the event, subsequent programs were clearly nothing but attempts to wrest more money from increasingly resentful coin collectors. The fact that several denominations might be authorized for a single program and that each was coined at multiple mints in both Proof and non-Proof editions often drove the annual cost of a complete collection above $1,000. At first, collectors went along with the game, dutifully buying each and every issue in all its variant forms, still buoyed by the sheer novelty of modern commemoratives. But when it became evident that these coins' mintages were too high to protect their values in the aftermarket, sales began to slide.

As these programs proliferated, once again the worthiness of their subject matter and funding recipients came into question. Commemorative coin sales quickly became the preferred means for funding the pet projects of special interest groups, their surcharges being added to whatever cost the Mint projected for producing, packaging, and distributing the coins. Indeed, unlike the marketing for the commemoratives issued from 1892 to 1954, these new coins were actually retailed by the Mint.

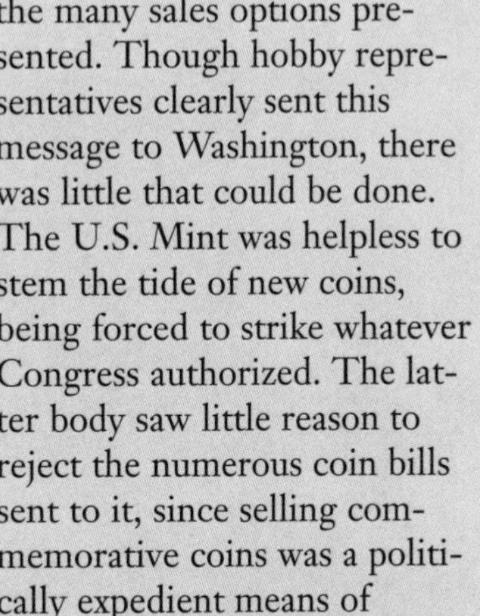

1987-W U.S. Constitution half eagle (21.6 mm)

By the end of the 1980s there was growing resistance among collectors to the large number of new commemorative coins and the many sales options presented. Though hobby representatives clearly sent this message to Washington, there was little that could be done. The U.S. Mint was helpless to stem the tide of new coins, being forced to strike whatever Congress authorized. The latter body saw little reason to reject the numerous coin bills sent to it, since selling commemorative coins was a politically expedient means of funding memorials and other projects that otherwise would have required tax appropriations. As sales of each new coin program continued to drop during the early 1990s, the Mint found itself actually suffering net losses after its costs and the recipients' surcharges were deducted.

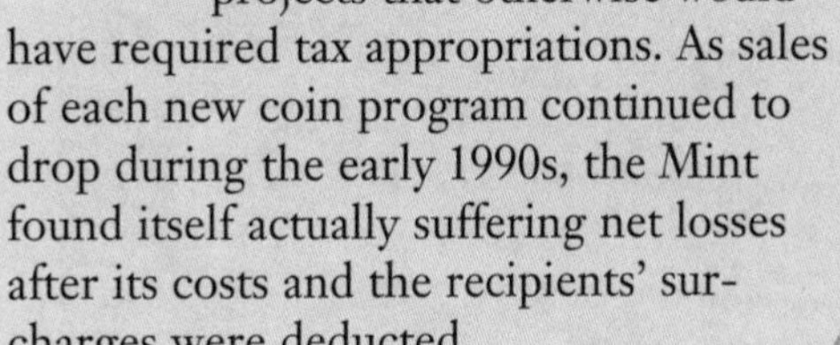

1992-S Proof XXV Olympiad commemorative silver half dollar (30.6 mm)

A Time of Reflection

As the 20th century drew to a close, the number of commemorative coin programs had successfully been reduced to two annually, though the pressure to lift this ceiling is always present. Of course, the generally lower sales of recent issues have somewhat diminished the appeal of these coins to fund-raising organizations.

While a number of truly attractive issues have resulted from the modern commemorative coin series, most are mediocre in both subject matter and execution. Often designed by committees or by graphic artists, they reveal the mistakes common to those not well versed in numismatic art. The Mint has contributed to this mediocrity by insisting on low relief to maximize die life, despite the fact that these coins are produced in very small numbers and may be struck more than once, if needed.

The long-term response to the modern commemorative series will be determined by later generations of collectors who have had no first-hand experience with their objectionable history. This has happened already with the vintage commemoratives, the marketing of which was usually no less controversial and often far more so. Ultimately, the coins will have to stand or fall on their own merits, the common fate of all numismatic issues.

1997-S Jackie Robinson silver dollar (38.1 mm)

The Mastery of Saint-Gaudens

Saint-Gaudens was diagnosed with cancer in 1900 and died in 1907 before his redesign of America's coins was complete.

Augustus Saint-Gaudens' first major commission was a statue of Civil War admiral David Farragut, unveiled in 1881. The work blended allegory with the realism then so prevalent in American sculpture, and it was this departure from the norm that launched his career. More commissions came his way, and his many successes established him as one of the nation's finest artists.

President Theodore Roosevelt was so taken with the inaugural medal Saint-Gaudens created for him in 1905 that he enlisted him as a partner in his "pet crime" – redesigning America's coins to meet a higher aesthetic standard.

Roosevelt wanted to achieve the high relief seen on ancient Greek coins, and Saint-Gaudens agreed that this was a worthy goal. Both men understood from the outset that there would have to be compromises between their vision and the harsh realities of a production process controlled by the Mint's formidable chief engraver, Charles Barber.

After Roosevelt suggested that producing these unusual coins might take its toll on Mint workers, Saint-Gaudens replied, "Whatever I produce cannot be worse than the inanities now displayed on our coins and we will at least have made an attempt in the right direction, and serve the country by increasing the mortality at the mint. There is one gentleman [Charles Barber] there, however, who, when he sees what is coming, may have 'the nervous prostitution' as termed by a native here, but killed, no. He has been in that institution since the foundation of the government and will be found standing in its ruins."

Ultimately, Saint-Gaudens created a magnificent high-relief double eagle that suffered mightily from being flattened by Charles Barber in an effort to simplify production. In Barber's defense, however, it must be noted that Saint-Gaudens' models were impractical for mass production.

Obverse of an extremely high-relief double eagle

A model for the obverse of the gold double eagle

CHAPTER TEN

New Coins for a New Age

On the same day Congress abolished the nickel three-cent piece, the gold dollar, and the $3 piece, another bill was passed that contained some very significant provisions. The first of these granted the Mint Director authority to change existing coin designs, subject to the approval of the Treasury Secretary, as soon as such designs had been in production for a minimum of 25 years. Interestingly, the law specifically exempted the current five-cent piece and silver dollar from this minimum requirement and urged their speedy replacement, implying that both designs were then considered objectionable. A final provision of this bill also proved to have far-reaching implications – it provided for the temporary hiring of outside artists whenever deemed necessary for the creation of new designs.

Ironically, this last clause was not immediately implemented for the two coins evidently considered most in need of redesign. Both Charles Barber's five-cent piece of 1883 and George Morgan's silver dollar of 1878 managed to exceed their minimum coinage period before replacements were sought. Instead, the push for new designs was directed at the three fractional silver coins. The seated figure of Liberty, which seemed so novel and impressive in 1836 and 1837, had since become the object of derision within both the numismatic community and

The Denver Mint, seen here under construction in 1904, became a powerhouse of coin production that helped stabilize the nation's coin supply.

Mint Director Edward O. Leech

It is not likely that another competition will ever be tried for the production of designs for United States coins. The one just ended was too wretched a failure.

– Edward Leech's comments following a public coin design contest, published in the July 31, 1891, *Boston Transcript*

1892-S Barber Liberty Head dime (17.9 mm)

1892 Barber Liberty Head half dollar (30.6 mm)

the general press. Aggravating this negative perception was the return to circulation in 1876 and 1877 of so many badly worn examples.

Seeking to take advantage of the new law, and yet obviously reluctant to pit Barber against Morgan, Mint Director Edward O. Leech dismissed the many splendid patterns created by these employees during the 1870s and '80s and instead launched an invitational competition for new designs. Among the 10 individuals solicited were such brilliant sculptors and medallists as Augustus Saint-Gaudens, Daniel Chester French, and Kenyon Cox. To a man, however, they rejected the restrictive terms and meager fees offered by the Treasury Department, issuing a joint rebuttal to the invitation:

> The undersigned, having been invited to prepare designs for a new coinage for the United States, beg respectfully to state that the conditions of the competition as given in the circular letter of invitation are such as to preclude the possibility of any good result from it. The time given for the preparation of designs is too short and the compensation altogether insufficient, while no assurance is given as to who will make the awards.

Also submitted by the artists was a list of recommended conditions for the coin design competition. Stunned by this rebuke, the Treasury Department discarded its plans for a contest among sculptors of proven merit and instead opted to solicit designs from any and all takers within the general public. These entries were to be judged by Charles Barber, Augustus Saint-Gaudens, and commercial engraver Henry Mitchell.

Though there was no lack of interest among the country's would-be artists, there did prove to be a certain deficiency of talent and skill, and the results of the competition were discouraging to say the very least. In its July 3, 1891, report to Treasury Secretary Charles Foster, the committee revealed this predictable outcome:

> We are of the opinion that none of the designs or models submitted are such a decided improvement upon the present designs of the silver coins of the United States as to be worthy of adoption by the Government.
>
> We would respectfully recommend that the services of one or more artists distinguished for work in designing and relief, be engaged at a suitable compensation to prepare, for the consideration of the Department, new designs for the coins of the United States.

Embarrassed and exhausted by this sequence of events, Director Leech simply instructed Chief Engraver Barber to prepare the requisite designs. The results of his labors debuted early in 1892 to mixed reviews. While the general press and public seemed satisfied with the new dime, quarter dollar, and half dollar, numismatists were either mildly disappointed with the coins or remained silent on the matter. Editor and publisher of *The Numismatist*, Dr. George Heath, remarked, "The mechanical work is all that could be desired, and it is probable, that owing to the conventional rut in which our mint authorities seem obliged to keep, that it is the best that could be done ... ." While his was faint praise indeed, these coins, commonly called the "Barber type" after their creator, found greater favor with later generations of collectors.

Barber fashioned a purely classical head of Liberty in the Roman style that is somewhat reminiscent of Morgan's silver dollar. He was guided in this direction by Mint Director Leech, who specifically requested that Barber furnish a near copy of the Ceres bust then current on French coinage. The goddess faces right wearing the Liberty Cap, as well as a crown fashioned from an olive branch and a small headband inscribed with her name. On the quarter dollar and half dollar, the motto IN GOD WE TRUST appears above her, while 13 stars arranged six left and seven right flank her portrait, with the date below. The reverse of these two coins depicts the Great Seal of the United States. The heraldic eagle is accompanied by the legend UNITED STATES OF AMERICA above and the value QUARTER (or HALF) DOLLAR below. The dime features the same bust of Liberty, but with the nation's identity in place of the stars and motto of the larger coins. Its reverse is a slight revision of the wreath in use on the dime since 1860, which depicts a collection of American flora including corn, wheat, oak, and tobacco. This encircles the value ONE DIME. On all three coins, Barber's initial B is found at the truncation of the bust.

The period during which the Barber silver coins were issued (1892 to 1916) was a very stable one for United States coinage in terms of the number of pieces made and their unrestricted circulation. In fact, aside from the political debate over silver dollars, there were no problems whatsoever with the coinage, and Americans enjoyed the privilege of a convenient and reliable supply. Despite the gradual introduction of non-circulating commemorative coins beginning in 1892, the designs and denominations of the regular types remained standardized through 1906, and production was fairly consistent at the four mints active during these years. In addition to the mints at Philadelphia and San Francisco, gold and silver coins were produced at the New Orleans Mint until it ceased coining in 1909, and at the new Denver Mint beginning in 1906.

Until 1906, the production of minor coins (cents and nickels) was confined by law to the parent facility at Philadelphia for reasons that had long ceased to be valid. This fact, combined with the growing popularity of these small coins in the western states, led to passage of the Act of April 24, 1906. This law authorized the production of minor coins at the two western mints and provided for the purchase of the necessary metals. Cents were first coined at San Francisco during 1908 and at the Denver Mint in 1911. Nickels from both mints made their debut in 1912, the final year of authorized production for Barber's old Liberty Head design.

Group portrait of the Philadelphia Mint's engraving staff, circa 1910. Chief Engraver Charles E. Barber is seated in the front row, second from left, and Assistant Engraver George Morgan sits to his left.

I was looking at some gold coins of Alexander the Great to-day, and I was struck by their high relief. Would it not be well to have our coins in high relief, and also to have the rims raised? The point of having the rims raised would be, of course, to protect the figure on the coin; and if we have the figures in high relief, like the figures on the old Greek coins, they will surely last longer.

– From President Theodore Roosevelt to sculptor Augustus Saint-Gaudens, November 6, 1905

The same year that the new silver coins debuted, America opened yet another chapter in its coinage history. The concept of using coins to honor important events and individuals was a familiar one to the Old World, but the first coin of a commemorative design to emanate from the United States Mint appeared in 1892. This was the half dollar designed by Charles Barber (obverse) and George Morgan (reverse). Honoring both the 400th anniversary of Christopher Columbus' discovery of the New World and the World's Columbian Exposition held at Chicago in 1893, these coins were issued to the exposition's sponsors at face value and then sold by them to the public at $1 apiece. Though some five million coins were struck dated 1892 and 1893, most of the latter remained unsold and were melted. A few years later, many pieces of both dates were dumped into circulation at face value by banks holding them as collat-eral against loans that were not repaid by the exposition.

President Theodore Roosevelt

This inauspicious beginning proved to be all too typical of such fund-raising coins, and most of the several dozen commemorative types produced over the next 60-plus years, however appealing they may be as artworks and collectibles, were considered exploitative at the time of issue. Continued abuses by the sponsoring agencies finally led Congress to reject all commemorative coin legislation introduced from 1952 through 1980. It was not until 1981 that a new bill was passed, this one authorizing a coin in honor of the 250th anniversary of George Washington's birth in 1982. The proceeds from sales of this issue were directed toward reducing the national debt, and in that respect the program was quite honorable. But most of the subsequent commemoratives, though mar-keted by the U.S. Mint itself, have been intended as fundraisers for various special interests. As with earlier commemorative programs, Congress has approved a number of coin bills of questionable merit, and the sales and popularity of these coins has generally declined since 1982.

The Act of 1890, permitting the Mint to temporarily employ outside artists to design its coins, had not been tested after the unsuccessful 1891 competition. But, as the nation entered the 20th century, this authority was about to be used to outstanding effect. Dissatisfaction among numismatists and those having an interest in public art grew after the adoption of Barber's staid designs in 1892. Though most of this frustration was focused on the minor coins and fractional silver pieces, it was the various gold issues that were first selected for upgrading. No less a figure than President of the United States Theodore Roosevelt championed this cause, an action he described as "my pet crime." Inspired by the bold medal that sculptor Augustus Saint-Gaudens had created for his inauguration in 1905, Roosevelt enlisted the artist's talents in what the two conceived as a complete reworking of the existing coinage. Being an individual who never did anything small, Roosevelt determined that the two highest denominations, the eagle and double eagle, would be the first coins touched by Saint-Gaudens' genius.

Though the great artist died before these new coins were completed, his assistant, Henry Hering, carried on the work, performing the sculpting himself. Several variants were produced of both the eagle and double eagle, employing differing heights of relief, but the actual production coins of 1907 and later years were issued from conventional, low-relief dies prepared by Chief Engraver Charles Barber. Though much of the original works' spirit was

1907 extremely high-relief Saint-Gaudens double eagle with the date expressed in Roman numerals (34 mm)

lost in this translation, the coins produced for circulation were still remarkably beautiful and a vast improvement over the aged Liberty heads by Gobrecht and Longacre.

For the eagle's obverse, Saint-Gaudens reworked his head of Nike from New York City's monument to General William T. Sherman. Whereas the original work, in keeping with classical portraiture, featured a laureate head, Roosevelt requested that this be replaced with a Native American feathered headdress. The band of this Indian bonnet is inscribed LIBERTY, and the date appears below the bust. On the reverse is a standing eagle, facing left and perched atop a bundle of arrows around which curves an olive branch. Above the eagle is E PLURIBUS UNUM. The legend UNITED STATES OF AMERICA is inscribed around the upper periphery, with the value TEN DOLLARS beneath the eagle. In place of the traditional reeded edge, this type has an edge design featuring 46 raised stars representing the states of the Union. (Two additional stars were included with the admission of New Mexico and Arizona in 1912.)

Midway through 1908, the motto IN GOD WE TRUST was added to the left of the eagle. This had been omitted at the specific instructions of President Roosevelt, who believed that its inclusion on money was blasphemous. Public opinion held otherwise, and Congress ordered that the motto be retrofitted to both the eagle and double eagle beginning in 1908. It has appeared on virtually every United States coin minted since that time, though the nickels of 1913 to 1938 are a notable exception.

1927 low-relief Saint-Gaudens double eagle (34 mm)

The new double eagle was even more magnificent than its little brother. In place of the traditional bust of Liberty, the Saint-Gaudens design features a facing figure of the goddess striding toward the viewer, bearing a torch in her right hand and holding aloft the olive branch of peace in her left. She stands on a rocky precipice with a sunburst behind her. To the left is a small representation of the U.S. Capitol, while an oak branch is seen at the right, beneath the date and the artist's monogram. Above Liberty is her name, serving as the nation's motto, and nearly the entire obverse is framed by 46 stars representing the number of states in the Union (two more were added in 1912). The reverse is quite simple and elegant. A soaring eagle flies left over the rising sun, with the legend UNITED STATES OF AMERICA and the value TWENTY DOLLARS above. The Latin legend E PLURIBUS UNUM appears on the edge in raised letters (a technique rarely used with United States coinage), flanked by 13 raised stars. On some of the 1908 double eagles and on all those that followed, the motto IN GOD WE TRUST appears just above the sun's sphere.

The death of Augustus Saint-Gaudens in August 1907 prompted the search for another sculptor of his caliber to con-tinue with the remaining gold coins – the quarter eagle and half eagle. In the meantime, an acquaintance of President Roosevelt, Dr. William Sturgis Bigelow, conceived a novel treatment for the new coins. Bigelow suggested that the relief elements be placed below the coins' fields, producing an

Continued on page 146

1926 Saint-Gaudens Indian eagle with IN GOD WE TRUST on the reverse (27 mm)

*I am so glad you like the head of Liberty with the feather head-dress. Really, the feather head-dress can be treated as being the conventional cap of Liberty quite as much as if it was the Phrygian cap; and, after all, it is **our** liberty – not what the ancient Greeks and Romans miscalled by that title – and we are entitled to a typically American head-dress for the lady.*

– From President Theodore Roosevelt to Augustus Saint-Gaudens, March 14, 1907

The U.S. Mint at Denver

By the first of June 1859, Gregory Gulch from North Clear Creek to the confluence of Eureka, Nevada and Spring Gulches was literally crowded with human beings huddled together in tents, wagons, log cabins, dugouts, houses made of brush, and of every conceivable material that promised shelter.

– From a Gilpin County, Colorado, history in the December 3, 1874, *Daily Central City Register*

The United States mint that opened for business in 1906 and remains in operation today traces it origin to the private minting establishment of Clark, Gruber & Company. Purchased *en bloc* by the federal government in 1863, this facility operated simply as an assay office for the next several decades, though it was always called a United States Mint. It was not until 1904 that the current structure was occupied, and two more years passed before it produced any coins.

Known as the Mile High City, Denver lies on a high plain through which runs the South Platte River. It is the capital of Colorado and its most populous city. Until 1857, however, there was no city, nor was there a settlement of any kind. Though the area was traveled and sparsely populated by Arapaho, Cheyenne, and Ute Indians, the plains of the central Rocky Mountains had mostly been bypassed by European explorers and, later, American settlers. The entire region seemed devoid of value.

Regarding the possibilities it offered to farmers, Americans venturing into the Colorado plains found them "wholly unfit for cultivation."

On May 6, 1859, John H. Gregory discovered gold and staked claims on what came to be known as "The Richest Square Mile on Earth," near Central City, Colorado. News of the find traveled fast, and prospectors quickly flooded the area. The resulting boomtown was called "Gregory's Gulch." (From Frank Leslie's Illustrated Newspaper, *December 15, 1860)*

The Lure of Gold

Known generally as the Great American Desert, the west-central region of the United States was viewed simply as a vast wasteland through which one had to pass on the way to the richer lands of Oregon and California. This perception changed only in 1858, when the first significant gold finds occurred alongside Cherry Creek near where it met the South Platte River. Though the yellow metal had been found in this area as early as 1850, these previous discoveries had failed to fire the imaginations of Easterners. Even so, responding to the prospect of finding gold, several parties of fortune-seekers traveled to the Pike's Peak Region in the spring of 1858.

William Green Russell

William Green Russell, who hailed from a family that mined gold during the nation's earliest gold rush in Georgia, was the first to achieve success. Near a tepee that comprised the home of John Smith, his Indian wife Wappola, and son Jack, Russell found his gold on July 9, 1858. Others who had been exploring farther south near what is now the city of Colorado Springs heard of his discovery and relocated to the Cherry Creek area. Among these adventurers was Charlie Nichols, who quickly claimed the land north of the creek. He made hasty plans for a town on the site, which he named St. Charles. Not wanting to be left out, a party of 180 laid claim to the land south of Cherry Creek on October 30. They named their proposed settlement after the Georgia hometown of William Russell and his two brothers – Auraria.

With both gold fever and land speculation now growing, it was not long before others joined in the rush to the area, giving rise to the slogan "Pike's Peak or Bust." (Though well south of the Denver area, this prominent geographical feature was associated with the entire region.) Among the most aggressive of these opportunists was General William Larimer, who jumped Charlie Nichols' claim when the latter returned temporarily to his home in Kansas. Seeking to curry favor for his unethical action, Larimer renamed the St. Charles settlement in honor of the man he believed to be the governor of Kansas Territory (of which the Cherry Creek area was then a part).

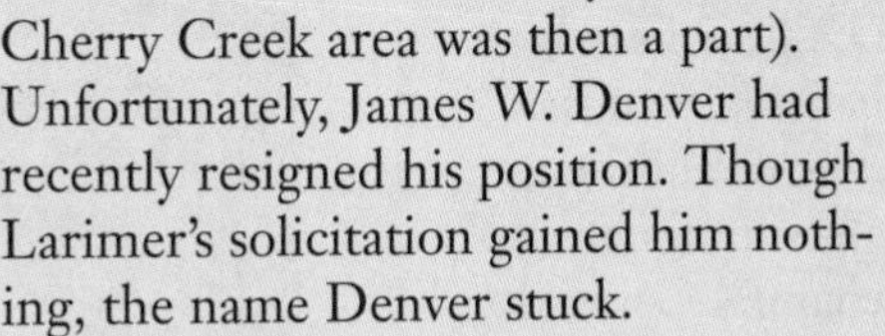

Unfortunately, James W. Denver had recently resigned his position. Though Larimer's solicitation gained him nothing, the name Denver stuck.

Initially, the gold discoveries were small placer finds in and around creek beds. Eventually, the mother lode was discovered in the area of Central City, west of Denver, but the potential for finding gold had already lured thousands to the region. As is usually the case in any gold rush, the greatest profits accrued not to those who panned or mined but to those who were in a position to provide goods and services to successive waves of prospectors.

The obverse of this $2\frac{1}{2}$-dollar gold piece shows a six-stamp quartz reduction mill, used to pulverize ore to make gold extraction easier. This denomination and \$5 gold pieces were minted by Dr. John Parsons in the back of a wagon parked in the Tarryall mining district near South Park. (17 mm)

Ten-dollar gold piece minted by bankers John J. Conway & Co. The firm converted gold dust into \$2.50, \$5, and \$10 pieces at its mint in Parkville, near present-day Breckenridge, in the early summer of 1861. (26 mm)

Denver's First Mint

1860 $20 gold piece by Clark, Gruber & Company. The cone-shaped image of Pikes Peak on the obverse, no doubt designed by someone who had never seen the mountains, was replaced in 1861 by a portrait of Liberty (below). (34 mm)

Among those who saw opportunity in the gold region were two brothers, Austin and Milton Clark. Originally from Ohio, they formed a partnership with Emanuel H. Gruber of Maryland in the spring of 1858, and the following year they commenced banking operations in Leavenworth, Kansas. Their plan was to assay and purchase raw gold from Western miners, then ship it east for coining at the Philadelphia Mint. While this scheme proved successful, it appeared that there was even greater profit to be made from coining the gold themselves, since coined money was always at a premium in frontier settings.

A precedent for this existed in the coinage of Templeton Reid and the Bechtler family in the Southeast, as well as the many privately minted issues from the California Gold Rush of 1849 to 1855. Commercial minting was still legal at the time, provided the coins were not in exact imitation of the federal issues.

In 1860 the firm of Clark, Gruber & Company relocated to Denver City in what was then the newly established Jefferson Territory (renamed Colorado Territory the following year). By that time, Denver had absorbed the old rival community of Auraria and occupied both sides of Cherry Creek. The company purchased three adjoining lots at the southwest corner of G Street (now 16th) and McGaa Street (now Market). Costing $5,000, their new building had two floors where it fronted the street and a basement at ground level in the rear only. This basement housed the minting equipment, while the first floor was used for the firm's banking business, and the upper floor was reserved for offices.

In December 1859, Milton Clark had gone east to order dies, presses, and associated machinery. The necessary equipment arrived on April 2, and by July 20 the partnership of Clark, Gruber & Company was ready to begin coining. $10 pieces came first, these bearing a distinctive design featuring some Eastern engraver's fanciful depiction of Pike's Peak as a perfectly conical mountain. This emission was followed by double eagles of similar design, as well as by half eagles and quarter eagles that shared the same design elements as federal coins but with appropriate legends identifying them as products of

Clark, Gruber & Company's Denver bank and mint in the early 1860s

Clark, Gruber & Company. Dated 1860, these pieces were followed by a second issue in 1861. Perhaps reacting to criticism of its odd, conical mountain peak, the 1861-dated coins were uniformly of the federal type. Following the precedent of earlier California coiners, the Denver operation dodged existing counterfeiting laws through use of its unique inscriptions.

The company's coins proved to be worth slightly more than their federal equivalents and were thus widely accepted. More than a half million dollars was coined of the four denominations. As with all such commercial coins, many of them ultimately were deposited at one of the federal mints as bullion and recoined, accounting for their scarcity today.

The little engine that drives the machinery was fired up, belts adjusted, and between three and four o'clock "mint drops," of the value of $10 each, began dropping into a tin pail with the most musical chink.

– The *Rocky Mountain News* describing minting at Clark, Gruber & Company, July 25, 1860

A Government Shop

Though pleased with the company's product, Denver citizens sought to replace the private minting firm with a branch of the federal Mint. The increased prestige and prosperity that such a transition would likely bring was not lost on Clark, Gruber & Company, and they approached the Treasury Department with a buyout offer as early as 1861.

Colorado's territorial representative, Hiram P. Bennet, introduced a bill to purchase the company in December of that year, and the necessary funding was approved by Congress on April 26, 1862. Due to some uncertainty over title to the land, the commission charged with completing the sale deliberated for almost a year. The United States finally took possession of the minting operation of Clark, Gruber & Company on April 16, 1863. Emanuel Gruber sold his interest in the firm's banking operation to his former partners, while the surviving Clark & Company was shortly thereafter merged with the new First National Bank of Denver.

Though it was anticipated that the federal branch mint would continue to produce coins in Denver, this did not come to pass for many years. It seems the Treasury Department preferred to run the facility as a mint in name only, initially citing hostile Plains Indians as a threat to the secure movement of coins. Over the next 40 years, the Denver Mint operated solely as a federal assay office, purchasing raw bullion and refining it into ingots. Though the existing structure was enlarged early on, the government made no further improvements. Even when Colorado attained statehood in 1876, it had no impact on the moribund operation.

Prospectors suffering from a particularly bad case of gold fever might have ordered the Magnetic Mineral Rod to help ensure their success, circa 1900.

The only excitement came on February 13, 1864, when a mint pay clerk named James D. Clarke absconded with gold and notes worth about $37,000. He was quickly apprehended, along with most of the stolen loot. Jailed in Denver, he briefly escaped before being recaptured. Though his was a serious federal offense, surprisingly he was simply banished from Colorado Territory.

A New Federal Mint

The 1906-D eagle was one of the first coins struck at the new Denver Mint. (27 mm)

At the turn of the century, as both Denver and the West in general grew in population and economic importance, a plan was laid to activate the Denver Mint as a federal coining facility. Silver had replaced gold as Colorado's primary mineral wealth, though a brief gold rush in the Cripple Creek area in the 1890s had brought this metal once again to the fore and had renewed calls for a real mint.

Congress approved funding for a new mint structure in 1895, restricting its coining operations to gold and silver. The following year, on April 22, a lot was purchased for $60,000 at West Colfax Avenue and Cherokee Street. The mint building was anticipated to have 100 rooms in a three-story structure measuring 100 by 200 feet. Even for that time, the dimensions seem needlessly conservative, and the passing of years would prove the folly of commissioning such a small building.

Misstruck coins were melted in this furnace so the metal could be re-used.

Construction was delayed until the summer of 1899, for reasons now uncertain. It took nearly five years to bring the building to completion at a cost of more than $800,000, some 60% over budget! It was occupied in 1904, the mint's staff relocating from the old 1860 structure, which was then sold for use as a

The Denver Mint with the Colorado State Capitol in the background

vegetable market. More valuable for the land upon which it stood, this historic building was demolished around 1909.

Coining did not commence until 1906, since the mint's brand-new machinery was loaned out for display at the 1904 Louisiana Purchase Exposition in St. Louis. The first emission of the new Denver Mint was a bronze, uniface medal with the simple legend DENVER 1905. This souvenir was issued to those attending the opening ceremony for the mint early in 1906.

When production began there on March 12, the first coins struck were gold eagles, each of which bore the mintmark D. (More than 40 years had passed since the last minting at Dahlonega, and there was no danger of confusing the two.) Before the year was out, the Denver Mint produced silver dimes, quarter dollars, and half dollars, as well as gold half eagles, and double eagles. Gold quarter eagles had not been struck at any mint other than Philadelphia since 1879, but the Denver Mint produced a small mintage of these in 1911, followed by larger numbers in 1914 and 1925.

A law passed on April 24, 1906, permitted production of minor coins (cents and nickels) at the Denver, San Francisco, and New Orleans mints and provided for purchase of the necessary metals. Denver did not exercise this option until 1911, when the first cents were coined on May 20 and released that same month. The coining of copper-nickel five-cent pieces commenced on February 5, 1912. The minting of silver dollars had been suspended in 1904, too late for Denver to participate. A new authorization led to a resumption of coining in 1921, and the Denver Mint struck silver dollars in 1921-23, 1926-27, and 1934. Also coined sporadically at the Denver Mint were various commemorative issues, the first of these being the Oregon Trail Memorial half dollar in 1933. The mint also has produced coins for assorted foreign countries, and it contributed mightily to the liberation coinage of the Philippines in 1944-45.

A mint crew in the melting room at the Denver Mint, circa 1906

Workers operating a rolling machine, circa 1906

An employee running a punching machine, circa 1906

Firing point-blank at Charles Linton, federal reserve bank employee, as he was loading packages of money into the reserve bank truck, the masked bandit who was the central figure of the spectacular holdup leaped from the running board of his car, seized the money from the bank truck, and threw it into the bandit machine [a Buick], according to Albert P. Kolquist, 24 South Emerson street, an eye-witness to the robbery.

– From *The Denver Post's* coverage of the December 18, 1922, theft of 5-dollar Federal Reserve notes

A Tempting Target

The Denver Mint was three times subjected to robberies. The first, at the old Clark & Company structure in 1864, has already been related. The second theft occurred in 1920 at the new mint. An employee named Orville Harrington concealed $80,000 in gold in his clothing over several successive trips, burying it underneath his backyard walkway. The gold was in the form of anode strips measuring 7 inches by 3 inches by 1 inch that were a byproduct of the refining process. A fellow employee suspected his activities and reported him to Rowland Goddard, supervisor of the Denver office of the U.S. Secret Service. Goddard actually witnessed Harrington in the act of burying the bars. Arrested and convicted, Harrington served 3½ years of his 10-year sentence, and all the stolen gold was recovered.

This sketch of the lead bandit was drawn by a woman who witnessed the theft. It was published in the December 18, 1922, Denver Post *so readers could be on the lookout for him.*

A far more dramatic episode occurred at the Denver Mint just two years later. While it was not the mint's money that was stolen, this is where the crime occurred. The Denver branch of the Kansas City Federal Reserve Bank occupied leased space in a commercial building, but possessed insufficient vault space for the currency it required. Thus, the bank entered into an arrangement whereby some of its money was stored in the nearby mint. On the morning of December 18, 1922, a transfer of $200,000 in new $5 Federal Reserve notes was taking place between the mint and the bank. Denver Mint Superintendent R.J. Grant was standing by with two guards to watch over the money when bank cashier J.E. Olsen pulled up in a truck accompanied by his driver, William Havenor, and a bank guard, C.T. Linton.

A mint employee taking gold bars out of the mold, circa 1906

Just as the money had been transferred to the truck, three men emerged from a large touring car and yelled, "Hands up!" Olsen and Havenor dove for cover, but Linton turned to face the attackers and was felled by a shotgun blast. A frenzied exchange of shots was fired between mint guards and the robbers, two of the latter being wounded. All three robbers escaped, however, while Linton died shortly thereafter.

The first clue did not emerge until 18 days later, when one of the robbers was found dead from his wounds, frozen in the abandoned getaway car. He was linked to a band of robbers known as the Harold Burns Gang, yet no one was ever apprehended or charged with the crime. Some $80,000 of the stolen money was recovered in St. Paul, Minnesota, but the crime was never officially solved. Even so, Denver Police Chief A.T. Clark declared in 1934 that the five men and two women responsible for planning and executing the crime were either dead or serving time for other offenses.

The Denver Mint, along with the San Francisco and Philadelphia mints, is striking coins for the United States Mint 50 State Quarters Program® (24.3 mm)

The Mint's Modern Role

When it was known that the San Francisco Mint would soon be replaced by a newer structure, $2.5 billion in gold and silver bullion was transferred to the Denver Mint for safekeeping in 1934. It was believed that San Francisco's location made it less defensible against threats, both foreign and domestic. To accommodate its expanded role as a bullion depository, the Denver Mint was enlarged from 1936 to 1938, the first of several such improvements. Today, the additions to the mint structure occupy more space than the original 1904 building.

The nationwide coin shortage of 1961 to 1965 taxed the mint to its limits, though at that time it was the larger of the U.S. Mint's two active facilities. Improvements made since 1945 to both the size of the mint and the arrangement of its equipment went a long way toward meeting the demands of that difficult period and have helped the mint maintain its position as one of the most productive coining establishments in the world.

In recent years the Denver Mint has been called upon to produce a wide variety of coins for both general circulation and the U.S. Mint's various collector and investor products. These include an assortment of commemorative coins in a variety of metals and finishes, as well as silver bullion coins for the metals market. Public tours were suspended after the September 11, 2001, terrorist attacks, but it is hoped that these will resume at some point. Tours remain available to select groups by appointment only.

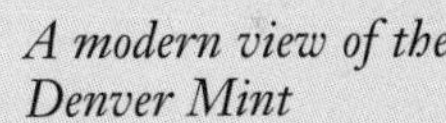

A modern view of the Denver Mint

1911-D Indian Head quarter eagle (18 mm)

Continued from page 137

effect similar to that of a wall carving. This style of modeling was known as "Egyptian relief," and Roosevelt was sufficiently smitten with the idea that he simply handed the project to Bigelow with a mandate to see it through. Dr. Bigelow selected Boston sculptor Bela Lyon Pratt to prepare models, and these were accepted with little fanfare; in fact, the Mint establishment seems to have been virtually bypassed in the creation of these coins, though the Treasury Secretary still retained the right of final approval.

Pratt's design is thematically linked to the $10 piece designed by Saint-Gaudens, but the Indian portrait that appears on Pratt's gold coins is a true representation of a male Native American, rather than the classical Liberty in native headdress employed on the eagle. The Indian faces left and is flanked by six stars left and seven right, with the motto LIBERTY above and the date below. The common reverse of the new quarter and half eagles is virtually identical to that of Saint-Gaudens' eagle, though the positions of the two mottoes are swapped.

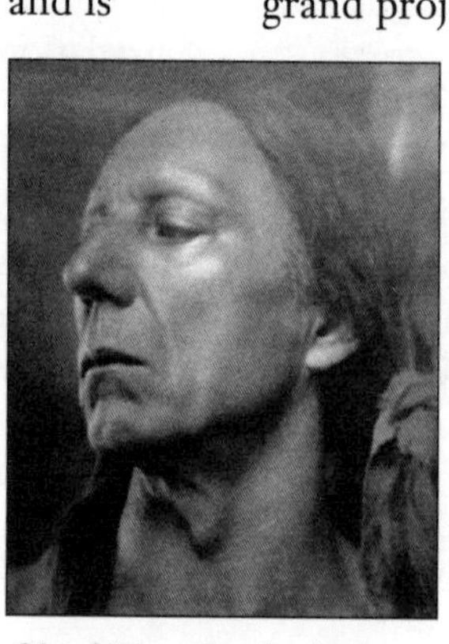

Chief Thundercloud, the model for Pratt's quarter eagle and half eagle coins

Debuting in 1908, the gold issues were absolutely identical to one another aside from their size and statement of value. They lacked borders and rims entirely, the flat fields of the coins serving as their only protection against wear. This was a radical departure for United States coins and one that drew much criticism from both numismatists and bankers. These protests were in vain, however, as the new coins remained in production as late as 1929. One bid to conventionality was a simple reeded edge, as opposed to the fancier treatment accorded to the $10 and $20 dollar pieces.

Victor David Brenner

Among the projects left unfinished at the time of Saint-Gaudens's death was a proposed redesign of the cent, which had borne the same imagery since 1859 – the familiar Indian Head of Liberty. In fact, the soaring eagle that appears on the reverse of the $20 dollar piece had been intended as the obverse for a new cent. The great sculptor admired the attractive but short-lived Flying Eagle cent of 1857 to 1858, and his new rendition was to serve as a tribute to that vintage coin. Sadly, this new Eagle cent was abandoned after Saint-Gaudens' death, though Roosevelt remained eager to proceed with a general redesign of the nation's coinage. All that was lacking was an artist with the right vision and skill.

In 1908, the president sat for his portrait with sculptor Victor David Brenner, who had been commissioned to create a medal that would be presented to those having two or more years' service in building the Panama Canal. As a prime mover behind this grand project, Roosevelt was to appear on the medal's obverse. During his visit to Brenner's studio in New York, Roosevelt was struck by the artist's bronze plaque of Abraham Lincoln. Brenner had created this profile bust just the year before, basing his depiction on a recently rediscovered photograph taken in 1864 by Anthony Berger of the Mathew Brady Studio. Pleased with the president's favorable comments, Brenner suggested that Lincoln be the subject of a new coin marking the centennial of his birth in 1909. Roosevelt was sold on this plan immediately, though at what point the cent was selected for this honor has not been recorded. Brenner himself preferred to have his work appear on the half dollar, but the law of 1890 made this denomination ineligible for redesign before 1916.

By early 1909, Brenner's models were complete, and it was hoped that the coins could be ready for distribution on the centennial of Lincoln's birth, February 12. This plan was overruled by Mint Director Frank A. Leach, who discovered that Brenner's reverse model was nearly an exact copy of a contemporary French coin. Leach's objections occasioned a delay, while the sculptor submitted a revised model depicting the two opposed ears of wheat that have since become so familiar to coin collectors. These models, both obverse and reverse, were quickly approved by President Roosevelt on February 18, 1909. By then, however, Roosevelt had become a "lame duck." His successor, William H. Taft, reportedly found further fault with the coin in that it lacked the motto IN GOD WE TRUST. The size of Lincoln's portrait was reduced to accommodate this inscription above the head, and the new cents were finally issued in August 1909.

Brenner's design is simple and very effective. A shoulder-length bust of Abraham Lincoln faces right, dressed in a suit of the period. The motto IN GOD WE TRUST appears above the bust, with LIBERTY to the left and the coin's date to the right. On the reverse, two stylized ears of wheat are placed at left and right in heraldic fashion. Between them are the value ONE CENT and the legend UNITED STATES OF AMERICA. The Latin legend E PLURIBUS UNUM is inscribed around the upper periphery.

The general press raised a loud cry against the placement of Brenner's initials "V.D.B." on the reverse just above the border at the bottom, and these letters were hastily dropped after just a few days' production. He was certainly not the first artist to sign his work, but the placement of his initials within the coin's field was perhaps too conspicuous, since this was widely denounced as a form of advertising. Brenner was hurt by all the negative publicity and declined to have any further involvement with the Mint. Though his initials reappeared without fanfare in 1918, their new placement at the truncation of Lincoln's bust is such that only coin collectors are aware of them.

Despite the furor over Brenner's initials, the general public took an immediate liking to the new cents. Their debut on August 2, 1909, had been widely heralded, and long lines formed outside banks and the Treasury. Supplies were quickly exhausted, and the few people who were lucky enough to get them enjoyed the option of selling the new coins at a profit to those who were disappointed. There were accounts of single coins bringing as much as a dollar, though most were sold at prices ranging from 2¢ to 5¢ apiece.

The novelty of the Lincoln cent soon wore off, but this long-running series, with its hundreds of date and mint combinations, has been the traditional point of entry for new coin collectors for several generations. When Brenner's original reverse design was replaced with a depiction of the Lincoln Memorial in 1959, the older issues began to gradually disappear from circulation. It seems that both collectors and the general public are drawn to obsolete coin types, and they seldom remain in circulation for very long.

The question of whether a real person should be depicted on a United States coin was debated in the press, but Abraham Lincoln's popularity typically overrode such concerns. In addition, this barrier had been broken long ago on the nation's paper money. The *Rochester Post-Express* was one newspaper that went on record as being in favor of historical portraits:

> If the Lincoln cent is a precedent, then American money may acquire an historical value. Why shouldn't other great Americans be nominated for similar distinction? Who knows but centuries and centuries hence, the archeologists will construct the fabric of this civilization on the coins found in the ruins of the nation.

Theodore Roosevelt was no longer in office after 1909, but his legacy lived on in the Treasury Department. Secretary Franklin MacVeagh wanted to replace Charles Barber's Liberty Head design on the nickel, one of the two coin types singled out by the Act of 1890 as candidates for remodeling. Rejecting the uninspired patterns creat-

1909-S V.D.B. Lincoln cent (19 mm)

Brenner's initials were quickly removed from the reverse of the 1909 Lincoln cent.

1970-S Lincoln cent (19 mm)

The denomination on the 1913-D, Type II Indian Head/Buffalo nickel was recessed in an exergue to improve wear. (21.2 mm)

He made his prayer after a night in a sweat lodge, having partaken of no food. He would go to the creek, bathe himself, put on a few strips of buffalo hide, place in front of him a buffalo skull, then build a fire of buffalo chips beyond and toward the east. A thick column of smoke would lift to the sky and the rising sun would shed a glow over the whole picture. The bronze color of the man, his black hair with bits of red wound into his braids, made an indelible picture in my mind.

– From Fraser's autobiography. His boyhood among the Sioux inspired his *"End of the Trail"* sculpture and the 1913 Indian Head/Buffalo nickel.

James Earle Fraser with versions of his sculpture, "The End of the Trail"

ed by Barber 1909 to 1910, MacVeagh sought an outside artist of greater imagination. Learning of this, sculptor James Earle Fraser volunteered his talents toward redesigning the nickel. Fraser had been a student of Saint-Gaudens's and had been singled out by the great sculptor as his most promising pupil. Initially, however, Mint Director George E. Roberts inexplicably distracted Fraser with the idea of a new Lincoln portrait for the nickel, seeming to disregard the improbability of two Lincoln coins circulating simultaneously. Once this obstacle was overcome, Fraser submitted his own concept for the nickel, which featured a realistic portrait of a Native American paired with an American buffalo, or bison. These models were approved, though numerous modifications were made to satisfy critics in the vending machine industry, who regarded the high relief of the nickel's new design as a threat to their lucrative enterprises.

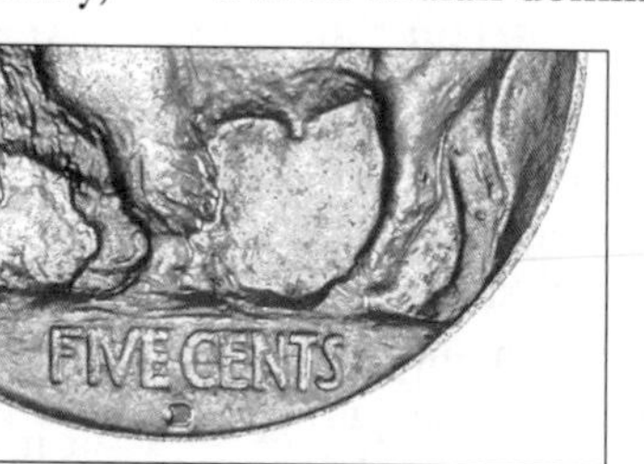

On the Type I 1913 nickel, the denomination was displayed on a mound. Once in circulation the letters wore away quickly.

Fraser's models for the new nickel are amazingly bold for a United States coin, as the principal relief elements take up nearly the entire surface area available to them. His right-facing portrait of a male Indian dominates the obverse. LIBERTY is inscribed to the right of the bust, with the date placed on the Indian's shoulder and Fraser's initial F appearing directly below it. A male bison is shown in full profile on the reverse, facing left. It stands on the prairie, with this feature providing a foundation for the value FIVE CENTS. The legend UNITED STATES OF AMERICA is placed around the upper periphery, with E PLURIBUS UNUM crowded into a small space directly above the bison's rump. The motto IN GOD WE TRUST was not included, yet this omission did not stir the controversy it had with the 1907 gold coins.

Fraser's Native American portrait is actually a composite of features taken from three models: Two Moons, of the Cheyenne tribe; Big Tree, a Kiowa; and Iron Tail, a member of the Oglala Sioux tribe. Of these individuals, Iron Tail bears a striking resemblance to the finished product. For the bison figure, Fraser selected Black Diamond as his model. This beast was a popular feature of the New York Zoological Garden until its death in 1915. Ignominiously slaughtered for its meat, which was marketed in cuts labeled "Black Diamond steaks," its hide was recycled as an automobile rug. As one consolation, Black Diamond's head was mounted for display in the butcher's shop. Now preserved in a private home, it remains an attraction to this day, groups of school children having their pictures taken with the famous buffalo from the nickel.

The new coins were issued to circulation on March 4, 1913, and were immediately hailed as superb representations of truly American themes. Once the usual criticisms aimed at any new coin type had run their course and been disproved, another very real problem arose. It quickly became evident that the value FIVE CENTS was placed in such a way that it was subject to rapid wear and eventual obliteration. This flaw was corrected by Chief Engraver Charles Barber, who simply placed the letters in an exergue cut into the plain on which the bison stands. The fact that the coin's date was equally vulnerable to quick erosion seems to have been overlooked at that time. In fact, this problem was never satisfactorily addressed, with the result that thousands of these nickels became dateless after just a few years of wear. Though a source of frustration to collectors seeking to build sets from pocket change, this flaw did not prevent the popular Indian Head/Buffalo nickel from circulating for many years. While these coins were last minted in 1938, they still turned up in ever-smaller numbers as late as the 1960s.

A lasting tribute to the Plains Indians and to the animal so closely linked to their survival, the Indian Head/Buffalo nickel is also an outstanding piece of medallic sculpture.

In 2001, Fraser's nickel design reappeared in the form of a commemorative silver dollar that became an instant sellout.

The U.S. Mint, so long a repository of conventional thinking in numismatic art, was seemingly enlightened during the early 20th century. New designs were appearing every few years. The fact that all of these models were the work of outside artists did not sit well with Chief Engraver Charles Barber, who revealed a tendency to make life difficult for anyone treading on what he considered to be his own soil. To his credit, however, Barber was usually correct in assessing technical matters that would affect the suitability of an artist's coin models for high-speed presses. Each of the designs submitted by outside artists between

The challenge in creating the 2001 Indian Head/Buffalo commemorative dollar was in maintaining the integrity of Fraser's nickel designs on a much larger coin. The buffalo has been reduced in size, its head is lowered and its front legs have been shortened to accommodate the motto IN GOD WE TRUST, which must now appear on all United States coins.

Two Moons was reportedly present at the Battle of the Little Bighorn, in which General George Armstrong Custer and his forces were defeated.

Iron Tail was an Oglala Sioux leader who later performed in Buffalo Bill Cody's Wild West Show.

Kiowa leader Big Tree (Adoeette)

Hermon MacNeil

1917 MacNeil quarter dollar, on which Liberty's breast is bare (24.3 mm)

1929-S quarter dollar with Liberty wearing chain mail

1907 and 1921 required additional fine-tuning by Mint personnel. This work was usually performed by Barber until his death in February 1917, after which time he was succeeded by George Morgan.

This lack of cooperation from Barber manifested itself again in 1916, when new designs were sought for the dime, quarter dollar, and half dollar. These coins had just achieved their statutory minimum production of 25 years, after which time they were eligible for design changes. In a most fortunate mistake, Mint Director Robert W. Woolley misinterpreted the 1890 law to read that he was *required* to replace Charles Barber's Liberty Head designs of 1892. As always, Barber dutifully submitted his proposed models for new coins, but once again he was politely dismissed in favor of outside artists. The winners of an invitational competition were Hermon MacNeil, whose models were chosen for the quarter dollar, and Adolph Weinman, selected to prepare the dime and half dollar. For the first time in its history, the Mint would produce three distinctive types for these denominations, which had previously been of similar design.

The complete story of the new silver coins of 1916 is complex and beyond the scope of this study, but it is worth noting that numerous delays were encountered as the artists fine-tuned their models while simultaneously avoiding obstacles thrown in their path by Barber. While his observations regarding many aspects of practical coinage were quite accurate, they clearly could have been presented in a more constructive manner. All three coins were ultimately produced for circulation in 1916, but only the dime was ready for widespread release before year's end; new quarters and halves dated 1916 debuted in January of the following year. Each of these attractive coins was received with acclaim by the press and the numismatic community.

Mistakenly called the "Mercury" type, Weinman's dime bears no relation to the winged messenger of the Roman gods. It actually portrays a youthful bust of Liberty facing left, with the Liberty Cap and wings on her head. Her wings are, in the artist's own words, intended to symbolize "liberty of thought." The motto LIBERTY is inscribed around the periphery. IN GOD WE TRUST is to the left of the bust, while the date appears beneath it. Weinman's monogrammed initials AW are above and to the right of the date. The dime's reverse displays a fasces, which is a bundle of rods wrapped around an ax and secured with leather thongs. The fasces was carried by Roman magistrates as a symbol of power and authority. Wrapped around it on the coin is an olive branch, the two elements symbolizing the tempering of force by the virtue of peace. Inscribed around the periphery are the legend UNITED STATES OF AMERICA and the value ONE DIME. To the right of the fasces is E PLURIBUS UNUM.

Hermon MacNeil's 1916 quarter dollar features the theme of the nation awakening to its own defense, a timely message given that the United States entered World War I just a year later. A partially nude, standing figure of Liberty is seen stepping toward the viewer through a waist-high gateway. She gazes to her left, her left arm holding up a shield bearing the national arms. Her right hand holds an olive branch and withdraws from the shield a long drapery. The gateway is flanked by seven stars to the left and six to the right, with the motto IN GOD WE TRUST inscribed on the wall. At the upper periphery is the motto LIBERTY, while the date appears on the lowermost step, with MacNeil's initial M to the right. On the reverse is seen an eagle in flight, flanked by seven stars left and six right. UNITED STATES OF AMERICA and the motto E PLURIBUS UNUM are above it, with the value QUARTER DOLLAR below.

Chief Engraver George Morgan made extensive modifications to MacNeil's quarter midway through 1917, the principal changes being the repositioning of the eagle and stars, the covering of Miss Liberty's bare bosom with chain mail and the application of a basin, or convexity, to the dies. It was anticipated that this last change would make the coins strike up better, but the exact opposite proved true, and most coins of this modified type were marked by poor definition in many details, particularly Liberty's hair and face. Like Fraser's nickel, the quarter dollar by Hermon MacNeil bore its date in a position that rendered it unreadable after only a few years' circulation. This was corrected in 1925, when the step bearing the date was cut away and the date set within the resulting depression. This was quite effective in preserving the dates of Standing Liberty quarters issued 1925 to 1930. Earlier coins, however, are often found dateless and are thus scarcer than their mintages would suggest.

Elsie Kachel Stevens with her daughter Holly in 1924

Numismatic lore has it that cladding Liberty's bare breast in chain mail was done as the result of a public outcry over nudity. No accounts have been located to support this story, and the decision was more likely prompted by objections from the Treasury Department. Morgan's changes to MacNeil's models were very extensive, and the result was almost an entirely new coin. A side-by-side comparison of both versions reveals just how many subtle differences exist.

In addition to his winning a commission for the dime, Adolph Weinman created models for the half dollar that also were selected. The resulting coin has been hailed as the most beautiful of our country's silver issues, and it remains among the most popular of all United States coins. The Liberty Walking half dollar portrays a figure of Liberty striding leftward toward the rising sun. She holds in her left arm an olive branch, while her right is raised in a bid toward the dawning of a new day. Liberty is draped in the American flag of stars and stripes, and she wears the Liberty Cap atop her head. (In fact, her head is the same one that appears on the dime, though on the half dollar it has no wings. This similarity is not a coincidence – Weinman's model for both coins was Elsie Kachel Stevens, the beautiful wife of acclaimed poet Wallace Stevens.) To Liberty's right is the motto IN GOD WE TRUST, while the date is placed in an exergue below her left foot. Completing the obverse is the motto LIBERTY, written in large letters around the periphery. For the reverse, Weinman selected an eagle facing left, perched on a mountain crag. A pine sapling projects from the rock face, and directly above it is E PLURIBUS UNUM. The legend UNITED STATES OF AMERICA appears around the upper periphery, with the value HALF DOLLAR below. The artist's monogrammed initials AW are seen to the right of the rock.

All three of the new silver coins introduced in 1916 were greeted with accolades from the numismatic community and the general public. Their popularity continues to the present day, long after they ceased to be in production. The dime was minted through 1945, while the half dollar survived another two years. Coining of the Standing Liberty quarter ended prematurely in 1930; it failed to achieve its statutory minimum of 25 years when Congress passed special legislation authorizing a new quarter dollar honoring George Washington in 1932. Still, all three coins continued to circulate for years afterward, the dime and half dollar remaining familiar sights in pocket change as late as the 1960s.

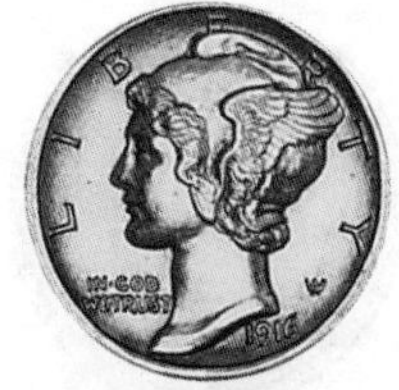

1916-D "Mercury" dime (17.9 mm)

1942-D Liberty Walking half dollar (30.6 mm)

The U.S. Mint at Manila

1908-S 20-centavo piece (20 mm)

1928-M 1-centavo piece (24 mm)

Here is a great way to win a bet. Ask a numismatic acquaintance to name all nine of the United States mints. While he or she may be clever enough to remember West Point, it is almost a certainty that Manila will remain elusive. Manila? That's right. The U.S. operated a mint in the capital of the Philippines from 1920 through 1941.

Little remembered today is that this archipelago was administered by the U.S. from 1898 until 1946. A legacy of the Spanish-American War, our adventure in the Philippines began with a decisive naval victory over the Spanish fleet in the Battle of Manila Bay on May 1, 1898. Shortly afterward, American troops landed and set up a military occupation. Formally ceded to the United States by Spain under the Treaty of Paris, the Philippines remained an American possession until granted full independence on July 4, 1946.

To-day The Press Prints 3674 Advertisements

The Press. 4 A.M.

VOL. XL. PHILADELPHIA, SUNDAY MORNING, MAY 8, 1898.—Copyright, 1898, by The Press Co. FIVE CENTS.

DEWEY'S MARVELOUS VICTORY.

NO AMERICAN SHIP OR MAN LOST.

COMPLETE MASTER OF MANILA.

DEWEY IS MADE ACTING ADMIRAL.

Secretary Long Promptly Cables Him Congratulations—He Will Probably Be Thanked by Congress and Made an Admiral.

Washington, May 7.—By direction of the President, Secretary Long sent the following cable despatch to Commodore Dewey:—

"Washington, May 7.—Dewey, Manila: The President, in the name of the American people, thanks you and your officers and men for your splendid achievement and overwhelming victory. In recognition he has appointed you Acting Admiral and will recommend vote of thanks to you as foundation for further promotion by Congress.

"LONG."

Chairman Boutelle, of the House Committee on Naval Affairs, says he will introduce from that committee Monday a resolution of thanks to Commodore Dewey.

He will also introduce a bill creating an additional rear admiral. Commodore Dewey cannot be named in the bill, but it will provide for the promotion of a commodore who has won honor for the United States.

LONG'S HIGH PRAISE OF DEWEY.

WASHINGTON, May 7.—Secretary Long, after reading the reports from Commodore Dewey and newspaper bulletins, copies of which had been furnished from the White House, said:—

"It will go down as one of the greatest battles in naval history. From what I can gather we were on the enemy before they realized it. Our guns poured such a deadly and steady stream of projectiles into the opposing fleet that they were almost prostrated from the start. Our courage, daring and quickness made the battle as quick as it was decisive.

"The department will make all haste in sending to Commodore Dewey reinforcements across the Pacific. There is apparently no need of a hospital ship. The main thing wanted is men. I cannot now say how soon the transports will start from San Francisco. They will co-operate with the War Department.

"It is very likely that we soon will have cable connections with Dewey. As he cut the cable, there will be no difficulties in locating the break. When the cable ship arrives repairs will quickly be made and communication will be opened at once."

ALL WASHINGTON REJOICES.

DEWEY'S REPORTS ON THE MANILA VICTORY.

ACTING REAR ADMIRAL DEWEY.

Washington, May 7—The splendid triumph won by Commodore Dewey in Manila Bay is thus modestly told in despatches received from the victorious commander:

"Manila, May 1—The squadron arrived at Manila at daybreak this morning. Immediately engaged the enemy and destroyed the following Spanish vessels: Reina Christina, Castilla, Ulloa, Isla de Cuba, General Lezo, Del Duero, Correo, Velasco, Mindanao, one transport, and the water battery at Cavite. The squadron is uninjured and only a few men were slightly wounded. The only means of telegraphing is to the American Consul at Hong Kong.

Cavite, May 4—I have taken possession of naval station at Cavite, on Philippine Islands, and destroyed its fortifications. Have destroyed the fortifications at bay entrance, paroling garrison. I control bay completely and can take city at any time. The squadron is in excellent health and spirits. Spanish loss not fully known, but very heavy. One hundred and fifty killed, including captain of Reina Christina. I am assisting in protecting Spanish sick and wounded. Two hundred and fifty sick and wounded in hospital within our lines. Much excitement at Manila. Will protect foreign residents. Signed "DEWEY."

WARSHIPS SIGHTED OFF MARTINIQUE.

London, May 7.—A despatch from Fort de France, capital of the Island of Martinique, French West India Islands, says

"THE DAILY PRESS" AHEAD AS USUAL.

First Philadelphia Paper to Print the Direct News of Dewey's Great Victory.

SPANISH LOSS SAID TO BE 2000.

Dewey's Victory Seems to Grow with Every Report—He Holds Cavite as a Base for Future Operations in Philippines

Hong Kong, May 7.—The long-looked-for vessels with despatches from the American squadron and Manila arrived at half-past 2 this afternoon. I have just interviewed the officer in command, who gives me the following story:—

"We left Mirs Bay at 2 o'clock April 27, steering straight for the Philippines. On sighting the coast the Boston, Baltimore and Concord went ahead in the Subic Bay, some thirty miles from Manila, found two small schooners and interrogated them. The occupants professed to know nothing, not even where Manila was.

"Here the line of battle was formed. The Olympia, Baltimore, Petrel, Concord and Boston were in the first line and the Raleigh, McCulloch, Vaughan and Zafiro in the second.

"We expected the batteries of Corregidor to open fire the first thing, but they did not do so until the second line got well in, when a shot was fired, going between the Boston and McCulloch, doing no damage.

"The Concord fired the first shot for the Americans. The McCulloch followed and the other vessels, which came in afterward, soon caused the flag on the battery, which only fired three shots, to be hauled down, there was no damage to the Americans.

"We then steamed slowly up the bay and in a small bay at Cavite we found the Spanish fleet. The Cavite battery of very heavy guns opened fire, the several Spanish vessels following, but all the shots went wide.

POURED IN A WITHERING FIRE.

Fourteen Spanish vessels lined up to receive the Americans. As Admiral Dewey's fleet, headed by the Olympia,

The front page of The (Philadelphia) Press *on May 8, 1898*

Monetary Problems Lead to a Solution

Following several years of guerilla resistance to the American occupation, a civil administration was finally established in 1901 under the Bureau of Insular Affairs. The first governor-general of the Philippines was William Howard Taft, who became the U.S. president in 1909 and, some years later, chief justice of the United States Supreme Court.

William Howard Taft

Under Spanish rule, the Filipinos had used coins and paper money denominated in *centavos* and *pesos*, respectively. Though this was a modern decimal system, the end of Spain's dominion rendered it obsolete. In addition, it was deemed important for reasons of sovereignty to replace Spanish money with something distinctively American. Shortly after taking over the islands, the United States attempted to introduce its own regular coinage in the form of dimes, quarter dollars, and half dollars. These were products of the San Francisco Mint and included the issues of 1898, 1899, and 1900. It was soon discovered that these coins were too valuable for the simple, mostly agrarian economy, and another solution was sought.

The answer was found in a hybrid coinage that combined the best elements of both systems. Retaining the Spanish peso as a unit of value, it was made exchangeable for the American dollar at the rate of two for one. Thus, a peso was worth 50¢ in U.S. money. A new series of coins debuted in 1903 that clearly proclaimed this duality. On each piece, the Spanish name FILIPINAS appeared on the obverse, as did the statement of value, while the reverse of each denomination bore the English legend UNITED STATES OF AMERICA and the date of coining. Like the Spanish coin that preceded it, the new peso was divided into fractional silver pieces valued at 50, 20, and 10 centavos. The five-centavos piece was coined from the same blanks used for U.S. nickels, while the series was completed with one-centavo and half centavo coins of bronze.

United States troops on the ramparts at Manila, circa 1898

Creating the Mint

The new coins were produced at both Philadelphia and San Francisco through 1908, after which time the mint in California handled this task exclusively. Seeking to transfer coining operations to the Philippines for reasons of economy, the Treasury Department advised officials in Manila of its desire. On February 8, 1918, the Philippine legislature passed an appropriation bill for 100,000 pesos to establish a mint at Manila. Eight days later the bill was signed into law by Governor-General Francis B. Harrison.

The requisite machinery was built at the Philadelphia Mint under the supervision of the Mint's chief engineer, Clifford Hewitt. Tested there in June 1919, it was then disassembled and shipped to the Philippines via the Panama Canal. The equipment arrived at Manila in November, and by the end of the month Hewitt was also on hand. He was assigned the task of both installing the machinery and training the Filipino staff.

1928-M 20-centavo piece (21 mm)

As the original appropriation had called for twice the figure received, there was need for economy. It was decided to install the mint in an existing structure rather than a purpose-built one. A relic from the Spanish period, the Intendencia Building would serve as the new mint's home. It fronted the Pasig River and was located inside the Intramuros, the old walled city that was part of greater Manila. While the mint occupied just the ground floor, the structure also housed the hall of the Philippine Senate and the offices of the Philippine Treasury. The United States Mint at Manila was formally opened on July 15, 1920.

The first denomination coined on opening day was the bronze one-centavo

1936-M peso (37 mm)

The "M" mintmark

An interior view of the mint on the ground floor of the Intendencia Building at Manila, circa 1921

The Mint of the Philippine Islands operated from 1920 through 1941 in the Intendencia Building.

1937-M five-centavos piece (19 mm)

piece. The very first coin was struck by Governor-General Harrison under Hewitt's supervision, with Mint Director A.P. Fitzsimmons observing. Medals were also struck that day commemorating the opening of the mint. The dies were by U.S. Mint Chief Engraver George T. Morgan, though some stock elements were employed. The obverse features a bust of President Woodrow Wilson, while the reverse is an adaptation of a much earlier medal from the U.S. Mint's annual assay ceremony. The first piece was made by Speaker of the Philippine House of Representatives Sergio Osmeña.

The mint included a modern refinery and was thus able to process both gold and silver into fine ingots, though no gold coins were issued under the American administration. A few examples of the commemorative medal were coined in gold, though it is not certain whether these were made at Manila or Philadelphia.

On October 11, less than three months after the mint's opening, fire raced through the upper floors of the building that housed the mint. While the other offices occupying this structure were almost completely destroyed, the mint survived without incident and resumed production the next day.

All of the denominations then current were struck by the Manila Mint. The half centavo had been discontinued after 1908, and the coining of pesos was suspended after 1912. The coins of 1920 and 1921 bore no mintmarks, and no pieces were issued during 1922 to 1924. When production resumed in 1925, each piece bore a tiny M on its reverse, the result of lobbying by numismatists in the Philippines who sought proper recognition for their coinage.

Various changes occurred in the U.S./Philippines coins over the years, including a reduction in the size and fineness of the silver pieces in 1907. The five-centavo coin was also reduced

Employees and officials of the U.S. Mint at Manila, circa 1921

in size in 1930 to avoid confusing it with the reduced-size 20-centavo piece. When the status of the Philippines changed to that of a commonwealth, a three-piece set of commemorative coins was issued to mark the occasion. Two one-peso coins and a single 50-centavo piece were included in this set, all dated 1936-M. These coins bore on their reverses the new arms of the commonwealth, and this design was adapted to the circulating coins the following year.

A burning building bombed during a Japanese air raid on the Philippine Islands, December 13, 1941 ▶

1936-M 50-centavo piece commemorated the establishment of the Commonwealth. Shown are the outgoing governor-general, Frank Murphy, and incoming President Manuel Quezon. (26 mm)

War and Ruin

The onset of World War II came quickly to the Philippines when Japanese airplanes bombed the American air base at Clark Field. The "Day of Infamy" there was December 8, 1941, since the Philippines is across the International Date Line from Hawaii. Japanese troops landed later that month and began their march toward Manila. The capital city fell early in January, but the American and Filipino defenders were able to ship all of the Treasury's gold and much of its silver to Pearl Harbor aboard the submarine U.S.S. *Trout*. The remaining supply of silver coins, more than 15 million pesos' worth, was crated and dumped into Caballo Bay off the fortified island of Corregidor when it became evident that Manila would soon fall.

The Manila Mint ceased operations under the Japanese occupation that lasted some three years. During the recapture of Manila by Allied forces, the mint building and nearly all of the surrounding Intramuros district were destroyed by the retreating Japanese army. Though the mint structure was later rebuilt and served as the headquarters of the new Central Bank of the Philippines, it never again minted coins. Instead, the pre-war issues were replaced with millions of new coins of the same types struck at the Philadelphia, Denver, and San Francisco Mints in 1944 and 1945. When the Philippines became an independent nation on July 4, 1946, the curtain was drawn on America's principal experiment in colonialism.

Chapter Eleven

World War I and Its Aftermath

It is a fearful thing to lead this great peaceful people into war, into the most terrible and disastrous of all wars, civilization itself seeming to be in the balance. But the right is more precious than peace ... .

– President Woodrow Wilson asking Congress for a declaration of war on Germany, April 2, 1917

Known in its own time as the Great War, and later as World War I, the conflict that broke out in August 1914 involved nearly all the nations of Europe and their far-flung colonies. Americans were very reluctant to become involved in this catastrophe, and Woodrow Wilson was re-elected to the presidency in 1916 on the slogan "He kept us out of war." This detachment was ultimately to end, as attacks on American merchant ships by German submarines drew the United States into the war in April 1917. Just as in 1861 to 1865, the onset of war had far-reaching economic consequences, though the effects on United States coinage were not as dire.

The regularity, some might even say monotony, of American coin production during the 20 years that preceded World War I was overturned by this global event. Among the casualties were United States gold coins, the production of which was suspended after 1916 and did not resume until 1920. This action was prompted by economic conditions in Europe, where many nations had already ceased coining gold or, at the very least, had suspended its payment in favor of paper money.

Perhaps the most visible impact of the war years, when viewed from a distance of nearly a century, was the tremendous increase in the coinage of all denominations from cent through half

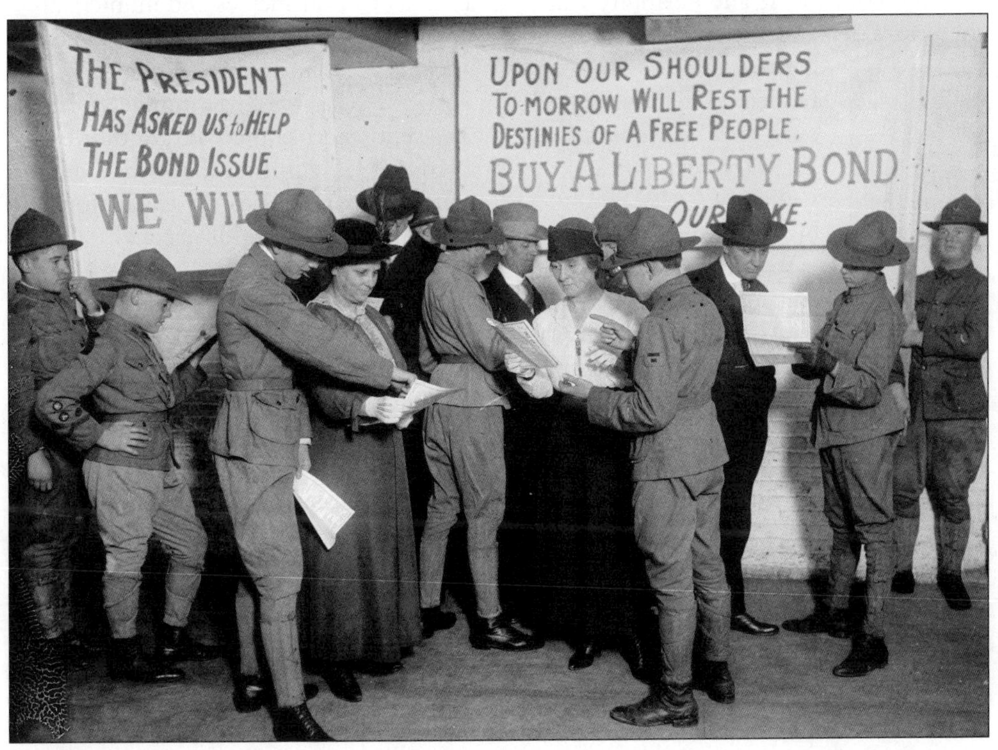

Boy Scouts dressed in United States Army uniforms sold Liberty Bonds in 1917 to support the war effort. Treasury Secretary William G. McAdoo financed World War I by awakening the patriotic feelings of the American people, who responded by buying government war bonds as an investment.

The medal honoring Mint Director Raymond T. Baker was designed by George Morgan. (76 mm)

dollar. The small coins in particular were always in short supply from 1916 through 1920. Between the country's economic vitality and the imposition of wartime sales taxes, the need for additional coins nearly overwhelmed the United States Mint. In 1915, for example, the Philadelphia Mint struck just over 29 million cents; by 1918 this figure grew to more than 288 million pieces; and in 1919 it peaked at a record 392,021,000 cents in a single year! This figure was not reached again until 1940, when World War II prompted a similar economic cycle.

Antonio De Francisci, seen here in mature years, was a young man when he won the honor of designing the new Peace dollar.

The shortfall of cents was particularly acute during 1917. At that time, and indeed until quite recently, the Mint worked on a fixed annual appropriation. This did not provide any flexibility when conditions demanded a sudden increase in production. Mint Director Raymond Baker expressed his concerns to Treasury Secretary William G. McAdoo in his 1917 annual report: "We are now considerably embarrassed by lack of funds to pay for sufficient copper and nickel to operate the mints to full capacity on minor coins."

Sheet music from 1917

Another factor in the growing demand for cents and nickels was a general inflationary pressure brought on by increased industrial activity and a shortage of labor. In addition, the assessment of temporary wartime taxes resulted in numerous payments in odd amounts, whereas previously most transactions had involved multiples of 5¢. As newspapers once priced at a cent rose in cost to 2¢ or 3¢, and streetcar fares jumped from 5¢ to 7¢, there were those in the business community who urged the minting of such odd-value coins. They failed to realize that some of these denominations had already been produced a couple generations earlier.

The shortage of cents was so severe and widespread toward the end of 1917 that there was even official discussion of a return to fractional paper money to supplement these coins. With the revival of this Civil War-era scheme, it seemed that history was set to repeat itself. Indeed, a number of businesses and municipalities actually issued scrip denominated in cents as a temporary expedient. Fortunately, as the huge numbers of one-cent pieces coined during the years 1916 to 1920 confirm, the Mint did ultimately manage to provide the nation with all the "pennies" it needed.

Another looming crisis, this one having a far greater potential impact on the economy, was the ever-increasing price of silver. During 1919, and again during 1920, the price of this metal briefly reached levels at which the bullion value of U.S. silver coins exceeded their face value. Had these levels been sustained for more than a few days or risen only a few cents higher, the catastrophic result would have been widespread hoarding and melting of silver coins. Just as in 1862, Congress failed to see this crisis coming and, when it was nearly upon them, failed to take effective action. Fortune smiled down on the innocent, however, and the price of silver returned to manageable levels, Americans narrowly dodging a deadly bullet.

One byproduct of the rising market for silver did have a lasting effect on United States coinage. It was generally assumed that the three new silver issues of 1916 had brought to a conclusion the complete updating of America's coins. Only the silver dollar had not been altered in many years. But, since it had gone out of production after 1904, everyone assumed that no more would ever be coined. Fate, however, stepped in. Early in 1918, Great Britain's urgent need to quell a potentially ruinous speculative silver market in India prompted London to appeal to its wartime ally, the United States, for a huge loan of silver, with which it would flood the market. This loan was accomplished through the Pittman Act of April 23, 1918. It called for melting up to 350 million silver dollars then held by the Treasury as a backing for silver certificates in circulation; these notes would be retired as they were returned in the normal course of operations.

Teresa Cafarelli De Francisci

The metal sold to Great Britain in 1918 should have realized an enormous profit for the U.S., as all of it had been purchased years earlier when the value of silver was much lower. Once again, however, political and economic interests prevailed. Among the provisions of the Pittman Act was one requiring that all silver dollars melted under its terms be replaced after the war with fresh ones minted from newly purchased, domestically mined silver. This represented yet another entry in a long and disgraceful series of subsidies to the silver mining industry. It resulted in the coining of many millions of unwanted silver dollars after the war's end, all of them made from metal purchased at or near the market's peak. Not all of the authorized silver was sold to Great Britain; only 270 million silver dollars were melted, and of this number some 11,111,168 were diverted to provide bullion for coining dimes, quarters, and halves.

When the minting of replacement dollars began in the spring of 1921, George Morgan's old Liberty head of 1878 was hastily resurrected. Morgan himself had to recreate master hubs for this design, since the originals had been destroyed in 1910 under the assumption that silver dollars would never again be coined! The old type was employed over the protests of numismatists, who wanted a new issue commemorating America's peace treaty with Germany. (Little remembered today is the fact that the United States did not sign the 1919 Treaty of Versailles, instead remaining in a state of war with Germany for another two years until a separate peace was finally negotiated.)

At the urging of the American Numismatic Association, an invitational design competition was hastily announced by the Treasury Department on November 19, 1921. All of the artists solicited had already created models for United States coins on other occasions or would do so in the future, yet these outstanding sculptors were given just three weeks to prepare designs. Their models were to be submitted to the Federal Commission of Fine Arts, a non-binding advisory board that since 1910 had been empowered to review all works of art created for the United States government (though it was not until 1921 that its scope was officially extended to include coins).

The winning design was that of Italian-American sculptor Antonio De Francisci, who used his wife, Teresa, as his model for Liberty's head. So pleased was she to appear on the coin that she wrote of her joy to her brother. "You remember how I was always posing

You will see that the Liberty is not a photograph of Mrs. De Francisci. It is a composite face and in that way typifies something of America. I did not try to execute an "American type" or a picture of any woman. I wanted the Liberty to express something of the spirit of the country – the intellectual speed and vigour and virility America has, as well as its youth.

– Antonio De Francisci to a columnist from the *Duluth Minneapolis Tribune*, January 12, 1922

1921 high-relief Peace dollar (38.1 mm)

I know you will be disappointed, but the pressure necessary to bring up the work was so destructive to the dies that we got tired of putting new dies in. In changing the date to 1922 I took the opportunity of making a slight change on the curvature of the ground. I anticipate at least 20 tons less pressure will be required to bring up the design. This could double the life of the die.

– From a letter sent by Chief Engraver George Morgan to Antonio De Francisci along with samples of Morgan's altered version of the Peace dollar, January 3, 1922

I have received a few of the Peace Dollars from the Philadelphia Mint and although the rush in which this coin had to be produced was too great to give a very perfect result, either artistically or mechanically, I feel now that something must be done since we will have more time for the 1922 issue. Primarily, I would suggest and with emphasis, that if possible, to forbid the mint engravers from touching in anyway the dies or hubs of said coins.

– De Francisci complaining to the Commission of Fine Arts about George Morgan's alterations, January 6, 1922

as Liberty, and how brokenhearted I was when some other little girl was selected to play the role in the patriotic exercises in school? I thought of those days often while sitting as a model for Tony's design, and now seeing myself as Miss Liberty on the new coin, it seems like the realization of my fondest childhood dream." Though the sculptor argued that his portrait was an idealized one, contemporary photographs of Teresa Cafarelli reveal a startling likeness to the lady on the coin. In viewing her charming features on the Peace dollar, collectors can now think of Teresa and share her dream of Liberty.

1926 low-relief Peace dollar (38.1 mm)

The obverse of this coin shows Liberty facing left with flowing hair. She wears a coronet with rays projecting upward from it, reminiscent of New York Harbor's Statue of Liberty. IN GOD WE TRUST is written to the left and right of Liberty's neck. The motto LIBERTY is inscribed around the upper periphery, with the date below the bust and the artist's AF monogram directly above the date. On the reverse, an eagle is perched atop a rock, facing right and grasping an olive branch in its right claw. Upon the rock is inscribed PEACE, and behind it are the rays of the rising sun. The legends UNITED STATES OF AMERICA and E PLURIBUS UNUM are around the upper periphery, while the value ONE DOLLAR is to the left and right of the eagle.

Production of the new Peace dollar commenced during the final weeks of 1921. The first specimen was presented to President Warren G. Harding, and the coins entered general circulation on January 3, 1922. The high relief of De Francisci's models did not strike up well in the single press stroke permitted for circulating coinage, yet more than a million pieces of the 1921 issue were coined. Another 35,401 examples of slightly lowered relief, dated 1922, were coined for circulation at Philadelphia in early January. These were not issued, and it was believed that all were destroyed until a single, worn example turned up in 2001.

To remedy the striking deficiencies of the Peace dollar, Chief Engraver George T. Morgan hastily prepared new master hubs of much lowered relief. Dies from these hubs were used to strike millions of Peace coins through 1928, when the recoinage of silver dollars melted under the Pittman Act was finally achieved. These low-relief dollars have poor details and very shallow lettering, leaving many of them with a worn look even when uncirculated.

George Morgan's crude efforts in lowering the relief of the Peace dollar hubs clearly revealed that Mint engravers still did not know how to properly use the Janvier reducing lathe acquired in 1905 at the urging of Augustus Saint-Gaudens. Considering such a machine mandatory for the execution of his models for the gold coinage, Saint-Gaudens had prompted President Roosevelt to order its purchase as a replacement for the aged Hill lathe used since the 1860s. Though this new machine permitted the reducing of hubs in varying heights of relief, Barber and Morgan failed to utilize it properly, a fact that prompted Saint-Gaudens' assistant, Henry Hering, to have the gold coin models reduced to hubs outside the Mint.

A NATIONAL TREASURE

America's Coin Collection

A largely forgotten action of the 1920s, but one that was quite controversial in its time and has since had far-reaching impact, was the Treasury Department's decision to transfer ownership of the U.S. Mint's collection of coins and other numismatica from the Philadelphia Mint to the Smithsonian Institution. This move was prompted by the death in 1922 of longtime Mint curator, Dr. T. Louis Comparette, and by the 1920 robbery at the Denver Mint that resulted in closing all three mints to the public for some years. With the collection thus inaccessible, there seemed no further point in housing it at the Philadelphia Mint. Treasury Secretary Andrew W. Mellon addressed this matter in his February 8, 1923, letter to the Smithsonian's secretary, Charles D. Walcott, reproduced here in part:

> There is an important and very beautiful selection of coins, tokens and medals, perhaps the largest and most complete numismatic collection owned by the Government. The logical place for this collection would seem to be in the National Museum in Washington, and I am writing to ask if you would consider it feasible to have the collection transferred there.

Dispatched to Philadelphia to inspect the Mint Cabinet, Curator Theodore T. Belote of the Smithsonian's Division of History remarked, "I found that the size and importance of the collection has been very materially increased since my last visit to the Mint in Philadelphia and that the acceptance of this collection will place the National Museum in the front rank of the museums of the world, so far as the science of numismatics is concerned."

Secretary Mellon's offer was gratefully accepted, and the accession was formally completed on June 13, 1923. It increased by many multiples the size of the Smithsonian's small numismatic holdings, among which already were two 1838 British gold sovereigns preserved from the original bequest of James Smithson. The popularity of this transfer was far from universal, as many Philadelphia resi-

The collection grew, year by year, by making exchanges to supply deficiencies, by purchases, by adding our own coin, and by saving foreign coins from the melting-pot – a large part in this way, at a cost of not more than their bullion value, though demanding great care, appreciation, and study.

– George G. Evans describing Cabinet specimens in his *Illustrated History of the United States Mint*, published in 1888

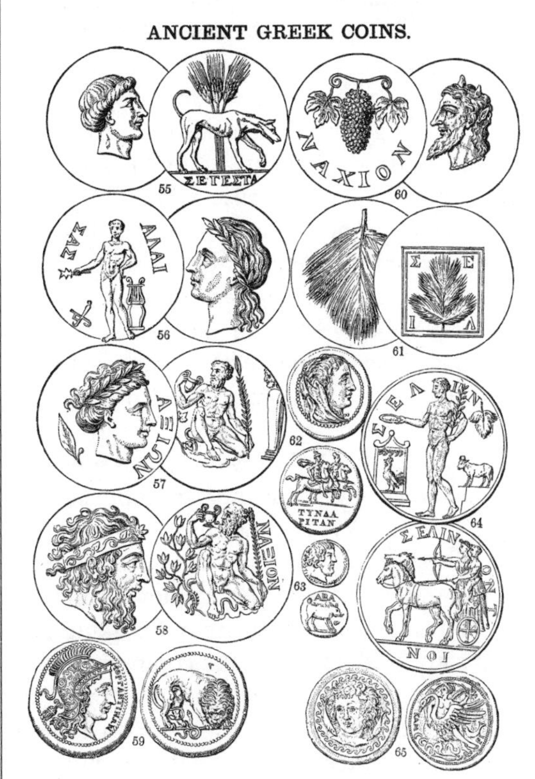

Greek coins in the Mint Cabinet, circa 1885 (From Visitor's Guide and History of the United States Mint, *published by A.M. Smith)*

The Mint Cabinet, circa 1885 (From Visitor's Guide and History of the United States Mint, *published by A.M. Smith)*

It was formerly a suite of three apartments connected by folding-doors, but the doors have been removed, and it is now a pleasant saloon fifty-four feet long by sixteen wide. ... The central section is lighted from the dome, which is supported by four columns. There is an open space immediately under the dome, to give light to the hall below, which is the main entrance to the Mint. Around this space is a railing and a circular case for coins.

– George G. Evans describing the Mint Cabinet in his *Illustrated History of the United States Mint*, 1888

dents expressed feelings that ranged from disappointment to outrage. Among the doubters was Philadelphia coin dealer Henry Chapman, who had been perhaps America's most esteemed professional numismatist for more than 40 years.

The Mint's collection, which had rarely received much in the way of encouragement and funding from the federal government, traced its origin to the individual initiative of long-ago Chief Coiner Adam Eckfeldt. This visionary had preserved (often at his own expense) specimens of old or unusual coins that were deposited at the Philadelphia Mint for recoining. These were later augmented by samples of the new federal coinage as it was produced, the whole being looked after by Assayer William E. DuBois, who served for a number of years as the part-time curator. The Mint's collection thus pre-dated the Smithsonian's own and held great sentimental value for Mint employees and Philadelphia numismatists. Speaking perhaps for the numismatic community as a whole, *The Numismatist* editor Frank G. Duffield cautioned, "Taking a broad view of the matter, the National Museum in Washington is the logical place for the coin collection. It has been termed the Mint collection, though, strictly speaking, it is the national collection. The National Museum already has a collection of medals, and the merging of the two collections will be advantageous. The construction of the Mint Cabinet is such that it would be impossible to enlarge the space for the collection without remodeling the entire rotunda. This fact would prevent the material growth of the collection ... ."

Duffield's words proved prophetic, as the Smithsonian's National Numismatic Collection has since been the beneficiary of splendid gifts of both important individual specimens and irreplaceable specialized collections. It is doubtful that such additions could have been secured without the prospect of their receiving the kind of international attention that is consistently directed toward the Smithsonian Institution's rich assembly of museums. Today, while only a fraction of the collection is on display at any given time, that which may be viewed at the National Museum of American History presents a fabulous panorama of numismatic history and technology.

Chapter Twelve

Changes at the United States Mint

So, first of all, let me assert my firm belief that the only thing we have to fear is fear itself – nameless, unreasoning, unjustified terror which paralyzes needed efforts to convert retreat into advance.

– Franklin Roosevelt trying to calm Depression-era jitters in his first inaugural address, March 4, 1933

Acquisition of the Janvier lathe was one of the many new developments occurring at the various United States Mint facilities at the turn of the 20th century. Another milestone was the transition from steam power to electric power. As early as 1817, steam-driven belts had provided remote power to the various pieces of machinery used in coin manufacturing, as they had in other industries. Beginning in the 1890s, however, steam was quickly phased out in favor of electricity, and individual motors soon powered each machine independently.

The elaborate system of belts and pulleys driven from a central steam engine, with its attendant hazards, faded into history. At the same time, coal power was also being supplanted by electricity for heating the furnaces, making the Mint factories quite a bit cleaner and more economical while also providing greater precision in maintaining desired temperatures.

These improvements and others less dramatic permitted production of ever-greater quantities of coins, though the average number of employees on the Mint payroll changed very little. The sole exceptions are found during the wartime periods of 1916 to 1920 and 1940 to 1945, when the number of employees rose dramatically, and during the worst years of the Great Depression, 1930 to 1933, at which time the roster of workers fell off almost as severely as the Mint's coin output.

Beginning in 1920, the production of gold coins was largely restricted to double eagles. This reflected the fact that gold was no longer achieving wide domestic circulation, but rather was produced almost solely for international exchanges. This largest denomination was preferred for the simple reason that it required the least amount of work for the mints to coin and for banks to count.

◀ *When Franklin Roosevelt took office in 1933, the United States was mired in the Great Depression, the worst economic crisis in the nation's history. More than 13 million people – almost a quarter of the American workforce – were jobless, and family farms were lost to foreclosure as commodity prices plunged. For many, the only option was to leave home and search for work elsewhere. Famous WPA photographer Dorothea Lange (no relation to the author) captured this image of an impoverished family on a New Mexico highway in August 1936. The parents were planning to sell their possessions and the trailer so they could buy food for their nine children.*

Eagles were struck only intermittently, while the quarter eagle and the

President Franklin Delano Roosevelt

All persons are hereby required to deliver on or before May 1, 1933, to a Federal Reserve Bank or branch or agency thereof or to any member bank of the Federal Reserve System all gold coins, gold bullion or gold certificates now owned by them or coming into their ownership on or before April 23, 1933, except the following: ... (b) Gold coins and gold certificates in an amount not exceeding in the aggregate $100 belonging to any one person; and gold coin having a recognized special value to collectors of rare and unusual coins.

– From Franklin Roosevelt's Executive Order 6102 forbidding the hoarding of gold coins, gold bullion, and gold certificates, April 5, 1933

half eagle were unofficially suspended after 1916. A substantial number of $5 pieces was coined in 1929, but few of these ever left the Philadelphia Mint or the Federal Reserve Banks, a fact made quite apparent by their pronounced scarcity today; evidently, most of this mintage was destroyed after the gold recall order of 1933.

Quarter eagles, on the other hand, remained quite popular with the public. They were rarely used in everyday transactions, but rather were acquired during the December holidays to be used as gifts, a practice for which silver dollars also drew some limited seasonal demand. Though the Liberty Head quarter eagles of 1840 to 1907 were consistently preferred for this purpose, these had acquired a slight premium after their discontinuance. As a consolation, Indian Head pieces were coined in fairly consistent numbers toward the end of each calendar year for the sole benefit of gift-givers. When existing pre-war stocks ran out, coinage resumed in 1925 and continued through 1929.

Realizing that these coins would only be returned to banks by those receiving them as gifts, the Treasury Department ordered a halt to their coining in 1930. The half eagle was likewise suspended, and both actions were shortly afterward formalized by law.

The severity of the worldwide economic depression that began in 1929 caused a widespread money shortage and a resulting fall in wages and prices. In an effort to combat gold hoarding and to induce a controlled inflation of the dollar, newly inaugurated President Franklin D. Roosevelt ordered the cessation of gold coinage and distribution in 1933. This was followed by a series of executive orders requiring all Americans to surrender their gold coins and gold certificate currency to the federal government, after which time the gold value of the dollar was legally revalued from $20.67 per ounce to $35 per ounce.

These executive orders also invalidated the gold payment clauses in existing contracts, which was almost certainly a violation of the Constitution, but one that was mostly overlooked due to the urgency of the economic crisis.

Instructions regarding the surrender of gold coins made some exceptions for coins of recognized collector value, and permitted Americans to retain a small quantity of gold coins not considered to be numismatic pieces. Widely misunderstood by nearly everyone, including the press, Roosevelt's actions prompted some Americans to surrender all coins and certificates without distinguishing between

NEW ORDER ISSUED TO TURN IN GOLD

Morgenthau Eliminates $100 Exemption and Sets Penalty at Twice Amount Held.

DEVALUATION STEP DENIED

Action Is Believed Taken to Correct Weaknesses in the Original Hoarder Edict.

Special to THE NEW YORK TIMES.

WASHINGTON, Dec. 28.—Drastic tightening of the government's regulations to bring all gold into the treasury with the exception of that legitimately held were issued today by Acting Secretary Morgenthau.

The new order, issued under authority of the Secretary of the

WARREN DEFENDS, KEMMERER ASSAILS OUR GOLD PROGRAM

Roosevelt's Adviser Says W Cannot Return to the Metallic Standard Now.

3,000 HEAR ARGUMENTS

New Group at Philadelphia Meeting Demands Halt in the Dollar Experiment.

By RUSSELL B. PORTER.

Special to THE NEW YORK TIMES.

PHILADELPHIA, Dec. 28.—Professor George F. Warren of Cornell University, monetary adviser to President Roosevelt and now the most influential member of the "brain trust," explained and defended the administration's gold policy at the annual meeting of the American Economic Association today. He read a paper prepared by himself and his colleague, Profes-

On December 28, 1933, Acting Secretary of the Treasury Henry Morgenthau, Jr. issued additional warnings and outlined new penalties for, those who hoarded gold. (From The New York Times*)*

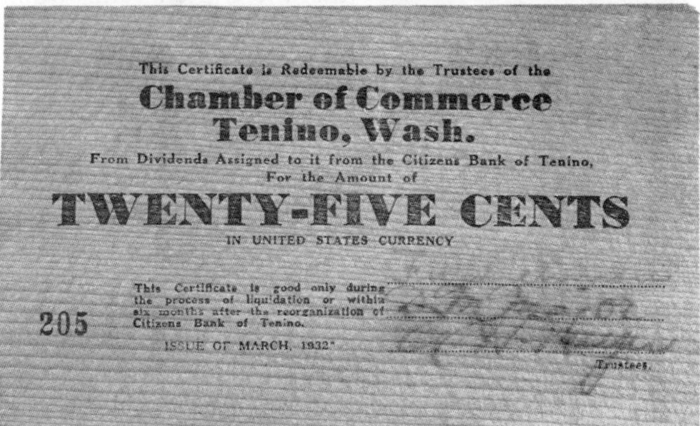

Wooden scrip issued in 1932 by the Tenino Chamber of Commerce

numismatic and non-numismatic items, while others hoarded everything they could lay their hands on, often hiding their stash behind walls or burying it in the back yard.

The coins recovered by the government were melted during the next two or three years, destroying many millions of America's gold pieces. For some of the later issues (1927 to 1933) not yet released in quantity, the destruction was nearly total, resulting in a number of key rarities. The final issue of double eagles dated 1933 was not released at all, and the few coins that were secured by collectors were later subject to seizure by agents of the Secret Service. For decades the only examples whose ownership was acknowledged publicly were the two pieces on display at the Smithsonian Institution's Museum of American History. These coins had been donated to the Smithsonian in 1934, when it became evident that all of their peers were about to be destroyed. Another example surfaced in 1996 and was promptly seized by the federal government. It was not until 2002 that the coin was auctioned, and it was sold that year with half of the proceeds going to the U.S. Mint.

The hard times of the early 1930s resulted in a severe cash shortage, as businesses shut down and banks called in their loans. With the value of stocks and other assets in decline, many of these loans were not recoverable. Thousands of banks collapsed, wiping out their depositors' savings in an era when such deposits were not insured by the federal government.

This shortage of money in circulation resulted in some odd substitutes that are only peripherally related to this history, but make for interesting reading. Taking advantage of materials at hand, the Chamber of Commerce in the town of Tenino, Washington, produced monetary scrip made of wood. This was redeemable only locally, of course, but it did fill a short-term need. Today, wooden scrip and coins are still being produced solely as collectibles on behalf of a wide variety of businesses and individuals, their practical value having long since passed.

Another example of an improvised coinage was that furnished by the town of Pismo Beach, California. Famous for its clams, the little hamlet painted clamshells with inscriptions giving them a legal-tender value! Though intended primarily as a publicity stunt to attract tourism, this action underscored the basic urgency of the economic situation.

Of a more lasting nature was the introduction by many states of sales taxes. Commonplace today, these were necessary but unpleasant innovations in the 1930s, when both cities and states were strapped for cash. In

Wooden money is a circulating medium in Tenino, Washington, as a part of the plan of its Chamber of Commerce, to thaw the frozen assets held in an insolvent bank. The Chamber of Commerce is accepting assignments up to 25 per cent of the depositor's account in the bank, that being the expected amount of the first dividend.

In return scrip is issued for the amount of the assignment, in denominations of $10, $5, $1, 50¢, and 25¢. Most of the business people have agreed to accept the scrip at face value so it serves as a medium of exchange … .

In order to protect the scrip from counterfeiting, the signatures of the three trustees are necessary, and the larger denominations are on lithographed forms, while the smaller currency is on two ply slicewood of Sitka spruce.

This unique Washington timber product is sliced to a thinness of 1-80 of an inch and is made strong and pliable by a sheet of paper pasted between the two surfaces.

– From an information sheet enclosed with each issue of wooden money mailed, starting in February 1932

1932 Washington quarter (24.3 mm)

combination with parking meters, another Depression-era invention, the use of sales taxes greatly increased the demand for cents, coinage of which rose dramatically beginning in 1934. Since a cent still represented some purchasing power during the 1930s, several states denominated their sales taxes in mils, each mil being equal to one-tenth of a cent. As a consequence, when sales taxes were added to purchases, the resulting figures often ended in mils. This required that states distribute aluminum or brass tokens valued at 1 and 5 mils. The onset of World War II, with its shortage of metals, largely spelled the end for tax tokens, merchants being instructed to simply round all figures to the nearest cent. Though not a product of the United States Mint, these tax tokens are nonetheless a part of the nation's coinage history.

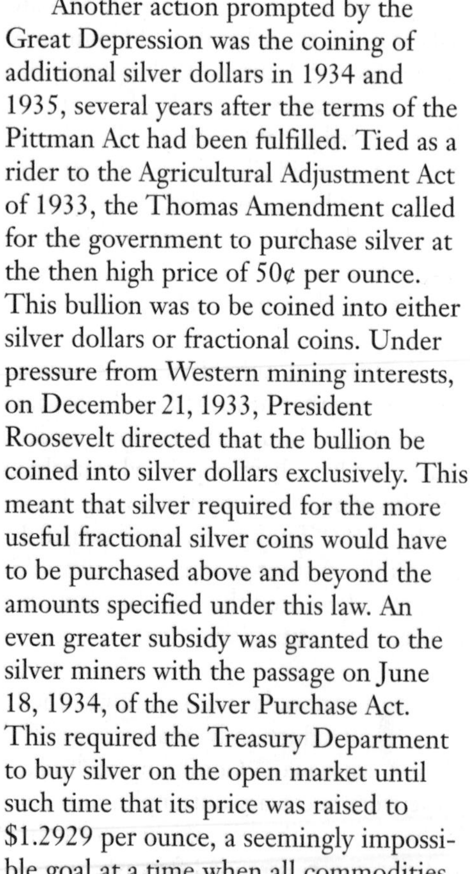

Bust of George Washington by Jean-Antoine Houdon

Another action prompted by the Great Depression was the coining of additional silver dollars in 1934 and 1935, several years after the terms of the Pittman Act had been fulfilled. Tied as a rider to the Agricultural Adjustment Act of 1933, the Thomas Amendment called for the government to purchase silver at the then high price of 50¢ per ounce. This bullion was to be coined into either silver dollars or fractional coins. Under pressure from Western mining interests, on December 21, 1933, President Roosevelt directed that the bullion be coined into silver dollars exclusively. This meant that silver required for the more useful fractional silver coins would have to be purchased above and beyond the amounts specified under this law. An even greater subsidy was granted to the silver miners with the passage on June 18, 1934, of the Silver Purchase Act. This required the Treasury Department to buy silver on the open market until such time that its price was raised to $1.2929 per ounce, a seemingly impossible goal at a time when all commodities had fallen drastically in value.

The coins mandated by these actions were minted during 1934 and 1935 using the Peace design adopted in 1921, but silver certificates actually circulated in their place. Recognizing the futility of such measures, legislation was subsequently passed by Congress that nationalized the purchasing of silver and revised the redemption clause printed on silver certificates. Each silver certificate now stated that the United States would pay the bearer "one dollar in silver" instead of "one silver dollar." The white metal could now be purchased in any quantity without the need for it to be coined into useless and unwanted silver dollars.

The slumbering economy of the early 1930s saw a drastic reduction in the number of coins issued from the three U.S. mints then in service (Philadelphia, Denver, and San Francisco). Some years witnessed the issuance of only one or two denominations (discounting gold coins, which did not actually circulate domestically). In fact, the only silver coins struck during 1932 were some 6 million quarter dollars issued to commemorate the bicentennial of George Washington's birth. Though both the Washington Bicentennial Commission and the Federal Commission of Fine Arts had selected the designs of Laura Gardin Fraser for the quarter, these were rejected by Treasury Secretary Andrew Mellon in favor of those submitted by New York sculptor John Flanagan. (Though set aside at the time, the Fraser models were not entirely forgotten. In 1999, the U.S. Mint used them for a commemorative half eagle marking the bicentennial of Washington's death.)

In compliance with the terms of the competition, Flanagan's portrait was based on the bust sculpted from life by Frenchman Jean-Antoine Houdon, a version of which remains one of the stellar attractions at Mount Vernon, Washington's home in Virginia. The

1933 medal honoring Mint Director Nellie Tayloe Ross (76 mm)

president faces left, the motto IN GOD WE TRUST appearing beneath his chin. LIBERTY is above the bust, the date of coining below. The reverse features a facing eagle with wings outstretched in a pose typical of architectural sculpture of the 1930s. The eagle is perched atop a bundle of arrows, with an olive branch below. UNITED STATES OF AMERICA and E PLURIBUS UNUM are stacked above the eagle, with the value QUARTER DOLLAR below it.

Unlike the Lincoln cent, which was intended from the outset as a replacement for its predecessor, the Washington quarter was originally conceived as a one-year-only circulating commemorative. Since the existing Standing Liberty type had been in production fewer than the 25 years mandated by the Act of 1890, introduction of the Washington quarter in 1932 required a special act of Congress. But this new coin was well received by the public, and the Mint favored it on purely practical grounds (Standing Liberty quarters struck up poorly and fared even worse after just a few years' circulation). When the minting of quarter dollars resumed in 1934, it was the Washington coin that appeared, and it has been in production ever since.

Monticello, Thomas Jefferson's home at Charlottesville, Virginia

The trend toward portrayal of real people on United States coins was confirmed in 1938 by the Treasury Department's announcement that it was holding an open design competition to replace the Indian Head/Buffalo nickel.

The terms of this competition specified that the new coin's obverse would depict "an authentic portrait of Thomas Jefferson," while the reverse would present a view of Monticello, the splendid house that Jefferson had designed for himself. A prize of $1,000 was to be awarded to the person submitting the winning models, this selection to rest with Mint Director Nellie Tayloe Ross and a judging panel of three sculptors.

The winner was German-American artist Felix Schlag of Chicago, who used as his model the fine bust of Jefferson by Jean-Antoine Houdon. Though his original perspective view of Monticello made for a superior work of art, the Mint opted to scrap it in favor of a straight-forward elevation (this depiction was presumably easier to coin). Jefferson faces left, dressed in a high-collar suit of the period. The mottoes IN GOD WE TRUST and LIBERTY are inscribed around the periphery at left and right, respectively. The date continues the arc formed by LIBERTY, the two elements being separated by a single star. A facing view of Monticello dominates the reverse, and the house's name is inscribed directly beneath it. Below this, arranged in an arc, are the value FIVE CENTS and the legend UNITED STATES OF AMERICA. The Latin legend E PLURIBUS UNUM appears around the upper periphery.

The Jefferson nickel was issued in November 1938, but contemporary accounts indicate that most of the new coins were hoarded by collectors and the general public. In fact, it was not until 1940 that they were commonly seen in circulation. Though slightly modified over the years to improve die life, the Jefferson nickel remains in production today, the only one of our current coins being struck in its original metallic composition. In 2003, a bill was passed that revised this coin's design to honor the bicentennial of the Louisiana Purchase while retaining a portrait of Thomas Jefferson.

Bust of Thomas Jefferson by Jean-Antoine Houdon

1939-D Jefferson nickel (21.2 mm)

2004 and 2005 reverse designs of the Westward Journey Nickel Series®

RECYCLING AND RATIONING DURING WWII

New Cents from Old Shell Casings

The United States Mint recycled salvaged cartridge cases to provide metal for 1944 to 1946 cents, a scheme that provided additional copper for military use by reducing the amount of new metal needed on the home front.

Ingots of pure copper were combined with 70% copper shell casings to produce an alloy of 95% copper and 5% zinc. Tin, in short supply due to the war, was eliminated during these years.

The color of uncirculated 1944 to 1946 cents was slightly different from that of pre-war copper cents, though after the coins became slightly soiled from use they were indistinguishable.

Some have suggested that the recycling program was designed primarily as a wartime morale booster – yet another way to sacrifice at home to support American troops abroad. Regardless of its intent, however, the program did deliver shell casings to the Mint for re-use as cents.

1944 cent made partly from shell casings

According to Chief Yeoman and Ship's Writer David C. Moser, who served on the destroyer U.S.S. *Greer* in 1943, "... a 'hot-shellman' wearing heavy asbestos gloves, would catch the burning hot empties as they were ejected from the breech and throw them quickly overboard. The new salvage operation, however, required that he pass the cases to a gloveless mate, who in turn stacked them some place out of the way ... ."

The OPA established price limits for many products. Here, a volunteer checks and posts ceiling prices in New York.

Wartime Food Rationing and OPA Tokens

During much of World War II, booklets of food rationing stamps were distributed to Americans on the home front to ensure the even distribution of commodities that were in short supply – sugar, cheese, meat, canned, goods, flour, fat and lard, coffee, and others. A pound of ham, for example, might cost 51¢ and 8 points.

In charge of this huge task was the United States Office of Price Administration (OPA), which established volunteer boards to control the buying and selling of rationed commodities in their communities.

The red, green, brown, or blue stamps were valued in points, and cardboard-fiber tokens issued in blue and red were used to make "change" for meat and processed food purchases. Both sides of the tokens contained the numeral 1 flanked by two initials. Though not a product of the U.S. Mint, OPA tokens were nonetheless a vital part of wartime commerce.

Red (top) and blue tokens (16.5 mm)

Chapter Thirteen

The Demands of World War II

The 1943 Lincoln cent was known as the "steelie" because it was made of steel with a thin zinc coating. This experiment, though ultimately a failure, was undertaken to free up copper needed to support the war effort.

The onset of another European war in 1939 stimulated economic activity in the United States, which was a nation then still at peace. The rapid growth in demand for additional coins prompted a hasty build-up of manpower at the three mints and set new production records with each succeeding year. This activity further intensified after 1941, when America joined the struggle. It was thus fortunate that a new San Francisco Mint had opened in 1937 to replace the 1874 structure, which had once been acclaimed as the most modern and productive mint in the world. Though quality took a back seat during the war years of 1941 to 1945, particularly with the quick hiring of so many inexperienced workers, productivity rose to levels then considered astonishing.

A number of innovations adopted during this period facilitated the growth in output. One of the most significant was the development by two San Francisco Mint employees of the dual-press, a single coining press set with two pairs of dies mounted in a single collar. In later years, this idea was expanded into the quad-press of four die pairs, used until quite recently.

The effects of World War II were felt at the mints in other ways as well. A shortage of certain metals prompted changes in the alloys used for cents and nickels. Early in 1942, tin was eliminated from the composition of the cent, since this metal had been supplied largely by the now Japanese-occupied Malaya. As this metal made up only about 1% of each coin's mass, the change went entirely unnoticed by the general public. But one of the other metals in critically short supply was copper. Cents of that time were made of a bronze alloy that was 95% copper, and minting billions of them each year used up a great amount of this metal. Throughout 1942, the Mint experi-mented with various substitutes for copper, even testing such materials as glass, plastic, and leather! As a result of these tests and of a law passed December 18, 1942, all of the cents

The U.S.S. Shaw *exploding during the Japanese attack on Pearl Harbor, December 7, 1941*

There is one front and one battle where everyone in the United States – every man, woman, and child – is in action, and will be privileged to remain in action throughout this war. That front is right here at home, in our daily lives, in our daily tasks. Here at home everyone will have the privilege of making whatever self-denial is necessary, not only to supply our fighting men, but to keep the economic structure of our country fortified and secure during the war and after the war.

– From Franklin Roosevelt's "Call for Sacrifice," April 28, 1942

The "war nickel" was made of copper, silver and manganese to save nickel for use by the military. (21.1 mm)

coined during 1943 were made of steel with a zinc coating. Shiny white when new, the steel cents were quickly confused with dimes and prompted many complaints from the public. When worn, the cents became dark and were sometimes mistaken for nickels. Being magnetic, they also jammed parking meters and other mechanical devices. It seemed that no one liked the steel cents, with the pos-sible exception of coin collectors.

The Mint returned to using bronze for the nation's cents in 1944. (Technically it was brass, since tin had been eliminated. Congress ultimately removed tin from the cent altogether in 1962, as its inclusion clearly served no purpose other than tradition.)

The steel cents were systematically withdrawn beginning in 1945, but they still turned up in circulation as late as the early 1960s. Though they had proved unpopular, the "steelies" saved a great deal of copper for the war effort, and Americans accepted this sacrifice as they did so many others during the difficult years of World War II.

A wartime worker flexes her muscles in this poster by graphic artist J. Howard Miller, who produced the piece for the Westinghouse Corporation in 1943. Note the fingernail polish, rouge, lipstick, mascara, and carefully plucked eyebrows.

After the steel cent debacle, the Mint gained much publicity from the fact that spent artillery shell cases were being retrieved and melted and their brass recoined into cents, making up a portion of the metal used from 1944 to 1946. Unlike the steel cents, which became increasingly scarce during the 1950s, the brass cents were commonplace until the early 1970s, when all Lincoln cents bearing the Wheat Ear reverse were hoarded.

The five-cent piece was also affected by wartime shortages. Though only 25% nickel, coinage of this denomination required enough of that vital metal to threaten the manufacture of armor plating for ships, tanks, etc. As of October 8, 1942, nickel was eliminated from the composition of the five-cent piece, and an alloy of copper, silver, and manganese was substituted through 1945. Though this alloy did not always mix properly, providing numerous error coins to delight collectors, it proved quite satisfactory in all other respects. It also carried the added virtue of a reduced copper content, this metal being even more crucial to the war effort than nickel.

To distinguish the so-called "war nickels" from those of the regular composition, each coin bore a greatly enlarged mintmark that was placed directly over Monticello's dome (the letter P was used for the very first time on a United States coin to identify pieces struck at the Philadelphia Mint). Such distinguishing marks were needed, it was believed, so these coins could be speedily withdrawn after the war. As it turned out, this action was never taken. Though the coins wore quickly and tarnished more readily than those of the regular copper-nickel composition, they remained in circulation until their silver value exceeded their face value in the late 1960s.

The various changes made to America's minor coins were permitted under the Act of March 27, 1942, which empowered the Mint to alter the composition of the cent and five-cent piece as needed. This authority terminated on December 31, 1946. By that time, of course, the war had ended and the crisis was past. Though production of five-cent pieces of the regular copper-nickel composition was resumed at the beginning of 1946, tin was not restored to the cent until later in the year, and many of those coined in 1946 and possibly into 1947 were struck on planchets of the wartime brass alloy. In an interesting footnote, the law of December 18, 1942, which specified the cent's steel-zinc composition, also permitted the minting of a three-cent piece to ease the demand for cents. As we now know, of course, this authority was never exercised.

Chapter Fourteen

New Designs for a New Age

1946 Roosevelt dime (17.9 mm)

Though the post-war American economy experienced a few recessions, most notably in 1948 to 1950 and 1957 to 1958, the general trend during the first couple of decades after World War II was toward sustained progress and economic growth. While not created as a direct result of this prosperity, a number of new coin designs debuted during this period that reflected changing trends in art and politics. These included a dime honoring President Franklin D. Roosevelt and a half dollar bearing the portrait of the great scientist and diplomat Benjamin Franklin.

Before the war, there had been some thought of replacing Weinman's Winged Head of Liberty on the dime with a portrait of Benjamin Franklin. This was a particular goal of Nellie Tayloe Ross, who served as director of the United States Mint throughout the administrations of Presidents Roosevelt and Harry S Truman (1933 to 1953). Franklin was considered a worthy and apolitical subject, and proponents of the Philadelphia sage were campaigning for a new dime when that coin became eligible for revision under the Law of 1890. The old dime achieved its 25-year minimum production in 1940, but the urgency of increased coinage during the war years forestalled any attempt at introducing a new design. Before this plan could be revived, the death of President Franklin D. Roosevelt in 1945 prompted the Treasury Department to announce that it would be his portrait that supplanted Miss Liberty on the 1946 dime. This denomination was chosen specifically because Roosevelt, a polio victim, was closely associated with the March of Dimes campaign to eradicate the dreaded disease. The new dime debuted early in 1946, and it continues in production to this day, though it has been coined of base metals since 1965.

The dime was created by U.S. Mint Chief Engraver John Ray Sinnock, though a compelling case was later made that his Roosevelt design was based on a bas-relief created by sculptor Selma Burke and presented to the president in 1943. The dime's design is fairly simple. Roosevelt's bust faces left on the obverse, the motto LIBERTY appears around the periphery at left, while IN GOD WE TRUST is below the president's chin. Beneath the truncation of the bust are the date and Sinnock's initials, JS. The reverse of this coin type features the

Joseph Stalin, Franklin Roosevelt, and Winston Churchill at the Russian Embassy in Tehran, Iran, November 28-December 1, 1943

1949-S Franklin half dollar (30.6 mm)

torch of freedom. It is flanked by an olive branch to the left and an oak branch to the right, symbolizing peace and strength, respectively. Across these elements, inscribed rather awkwardly, is the motto E PLURIBUS UNUM. Around the periphery are the legend UNITED STATES OF AMERICA at the top and the value ONE DIME below.

There is one episode associated with the adoption of the Roosevelt dime that is worth retelling only because it is so reflective of the times. The end of World War II saw the United States fighting a new battle of nerves in what came to be known as the Cold War. Americans feared and mistrusted their former ally, the Soviet Union, and many people saw communist conspiracies in every aspect of American life. One of the silliest involved the new dime. John Sinnock unwittingly set off a nationwide controversy when rumors were spread that his initials JS on the dime actually stood for Joseph Stalin! So persistent were these reports that the Mint was moved to issue a press release identifying its artist and refuting any "red" connection.

Bust of Benjamin Franklin by Jean-Antoine Houdon

Though the dime had been claimed for Franklin D. Roosevelt, old Ben Franklin was not entirely forgotten. Mint Director Ross selected the half dollar to bear his portrait beginning in 1948. It was then the only United States coin eligible for a face-lift under the 1890 law, with the exception of the Lincoln cent. Since Ross did not want to be responsible for displacing the beloved Lincoln, and Weinman's 1916 half dollar now seemed antiquated, the choice was a natural one. John R. Sinnock had already commenced work on a Franklin portrait, basing it on yet another Houdon bust, when he died in office in 1947. This portrait was completed by Gilroy Roberts, who succeeded Sinnock as chief engraver and designed the coin's reverse.

Like the Roosevelt dime, the Franklin half dollar has a simple and spare composition. Franklin faces right, dressed in a suit of the period. Around the periphery are the mottoes LIBERTY above and IN GOD WE TRUST below, while the date appears to the right beneath Franklin's chin. The central device of the reverse is a profile view of Philadelphia's Liberty Bell. UNITED STATES OF AMERICA is above it, with the value HALF DOLLAR below. The Latin legend E PLURIBUS UNUM is to the left of the bell, and a tiny eagle, somewhat similar to that on the Washington quarter, is to its right. As its diminutive size suggests, the eagle was an afterthought. After the main themes had been chosen, someone belatedly recalled the Mint Act of 1837, which clearly specifies that the half dollar must depict our national symbol on its reverse.

In its first few years of production, the Franklin half was coined in relatively small numbers, as compared to the preceding type. Mintages began to rise more or less steadily in 1957, and they took a tremendous upswing in 1962 and 1963 with the onset of a nationwide coin shortage. By that time, however, the half dollar was already becoming an unfamiliar coin in most of the nation, though the Western states still fancied large silver halves and dollars. While it proved to be a suitable coin in most respects, minting of the Franklin half dollar was terminated in 1963 before it achieved the statutory minimum of 25 years.

This move was prompted by the death of yet another president in office, John F. Kennedy.

By the 1950s, each of the five current coin denominations had received new designs featuring prominent Americans, all but one of them a president of the United States. It seemed that the redesigning process would have stopped at that point, and indeed, most of the coins in use today bear the same images they did 50 years ago. Exceptions are the half dollar, the Washington/ Statehood quarters and the Westward Journey Nickel Series™.

A partial revision of the cent occurred in 1959, when its reverse was changed to mark the sesquicentennial of Abraham Lincoln's birth. This movement had begun four years earlier at the American Numismatic Association's convention in Omaha. A resolution was passed calling for replacement of the Lincoln cent with a new type entirely, as this coin was already more than 40 years old. Acting Mint Director Leland Howard responded that there was little enthusiasm within the Treasury Department or Congress for changing any of the existing coin designs. There the matter rested until the formation of a Lincoln Sesquicentennial Commission in 1958 renewed pressure for a redesign of the cent's reverse alone. Though the commission's original plan was to depict Lincoln's birthplace cabin in Hodgenville, Kentucky, this soon evolved into a movement to portray Washington, D.C.'s Lincoln Memorial, built in 1922. While the selection of coin designs was legally at the sole discretion of the Mint Director and the Secretary of the Treasury, President Dwight Eisenhower nonetheless signed an executive order authorizing this change on December 20, 1958.

French's statue at the Lincoln Memorial in Washington, D.C.

All of the cents dated 1959 and later have borne the new reverse designed and sculpted by U.S. Mint Assistant Engraver Frank Gasparro. It shows a front elevation of the Lincoln Memorial, which was the work of architect Henry Bacon. The legend E PLURIBUS UNUM is directly above the structure, while UNITED STATES OF AMERICA and the value ONE CENT are inscribed around the periphery, above and below the memorial building, respectively. Gasparro's initials FG appear just to the right of the Lincoln Memorial. Daniel Chester French's seated figure of Lincoln is visible within the building, making the Lincoln Memorial cent one of only two circulating United States coin to portray the same individual on both sides (the 1999

The Lincoln Memorial reverse (19 mm)

The new design ... copies the reverse of the five-dollar bill. Unfortunately, the conception is ill-suited to a small coin. On the bill, the regularity of the outlines is broken up by a chiaroscuro within and surrounding the building. There are no shadows on the coin, and there is no feeling of depth. The details are lost, and what remains looks at a glance more like a trolley car.

– Don Taxay critiquing the design of the Lincoln Memorial reverse in his book *The U.S. Mint and Coinage*, 1966

President John F. Kennedy

1965 Kennedy half dollar (30.6 mm)

New Jersey State Quarter depicts George Washington twice).

The assassination of President John F. Kennedy in November 1963, prompted a nearly immediate plan to memorialize him on a circulating United States coin. The only denominations then eligible for redesign under the 25-year-minimum rule were the Jefferson nickel, the Washington quarter, and the Peace silver dollar. As there was no demand for additional silver dollars, this meant that some hard political choices would have to be made. The Democratic majority in Congress was reluctant to remove Jefferson, one of their own, and the president's widow, Jacqueline Kennedy, balked at displacing the revered George Washington. Since he was not associated with any current political party, it was poor Ben Franklin who got the boot when the half dollar was chosen to bear the portrait of President Kennedy. This selection required congressional action, since the Franklin half dollar was then only 15 years old. A bill was passed on December 30, 1963, enabling the change, though this work had already been authorized by Mint Director Eva Adams as early as November 27 in anticipation of its passage.

Chief Engraver Gilroy Roberts was pressed to hastily modify his Kennedy presidential medal of 1961 and adapt the portrait to the half dollar. Assistant Engraver Frank Gasparro prepared the reverse of the new coin utilizing the Presidential Seal. Both models were completed in record time, and the new coins were in production only two months after the president's assassination. Kennedy faces left, with the motto IN GOD WE TRUST appearing beneath his bust. Around the periphery are the motto LIBERTY and the date, which is at the bottom. Gilroy Roberts' monogram, which some very imaginative Americans believed to be the Soviet Union's hammer and sickle insignia, is at the truncation of Kennedy's bust. The reverse is dominated by the Presidential Seal, which contains the same basic elements as the Great Seal of the United States, used on earlier generations of U.S. coins. The only additions to it are the nation's identity, the value HALF DOLLAR and Gasparro's initials FG just above and to the right of the eagle's tail.

Debuting in March 1964, the Kennedy half dollar became an instant collectible worldwide, and precious few of them saw any real circulation. In fact, these coins were so completely hoarded that the half dollar as a circulating coin has been effectively obsolete ever since. Even though all traces of silver were removed from the half dollar beginning in 1971, this coin was rarely seen outside of gambling casinos. In recent years, casinos have phased out half dollars in favor of their own more profitable 50¢ tokens, which they can have manufactured at significantly below face value. This falling demand for halves is reflected in their declining mintages and slow distribution. It appears that this denomination may soon become a coin produced solely for collectors.

Chief Engraver Gilroy Roberts and his design for the obverse of the John F. Kennedy half dollar

Chapter Fifteen

The Challenges of Modern Minting

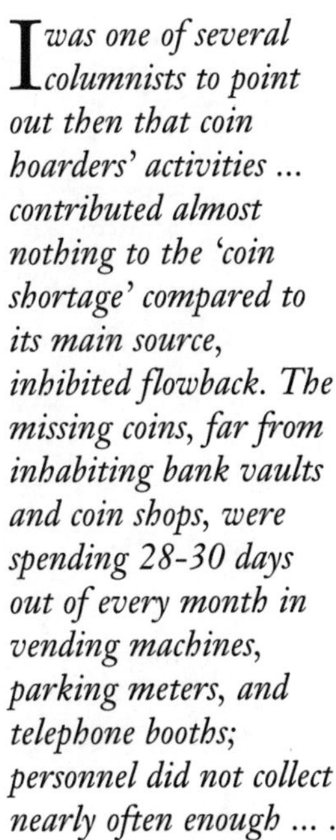

I was one of several columnists to point out then that coin hoarders' activities ... contributed almost nothing to the 'coin shortage' compared to its main source, inhibited flowback. The missing coins, far from inhabiting bank vaults and coin shops, were spending 28-30 days out of every month in vending machines, parking meters, and telephone booths; personnel did not collect nearly often enough ... .

– Walter Breen criticizing the Mint's claim that hoarders and coin collectors were responsible for the coin shortage of the 1960s, in his *Complete Encyclopedia of U.S. and Colonial Coins*, 1988

After 1909, when the New Orleans Mint ceased production, there were just three federal mints in operation. These were located at Philadelphia, Denver, and San Francisco. Though it was originally built in 1906, repeated additions to the Denver Mint had made it the most productive of the three. By the mid-1950s, it was more cost-effective to produce coins at Denver and ship them to the western states than it was to mint them in San Francisco. The San Francisco Mint thus ceased all coining operations after March 31, 1955, though it continued to function as an assay office. This partial closure would come back to haunt the Mint and the Treasury Department just a few years later during a severe nationwide coin shortage.

Mint Director Eva Adams

The coin crisis of 1961 to 1965 was prompted by the rapidly expanding American economy and an even greater growth in the mechanical vending industry. The mints stepped up production dramatically during these years, but the supply of fresh coins still fell short of demand. The Treasury Department had made repeated requests throughout the 1950s and early '60s for a new Philadelphia Mint to replace the aged structure in use since 1901, but these had fallen on deaf congressional ears. It was not until banks began paying premiums over face value for coins returned by the public that action was finally taken in Washington.

Embarrassed by being caught unprepared, Congress sought both solutions and a scapegoat; while the former were some time in coming, assigning blame for the coin shortage was a task more easily completed. The enormous popularity that coin collecting enjoyed during 1955 to 1964 was attracting media attention and prompted a speculative market in rolls and even bags of newly released coins. Coin collectors, Congress believed, were the cause of the severe coin shortage. This view was reinforced by a Mint establishment desperate to relieve some of the pressure it was feeling from angry bankers and business owners.

To discourage coin speculators, Congress authorized a freeze on the date 1964, so that all coins would be alike regardless of when they were made. As a result, cents through half dollars bearing the date 1964 were coined as late as 1966, accounting for the tremendous mintage figures recorded. Mint Director Eva Adams took this a step further by announcing a suspension of mintmarks until further notice. For coins dated 1965 to 1967, only a study of the Mint Director's annual reports will reveal where these were actually coined and in what respective numbers; the coins themselves are indistinguishable as to their origin. Finally, the production and sale of proof coins for collectors was suspended from 1965 until 1968. In its one positive move, Congress finally appropriated the funding needed for the construction of a new Philadelphia Mint building. Though this structure would prove useful down the road, its completion came too late to address the coin shortage of 1961 to 1965.

In the meantime, the Mint came up with some innovations to speed production at existing facilities. The positioning of machinery in each mint was revised to allow ingots to be rolled into much longer strips (the cramped quarters of the San Francisco facility had precluded this and led to its closure). The manufacture of press-ready planchets for minor coins was partially contracted out to private industry, a practice that had been used intermittently in the past. The dual-press collar devised during World War II was expanded to quad-press operation. This was accomplished by fitting presses with even larger collars having four openings, thus permitting four pairs of dies to strike coins with each blow. Though limited to pieces of smaller size, such as cents and dimes, this move greatly increased the number of coins produced per eight-hour shift. Since the mints were operating three shifts a day during the mid-1960s, this resulted in an unprecedented output of coins.

To accelerate the manufacture of coin blanks, the Mint acquired some old ammunition presses from the Defense Department, and the San Francisco Assay Office (formerly the mint) began producing blanks in 1964 for shipment to Denver. It began minting its own coins (without mintmarks) in September of the following year.

At the same time when coins of all types were in short supply, still another

The Ill-Fated 1964-D Silver Dollars

A bill passed by Congress on July 28, 1964, and signed by President Lyndon B. Johnson on August 3, authorized the coining of 45 million silver dollars at the traditional standard of .900 fine silver. Coming during the very height of the coin crisis of 1961 to 1965, the contradictory nature of this legislation was criticized in many circles. To divert so much silver, machinery, and manpower to minting silver dollars that would almost certainly be hoarded was a foolish move under any circumstances. Because this bill was an obvious concession to the owners of gambling casinos, who were finding it increasingly difficult to keep these popular coins in-house, the move was even more difficult to jusify. In fact, the Treasury had only months earlier suspended the exchange of silver dollars for silver certificates, when it became obvious that the coins were being obtained primarily for the purpose of profit. Casino owners attempted to destroy the numismatic appeal of their silver dollars by filing off their dates, but this labor-intensive effort was both impractical and largely ineffective.

Here is what happened: silver dollars dated 1878 and later had never enjoyed much popularity with collectors, and coins that old could still be found in general circulation in the western states. A collector market gradually developed during the 1950s on the rising popularity of coin collecting in general, and increasing numbers of silver dollars were withdrawn from Treasury vaults beginning around 1958. As the withdrawal of these coins finally reached the deepest recesses of the Treasury Building in Washington, rare dates of recognized collector value began to appear, and that is when Treasury Secretary C. Douglas Dillon ordered a halt to the raids in March 1964.

With the existing supply of silver dollars thus threatened, the Western Governors Conference appealed to Congress that May for a new edition of 150 million more. This motion was supported in the Senate by Mike Mansfield (D-Montana). Treasury Secretary Dillon first reduced the request to 100 million coins, before settling on the more reasonable figure of 45 million. Mint Director Eva Adams gave her approval to the plan, perhaps because she, as a native Nevadan, sympathized with both the casino owners and silver producers. She gave as her argument in favor of silver dollars that each one minted would take the place of four quarters or two halves, thus reducing the need for so many coins!

crisis loomed, particularly for the three silver denominations. By 1964, it was apparent that at the rate these pieces were being produced, the United States Mint would exhaust the supply of available silver in just a few years. In addition, the price of silver was slowly rising: the bullion value of silver dollars was already close to face, while the fractional silver coins, with their slightly lower standard, were not far behind. Though reluctant to debase the nation's coinage, Congress could not simply wish the crisis away, and some action had to be taken soon. On July 23, 1965, legislation was passed eliminating precious metal from the dime and quarter dollar, while substantially reducing the percentage of silver in the half dollar. This last provision was a pointless gesture toward maintaining some recognizable standard, even though the value of America's coinage had not been dependent on its bullion content for generations.

The new silverless dimes and quarters were composed of copper and nickel in three layers of metal bonded together under high pressure. The two outside layers consisted of an alloy of 75% copper and 25% nickel, the same composition used for the five-cent piece. Inside, however, was a core of pure copper. While giving the finished coins the same electromagnetic properties as the silver pieces (critical to the vending machine industry), this feature also imparted a bright red edge that turned a dark rust color as the coins aged.

The new "clad" quarter dollar debuted in November 1965, the dime in January 1966. The copper-nickel clad

Though the authorization for additional silver dollars had passed nearly a year earlier, and some $600,000 had been appropriated for their production, the urgent demand for minor coins and fractional silver delayed the coining of the new dollars until May 1965. Both dies and collars for the silver dollar had been on hand since January, but it was the impending end of the Mint's fiscal year on June 30 that at last prompted their production. During the first two weeks of May, some 316,076 Peace dollars of the 45 million authorized were coined at the Denver Mint. These were all dated 1964-D in compliance with the standing date freeze (see page 165).

Because space at the Denver Mint was at a premium, the dollars were coined in an adjacent structure connected to the Mint building by an enclosed walkway. This auxiliary mint had originally been built as a substation for Denver's electric street railway, but the retirement of streetcar service permitted the overtaxed Mint to purchase the structure from the Denver Tramway Corporation in the 1950s. At first used for general storage, the building was quickly refitted as a supplemental coining room to help ease the coin shortage of the early 1960s. The tramway building was fitted with 12 ammunition presses that had formerly produced shell casings, acquired from the Department of Defense. Old and slow, they nevertheless were used to produce several coin denominations, including the 1964-D silver dollars. The difficulty in using these presses to strike silver dollars accounts, at least in part, for the small number that were coined before a phone call from Washington halted the entire program.

Before the coins were even struck, dealers were offering to buy any and all offered at sharp premiums, and ads appeared committing to sell them at even higher markups. Stung by harsh criticism of this ludicrous activity, President Johnson directed the Treasury Department to withhold the coins from release and destroy them. Mint employees involved with the silver dollar project were asked to sign statements attesting that none were in their possession and that all of the coins had indeed been destroyed. So embarrassing was the whole episode that the Act of July 23, 1965, which primarily eliminated silver from the nation's coinage or reduced its content, included as well a specific provision prohibiting the coining of dollar coins for a period of five years! The U.S. Mint's Division of Technology reportedly held two specimens of the 1964-D silver dollar for several years before these, too, were destroyed.

alloy was harder than the traditional silver and copper mix, and the new coins did not strike up very well. This problem was overcome in time by lowering the relief of the dies. While coins minted today are struck to the same standards for size, weight, and composition as those dated 1965, they differ dramatically in their sculptural appearance, as a side-by-side comparison will reveal.

The new half dollar was made of a different composition, though it too was bonded in three layers. Outside were two strips comprised of 80% silver and 20% copper, close enough to the traditional .900/.100 alloy to simulate the old coins in appearance. Inside was a core of 21% silver and 79% copper, resulting in a net silver content for each coin of 40%. The new halves were first released

Technological Advances

The need for additional dies has grown during recent decades, due to the tremendous increase in regular coinage and the addition of numerous commemorative and bullion coin programs. The United States Mint is thus constantly improving its production techniques. The need for ever-higher mintages requires the manufacture of thousands of dies annually, and several recent developments have greatly enhanced the Mint's ability to increase its die-making capability and extend die life.

During the 1970s the Mint began plating the faces of its dies with chromium to make them more resistant to wear. This had been done for some years with the proof dies, but it was new to regular production dies. When engravers and die-setters found that such plating made it difficult to address flaws that occurred in the dies during use, a solution was found in chemically stripping the plating, repolishing the dies, and then plating them again.

Since 1991, all mintmarks have been included in the master matrices for each denomination, eliminating the tedious process of hand-punching them into each working die. Typically, the master hubs are reduced from a sculptor-engraver's model already bearing the upcoming year's date and San Francisco's S mintmark. These are used to produce master dies for the S-Mint proof coinage of that year. The mintmark is then removed from the master hub, whereupon master dies are sunk for the Philadelphia and Denver mints, and into each of these is engraved the appropriate mintmark. From the master dies are raised working hubs, each of which is then used to sink working dies for the coin presses.

In 1996, the Denver Mint began manufacturing its own working dies in-house from hubs furnished by the Philadelphia Mint, an activity that historically had been limited to Philadelphia. One of the principal advances in die making debuted with this new Denver installation. For the first time in U.S. Mint history, dies were sunk with just a single impression from the hub. Previously, all working dies had to be annealed (heat-softened) after a first impression and then hubbed a second time to achieve a complete transfer. Between the lowering of the relief in our current coin dies and the use of more powerful presses, the goal of single-hubbing each die became a reality. Since extended to the Philadelphia Mint, this practice has greatly lessened the pressure to produce adequate numbers of dies.

The design on the 1955 cent is in much higher relief than that of the 1995 coin. Lowering the relief reduced the cost of the minting process.

Modern coin presses differ tremendously from the first steam-driven, knuckle-action press installed in 1836. Updated several times and converted to electric power during the 1890s, the vertical-stroke presses have recently been joined by presses striking coins in a horizontal motion. Though these strike just a single coin at a time, as opposed to the quad action of vertical presses, their movement is extremely fast. The slower, vertical-motion presses are now used solely for striking commemoratives and bullion coins, for which quality is more critical than speed.

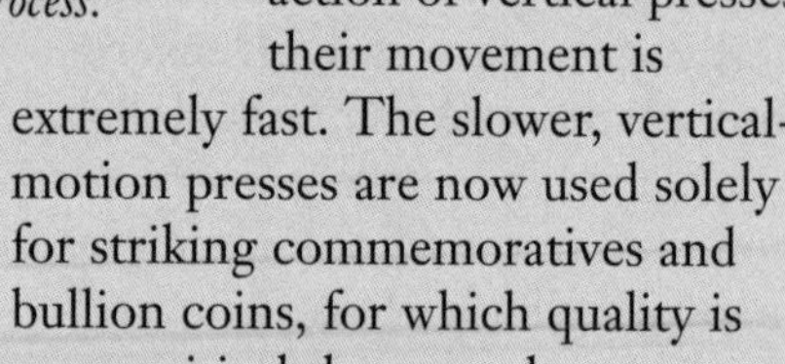

in March 1966, though most of the 1965-dated coinage was produced from 1966. Coins of this composition were produced through 1970, at which time silver was eliminated altogether. Since 1971, the half dollar has been coined of the same base metals used for its little brothers.

While President Lyndon Johnson reassured Americans that the old silver coins would circulate freely alongside the new clad issues for years to come, the Mint took no chances. It produced billions of the replacement coins from 1965 to 1967, taking full advantage of its suspension of mintmarks to make these coins unappealing to collectors and speculators. Silver dimes, quarters, and halves dated 1964 were minted simultaneously as late as 1966 to maintain the illusion that such coins were not being hoarded. The reality is that most of the newly minted silver coins went straight to speculators, who were already withdrawing the earlier issues. While silver coins continued to circulate in ever-dwindling numbers as late as 1970, only the most common issues were seen after 1967.

Cents, too, were a source of frequent concern for the U.S. Mint. When the new Philadelphia Mint opened for business in 1969, the great coin shortage of the early 1960s was already history, yet periodic shortages of cents continued to occur every few years through the 1980s. The reason for these shortages is found primarily in the cent's diminished purchasing power. The value of this little coin had become so slight by the 1970s that Americans seldom bothered to carry them around when going about their shopping. After being dispensed by store clerks providing exact change, cents were routinely taken home and dropped into a jar or some other receptacle until enough had accumulated to justify the effort of rolling and cashing them. This idleness meant that dozens or evenhundreds of cents needed to be produced annually for every person in America just to meet the requirement for exact change in retail transactions.

Seasonal shortages frequently occurred around the December holidays, merchants and banks sometimes offering premium prices for the return of cents by their customers. Aggravating this situation to some degree, though not a major factor, was the inclination of hoarders to save all cents bearing the original Wheat Ears reverse design terminated after 1958. Though most of these coins were no more valuable than the Lincoln Memorial cents that superseded them, the mere fact that they were different provided the impetus for hoarding, and this became widespread during the early 1970s.

Also subject to irrational hoarding were all cents coined at the San Francisco Mint. When mintmarks were restored to the nation's coins in 1968, after a suspension of three years, among the new pieces seen in circulation were cents and nickels bearing the popular S mintmark. This mint's coins had long held an added appeal for collectors, most of whom lived in the East, because their distant point of origin and generally lower mintages made them scarce in circulation. While those minted in 1968 and subsequent years were made in large enough numbers to eliminate any element of rarity, they still traded at a slight premium and were thus subject to hoarding by speculators. To combat this trend, the Mint suspended the coining of nickels for circulation at the San Francisco Mint after 1970 and removed the mintmark from cents coined there after 1974.

Inflation continued to plague the lowly cent, as its metallic value periodically approached its face value. Though the cost of recovering this copper negated any potential profit, the threat of rising copper prices prompted Congress to grant the Mint permission to change the cent's composition whenever needed to avert a crisis. One outcome of this development was a run of experimental aluminum cents of the regular design dated 1974. These were actually coined late in 1973, at a time when the price of copper was enjoying one of its occasional run-ups, but none were placed in circulation. After the crisis passed, almost all of

Evidence that the new clad coins were not universally popular can be seen on this satirical brass token directed at President Lyndon B. Johnson. (26 mm)

In adopting this concoction, the Mint Bureau abandoned counterfeit-detection methods thousands of years old, perhaps cynically recognizing that the purchasing power of dimes and quarters had already become low enough that these coins would no longer attract counterfeiters' attention.

– Walter Breen discussing the clad issues in his *Complete Encyclopedia of U.S. and Colonial Coins*, 1988

them were destroyed, though the Mint continued to experiment with alternative compositions for the "penny."

Time finally ran out for the brass cent in 1981, when the Treasury Department announced that the mints would soon start coining cents made almost entirely of zinc, with just a slim copper plating. This not only saved money on metal (zinc costing less than copper), but it also enhanced the durability of working dies to the point where up to two million impressions could be struck from each die. Both the old and new compositions were coined in 1982, but only copper-plated zinc cents have been minted since that time. How long this composition will remain practical is uncertain, as the cent is now worth so little that it is difficult to imagine it costing less than that amount to manufacture, regardless of the material used.

Dwight D. Eisenhower in uniform as Supreme Allied Commander during World War II

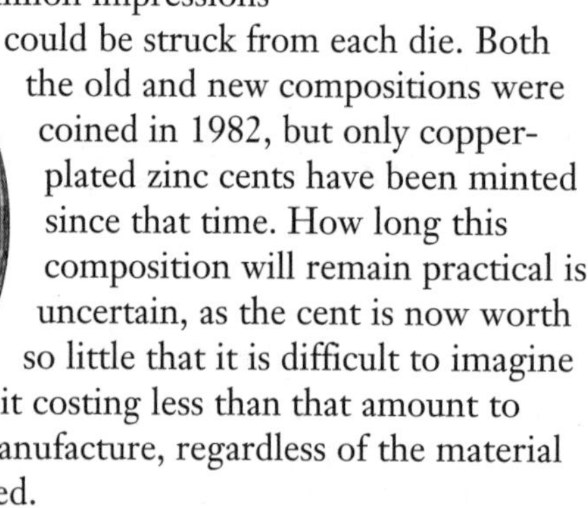

1971-D Eisenhower dollar (38.1 mm)

Many people have argued that the real solution to the cent problem lies in eliminating this denomination altogether, and this action has more than once been recommended to Congress by independent consultants. One important factor weighing in favor of continued cent coinage is the economic implication of its demise. The act of eliminating the cent would be seen by many people as tacit acceptance of inflation, though most would agree that this coin no longer possesses any individual purchasing power. The same people who will not stoop to pick up a "penny" off the street will be the first to complain, should the government attempt to deprive them of their exact change!

At the other end of the coinage spectrum is the one-dollar piece, a coin that has had many ups and downs since it was first minted in 1794. As the five-year ban on dollar coinage imposed in 1965 drew to a close in 1970, agitation resumed for the minting of these coins. Once again, this plea was made primarily by gambling casino owners. Since 1965, the casinos had been using tokens made of nickel and valued at $1.00, but it was clear that real "silver" dollars carried a psychological edge with their customers. Legislation creating a new dollar coin of traditional size but coined in the current copper-nickel clad composition was debated throughout 1970 and was finally passed late in the year,

Former first lady Mamie Eisenhower received the first Eisenhower dollar from President Richard M. Nixon on July 27, 1971.

December 31st to be exact! These bear the portrait of war hero and former president Dwight D. Eisenhower, then recently deceased. The reverse depicts the emblem of Apollo XI, humankind's first landing on the moon.

The new coin was designed and sculpted by U.S. Mint Chief Engraver Frank Gasparro. He had succeeded Gilroy Roberts when Roberts resigned in 1965 to take a position with the commercial Franklin Mint which produced, among its other items, casino tokens. On the dollar, Eisenhower faces left, with the motto IN GOD WE TRUST appearing below his chin. LIBERTY and the date are inscribed around the periphery, in conformance with most of our current coins. The reverse portrays the Apollo XI emblem of an eagle landing on the moon, with Earth seen in the distance. The eagle grasps an olive branch in its claws, while an arc of 13 stars surrounds it. UNITED STATES OF AMERICA and ONE DOLLAR are inscribed around the periphery, with E PLURIBUS UNUM directly above the eagle. Frank Gasparro's initials FG are seen at the truncation of Eisenhower's bust and again below the eagle's tailfeathers.

S-Mint Eisenhower Bicentennial dollar (38.1 mm)

Production problems delayed the release of the new coins until November 1, 1971. Though successful in their casino role, the huge "Ikes" failed to achieve general circulation for the same reason that their predecessors had – the public simply preferred paper dollars for their lighter weight and ease of use. After the first two years of production, the dollars of 1973 were coined solely for inclusion in sets sold to collectors on the Mint's mailing list. Production was halted after 1978 to make way for a new dollar coin of reduced size and different design. Though they continued to be used in casinos through the 1980s, Eisenhower dollars soon thereafter acquired a slight premium value and have all found their way to hoarders.

The minting of Eisenhower dollars coincided with the nation's bicentennial, and the dollar, became one of three coin types modified to mark this occasion. An open design competition for commemorative images to grace the reverses of the quarter dollar, half dollar, and dollar was announced by the Treasury Department in 1973, pursuant to a special act of Congress authorizing such changes. The Coinage Act of October 18, 1973, called for the dual dating of quarters, halves, and dollars issued from July 4, 1975, through 1976, and the replacement of their normal reverse designs with those bearing Bicentennial themes. The winners were Jack L. Ahr, whose colonial drummer was used for the quarter; Seth G. Huntington, who submitted an elevation view of Independence Hall ultimately adapted for the half; and Dennis R. Williams, for his depiction of the Liberty Bell superimposed on the moon. Though all of these concepts are appealing, only Ahr's drummer transferred well in the finished product, the larger coins appearing somewhat flat and featureless.

A bill passed on December 26, 1974, permitted the 1974 date to remain frozen on quarters, halves, and dollars minted well into 1975, while no coins of

S-Mint Washington Bicentennial quarter (24.3 mm)

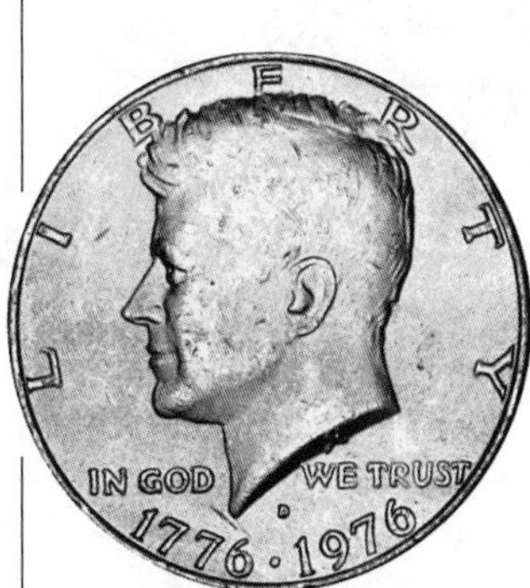

D-Mint Kennedy Bicentennial half dollar (30.6 mm)

NEW YORK

The U.S. Mint at West Point

The 2002-W West Point commemorative silver dollar honors the military academy's bicentennial. (38.1 mm)

The piece was struck at the West Point Mint in New York (below).

In 1973, America faced a severe shortage of cents, due primarily to speculation in the rising price of copper. To augment the Philadelphia Mint's production, a mint was installed at the United States Bullion Depository at West Point on the grounds of the U.S. Military Academy. This authority came under Public Law 93-127, passed October 18, 1973, which permitted "the use of any Mint facility for the manufacture and storage of medals and coins." While easily the smallest of the active mints, West Point enjoys perhaps the most scenic view, as it overlooks the beautiful and historic Hudson River.

Coinage operations commenced at West Point on July 29, 1974, and until 1984 the mint's coin production was limited to cents and quarter dollars. As these bore no mintmarks, they were thus indistinguishable from coins made at the Philadelphia Mint. While the *Annual Report of the Director of the Mint* has included separate figures for this mint's production, its circulating coinage is included in the Philadelphia Mint totals in most coin catalogs. Cents were coined at West Point every year from 1974 through 1985, though its annual production peaked at 2,036,215,000 pieces in 1984. Quarter dollars without mintmarks were struck at West Point from 1976 through 1979, with production peaking in 1978 (521,452,000 pieces).

Also minted at West Point during 1980 to 1984 were the American Arts 1-ounce and half-ounce gold bullion medals, the precursor of the U.S. Mint's current American Eagle bullion coins. The first coins made at the West Point Mint other than cents and quarters were the 1984-dated $10 pieces commemorating the 23rd Olympiad at Los Angeles. Also a first for this mint was the inclusion of its W mintmark.

Since that time, West Point's W has appeared on numerous commemoratives, as well as the American Eagle bullion coins. In 1996 a 50th anniversary edition of the Roosevelt dime was struck bearing the W mintmark for inclusion in that year's annual Uncirculated Mint set. To date, however, the only coins struck for general circulation at the West Point Mint have been cents and quarter dollars, as noted above.

West Point is unique among the four active mints in that it never offered public tours. This was due to its specialized role as a bullion depository and its limited space. In the wake of the September 11, 2001, terrorist attacks, both the U.S. military academy and the mint remain off-limits, and security there is especially tight.

these denominations were to be struck with the date 1975. The dual-dated Bicentennial coins went into production early in 1975 to enable their release to circulation by July 4 of that year. As a result, coins dated 1974 and 1776-1976 were in production simultaneously during part of 1975.

The Bicentennial coinage was only partially successful as a circulating commemorative program for the simple reason that, of the three denominations employed, only the quarter dollar was in general use. Halves and dollars of the regular types were seldom seen, so few outside the collecting community ever knew of their Bicentennial editions. As for the quarters, most were saved by the general public as novelties, and they are now rarely encountered in circulation.

When normal coinage resumed in 1977, a replacement for the unwieldy and unpopular Eisenhower dollar was already in the works. An extensive study of the country's future coinage needs to the year 1990 by the Research Triangle Institute (RTI) had suggested eliminating the half dollar and dollar denominations or replacing the traditional dollar coin with a much smaller piece. While many favored the discontinuance of dollar coins, it was projected in RTI's report that a successful 1-dollar coin would save millions of dollars over a period of years through elimination of the less-durable paper dollar. Congress was indeed moved to adopt a smaller dollar coin, but they sealed the coin's fate by not providing for the gradual withdrawal of paper dollars.

The Act of October 10, 1978, made the mini-dollar coin a reality, and the first test strikings with the adopted design were run off the following month. Earlier tests had been made with a very attractive flowing-haired portrait of Liberty on one side and a soaring eagle on the other. Dated 1977, this coin design by Chief Engraver Frank Gasparro, though popular with the numismatic community, succumbed to political pressure when it was directed that a real American woman must appear on the new coin. A number of candidates for this honor were presented by interested parties, but the ultimate winner was women's rights pioneer Susan B. Anthony. Gasparro's soaring eagle reverse design was also rejected in favor of the Apollo XI insignia, salvaged from the Eisenhower dollar.

The obverse of this coin portrays a bust of Susan B. Anthony facing right in late 19th-century dress, her hair tied back in a bun. LIBERTY is above the bust, with the date below. An arc of 13 stars appears around the border, arranged seven left and six right. The motto IN GOD WE TRUST is to the right of Anthony's chin, with Frank Gasparro's initials FG below the truncation of her bust. Mintmarks appear above her right shoulder, and these include, for the first time since World War II, a letter P for Philadelphia. This mintmark was subsequently added to all of that facility's coins except the cent beginning in 1980. Also appearing on a circulating coin for the first time since 1974 was the S mintmark of San Francisco.

Susan B. Anthony, circa 1890

1979-P Susan B. Anthony dollar (26.5 mm)

Galvanos of Frank Gasparro's rejected design for the dollar coin

As first conceived, the Anthony dollar was to have a multi-sided shape enabling it to be readily distinguished from the quarter dollar. This was a critical provision, since the two coins differed in diameter by only a few millimeters and were made of the very same composition. Such a radical departure from traditional U.S. coinage was rejected in favor of a multi-sided inner border within a conventional round shape. This compromise proved a fatal mistake, as the coin's size, shape, and color rendered it a near twin to the quarter. Its confusing appearance, combined with the high rate of inflation at the time of its release on July 2, 1979, earned it the derisive moniker of "the Carter quarter," a reference to then-president Jimmy Carter. Worse still, Congress lost its nerve and failed to eliminate the dollar note. With the option of choosing one tender over the other, the general public flatly rejected the dollar coin. Businesses followed suit, as plans to convert vending machines and turnstiles to accept the new coins were quickly cancelled.

The obvious failure of the new coin caused its minting for circulation to be discontinued after only two years of production, 1979 and 1980. Those struck the following year were minted exclusively for sale to collectors, and none were issued for general circulation. The coinage of Anthony dollars was then suspended for nearly 20 years. Embarrassed by its unshrinking stockpile of coins, the

The U.S. Mint's Bullion Coins

Among the many peripheral programs undertaken by the United States Mint in recent years is its lineup of silver, gold, and platinum bullion coins. Though they do not circulate as money, these coins do have a stated legal-tender value.

The silver coin is slightly larger than the traditional silver dollar. It is comprised of .999 fine silver, weighs 1 ounce and carries a face value of $1. The gold issues are denominated at $5, $10, $25, and $50, and they weigh one-tenth ounce, one-quarter ounce, one-half ounce and 1 ounce, respectively. Not pure gold, the bullion pieces are comprised of 91.67% gold, 3% silver and 5.33% copper.

These silver and gold bullion coins have been minted annually since 1986, and were joined in 1997 by platinum coins denominated at $10, $25, $50, and $100. Like the gold pieces, they are in units of one-tenth ounce, one-quarter ounce, one-half ounce, and 1 ounce, respectively. Their fineness is .9995 platinum.

1986 1-dollar silver bullion coin (40.6 mm)

For the obverse of the silver bullion coin, the Mint revived Adolph Weinman's 1916 Walking Liberty. The reverse features Mint Sculptor and Engraver John M. Mercanti's interpretation of the Great Seal. Augustus Saint-Gaudens' acclaimed Striding Liberty from the 1907 to 1933 double eagle was selected for the obverse of the four gold issues, while artist Miley Busiek created the reverse design with "Family of Eagles" as its theme.

The platinum coins bear designs by two Mint sculptor-engravers. John Mercanti's bust from New York Harbor's "Liberty Enlightening the World" serves as the obverse, while Thomas D. Rogers Sr. provided the reverse design of an eagle soaring over a rising sun.

For the Proof editions of the platinum coins, the reverse is changed annually to depict the American bald eagle in various natural settings. The theme for these designs is "Vistas of Liberty."

Treasury tried to force the circulation of Anthony dollars wherever their recipients had no option. American military personnel stationed overseas were paid in "Susies," which their European hosts soon discounted, leaving the Americans and their families to absorb the loss.

The use of Anthony dollars did accelerate a bit in the waning years of the 20th century. A few metropolitan transit systems still accept these coins, but they remain the exception. The primary demand has come from the nation's post offices, which return these coins as change to those using its stamp-dispensing machines. Recipients are either annoyed or amused when these oddities come into their possession, and the coins are kept as novelties or quickly spent and returned to the Federal Reserve System in bank deposits. They are almost never re-circulated by retailers.

Despite its failure with the Susan B. Anthony dollar, Congress, under pressure from the vending industry, decided in 1997 that the time was right for another try at introducing a one-dollar coin. Public Law 105-124, signed by President William Jefferson Clinton on December 1, specified the properties that the new coin must possess, though it made no mention of the design it would bear. To maintain continuity with the still-current Anthony dollar, the size, weight, and magnetic signature of the new coin would be the same, though it would have a plain edge. Also distinctive was its composition, consisting of a center core of pure copper sandwiched between outer layers of manganese brass. The specific composition of the outer layers is 77% copper, 12% zinc, 7% manganese, and 4% nickel. This produced a brassy yellow "golden" coin that would certainly never be mistaken for a quarter dollar, unlike the ill-fated Anthony dollar.

A design competition that included artists both within and outside the U.S. Mint resulted in a compromise. The model by New Mexico sculptor Glenna Goodacre was approved for the obverse, which depicts an idealized, shoulder-length bust of the Shoshone woman Sacagawea, who accompanied Lewis and Clark on part of their historic 1804 to 1806 exploration of the Louisiana Territory. She is shown looking over her shoulder at the viewer, while carrying upon her back the infant Jean-Baptiste, her son with French-Canadian fur trapper Toussaint Charbonneau. Goodacre's model for Sacagawea, of whom no authentic portrait is known, was Randy'L He-dow Teton, then a 22-year-old student at the University of New Mexico.

The reverse of the Sacagawea dollar was created by U.S. Mint Sculptor and Engraver Thomas D. Rogers, Sr. His depiction of the American eagle in soaring flight is an attractive complement to the coin's obverse. One unsettling element, however, is the presence of 17 stars in place of the traditional 13. This higher figure represents the number of states in the Union at the time the Lewis and Clark Expedition began in 1804, though no explanation of this appears on the coin. The extra stars have a crowded appearance, and they disrupt an important element of continuity in United States coinage.

Randy'L He-dow Teton (left) and Glenna Goodacre

It was anticipated that the new dollar coins, dated 2000, would not be issued until March of that year. Stating that its

Continued on page 187

2002-P Sacagawea golden dollar (26.5 mm)

The CCAC advises the Secretary of the Treasury on themes and design proposals relating to circulating coinage, bullion coinage, commemorative coins and medals. The CCAC also makes commemorative coin recommendations to the Secretary and advises on the events, persons, or places to be commemorated, as well as on the mintage levels and proposed designs. The CCAC submits an annual report to Congress and the Secretary describing its activities and providing recommendations.

– From a United States Mint news release explaining the functions of the Citizens Coinage Advisory Committee, established by Public Law 108.15 on April 23, 2003

The 50 State Quarters® Program

Beginning in 1999, the nation embarked on an epic program of commemorative coins intended specifically for circulation. With the statutory mottoes and legends transferred to its obverse, the Washington quarter will play host to no less than 50 commemorative reverses, each one honoring a member state of the United States of America. Produced at a rate of five new issues per year, this program extends through 2008 and includes all of the quarter dollars minted at Philadelphia, Denver, and San Francisco.

To implement this program, U.S. Mint Sculptor and Engraver William Cousins modified the obverse design of John Flanagan's 1932 Washington quarter dollar. His stylized initials, WC, now appear alongside JF at the truncation of Washington's bust. Both the coin's value, QUARTER DOLLAR, and the legend UNITED STATES OF AMERICA have been transferred to the obverse, providing more room for the commemorative themes on its reverse. The design theme for each state is furnished by a committee appointed by that state's governor, and the modeling of the approved design is performed by one of the Mint's engraving staff. With five new designs per year, each coin is minted for about 10 weeks.

Since the quarter is currently our most popular and widely used denomination, the effects of this program will be far-reaching in creating awareness of both our nation's history and the rich panorama of its coins. Both the United States Mint and the numismatic community are behind this vast undertaking. Many thousands of Americans who had never previously thought about collecting coins are now searching through their change or ordering the needed pieces directly from the Mint and various commercial suppliers. After a lapse of more than 30 years, coin-collecting folders have once again become a common sight in retail stores, as everyone jumps on the bandwagon.

Common obverse · *Delaware, 1999* · *New Jersey, 1999*

Georgia, 1999 · *Connecticut, 1999* · *New York, 2001*

Illinois, 2003 · *Maine, 2003* · *Missouri, 2003*

Release Schedule for the State Quarters

1999: Delaware, Pennsylvania, New Jersey, Georgia, Connecticut

2000: Massachusetts, Maryland, South Carolina, New Hampshire, Virginia

2001: New York, North Carolina, Rhode Island, Vermont, Kentucky

2002: Tennessee, Ohio, Louisiana, Indiana, Mississippi

2003: Illinois, Alabama, Maine, Missouri, Arkansas

2004: Michigan, Florida, Texas, Iowa, Wisconsin

2005: California, Minnesota, Oregon, Kansas, West Virginia

2006: Nevada, Nebraska, Colorado, North Dakota, South Dakota

2007: Montana, Washington, Idaho, Wyoming, Utah

2008: Oklahoma, New Mexico, Arizona, Alaska, Hawaii

Continued from page 185

existing stockpile of Anthony dollars was not sufficient to meet the demand until that time, the Mint produced millions more dated 1999 during the final quarter of that year. This issue proved unnecessary, as post office vending machines were still distributing 1979 and 1980 dollars well into 2000, while the 1999 pieces were mostly hoarded by speculators.

The new Sacagawea dollars were actually issued as early as the last week of January in the opening move of an innovative and highly visible marketing campaign. The principal distributors were not the nation's banks, but rather it was the retailer Wal-Mart that undertook an exclusive arrangement with the Mint and the Federal Reserve. Despite such efforts, millions of Sacagawea dollars issued have been hoarded by collectors and speculators or remain idle in vaults. This writer has never actually received one in change, and it is likely that future mintages may be solely for collectors. The fact that one-dollar Federal Reserve Notes are still being produced, without any plan to discontinue their issue, does not bode well for the coin's future. Americans are creatures of habit, and they resist change in something as fundamental as money.

The successful circulation of a one-dollar coin will be a crucial test for the adaptability of United States coinage to this new millennium. While other advanced economies of the world have gradually introduced coins of higher values to keep in step with normal inflation, simultaneously eliminating the lower denominations, the United States soldiers on with the same lineup it has had for generations. Americans seem oblivious to the inconvenience of needing so many small coins to complete each transaction.

Recognizing the changing needs of the American economy is not the responsibility of the U.S. Mint, as it only provides that which Congress has ordered. In the hands of our senators and representatives lies the future of United States coinage, and Congress will have to determine which pieces of money are most useful to the American people. It is a responsibility that requires the likes of Thomas Jefferson, Alexander Hamilton, and Gouverneur Morris, those Founding Fathers who created our national mint more than two centuries ago. Whether our current leaders can rise to the task is a question whose answer will be found in coins not yet minted. As numismatists, perhaps we can provide them with the historical perspective on coinage that is so crucial to understanding where we've been and where we are going.

◀ *There are no images of Sacagawea, but this circa 1884 photograph of Mary Enos, a young Shoshone woman with a baby in a cradleboard, gives us an idea of how she might have looked.*

Mint Director Henrietta Holsman Fore was appointed to a five-year term in August 2001. There was no fixed length of service for the Mint Director before 1873, when Congress established the five-year term. Directors, however, may serve more than one term.

Bibliography

Adams, Eugene H., Lyle W. Dorsett and Robert S. Pulcipher. *The Pioneer Western Bank – First of Denver: 1860-1980.* First Interstate Bank of Denver, N.A. Denver, Colo., 1984.

Alexander, David T., and Thomas K. Delorey, Editors. *Comprehensive Catalog & Encyclopedia of United States Coins. Coin World,* Sidney, Ohio, 1995.

Birdsall, Clair M. *The United States Branch Mint at Charlotte, North Carolina: Its History and Coinage.* Southern Historical Press, Inc., Easley, S.C., 1988.

Birdsall, Clair M. *The United States Branch Mint at Dahlonega, Georgia: Its History and Coinage.* Southern Historical Press, Inc., Easley, S.C., 1984.

Bowers, Q. David. *The History of United States Coinage, as Illustrated by the Garrett Collection.* Bowers & Ruddy Galleries, Los Angeles, Calif., 1979.

Bowers, Q. David. *Silver Dollars & Trade Dollars of the United States: A Complete Encyclopedia.* Bowers & Merena Galleries, Wolfeboro, N.H., 1993.

Bowers, Q. David. *United States Gold Coins: An Illustrated History.* Bowers & Ruddy Galleries, Los Angeles, Calif., 1982.

Breen, Walter. *Walter Breen's Complete Encyclopedia of U.S. and Colonial Coins.* F.C.I. Press, Inc. and Doubleday, New York, N.Y., 1988.

Breen, Walter. *Walter Breen's Encyclopedia of United States Half Cents: 1793-1857.* American Institute of Numismatic Research, South Gate, Calif., 1983.

Breen, Walter, and Ronald J. Gillio. *California Pioneer Fractional Gold, Second Edition.* Bowers & Merena Galleries, Inc., Wolfeboro, N.H., 2003.

Carothers, Neil. *Fractional Money: A History of the Small Coins and Fractional Paper Currency of The United States.* John Wiley & Sons, Inc., New York, N.Y., 1930.

Catton, Bruce. *The Civil War.* American Heritage Publishing Company, Inc., New York, N.Y., 1971.

Clain-Stefanelli, Vladimir. *History of the National Numismatic Collections.* U.S. Government Printing Office, Washington, D.C., 1968.

Cline, J.H. *Standing Liberty Quarters, Third Edition.* Published by the author, Palm Harbor, Fla., 1997.

***Coin World* Staff.** *Coin World Almanac.* Amos Press, Sidney, Ohio, 2000.

Crosby, Sylvester S. *The Early Coins of America.* Quarterman Publications, Lawrence, Mass., 1983.

Dewey, Davis Rich, Ph.D. *Financial History of The United States.* Longmans, Green and Co., New York, N.Y., 1934.

Doty, Richard. *America's Money, America's Story: A Comprehensive Chronicle of American Numismatic History.* Krause Publications, Inc., Iola, Wis., 1998.

Eitemiller, David J. *The Denver Mint: The Story of the Mint from the Gold Rush to Today.* Jende-Hagen Book Corporation, Frederick, Colo., 1983.

Fox, Bruce. *The Complete Guide to Walking Liberty Half Dollars.* DLRC Press, Virginia Beach, Va., 1993.

Ganz, David L., Editor. *Coinage Laws of The United States 1792-1894.* Committee on Finance of the United States Senate, Washington, D.C., 1894. Reprinted by Bowers & Merena Galleries, Inc., Wolfeboro, N.H., 1990.

Head, Sylvia Gaily, and Elizabeth W. Etheridge. *The Neighborhood Mint: Dahlonega in the Age of Jackson.* Mercer University Press, Macon, Ga., 1986.

Hepburn, A. Barton. *History of Coinage and Currency in The United States and the Perennial Contest for Sound Money.* Greenwood Press, New York, N.Y., 1968.

Hickson, Howard. *Mint Mark "CC": The Story of the United States Mint at Carson City, Nevada.* Nevada State Museum, Carson City, Nev., 1972.

Kagin, Donald H. *Private Gold Coins and Patterns of the United States.* Arco Publishing, Inc., New York, N.Y., 1981.

Lange, David W. *The Complete Guide to Buffalo Nickels, Second Edition.* DLRC Press, Virginia Beach, Va., 2000.

Lange, David W. *The Complete Guide to Lincoln Cents.* Bowers & Merena Galleries, Wolfeboro, N.H., 1996.

Lange, David W. *The Complete Guide to Mercury Dimes.* DLRC Press, Virginia Beach, Va., 1993.

Leach, Frank A. *Recollections of a Mint Director.* Bowers & Merena Galleries, Inc., Wolfeboro, N.H., 1987.

McGinty, Brian. *Haraszthy at the Mint.* Dawson's Book Shop, Los Angeles, Calif., 1975.

Morgan-Webb, Sir Charles. *The Money Revolution.* Economic Forum, Inc., New York, N.Y., 1935.

Mossman, Philip L. *Money of the American Colonies and Confederation: A Numismatic, Economic and Historical Correlation.* The American Numismatic Society, New York, N.Y., 1993.

Nugent, Walter T.K. *The Money Question During Reconstruction.* Norton & Company, Inc., New York, N.Y., 1967.

Perez, Gilbert S. *Numismatic Notes and Monographs No. 8: The Mint of the Philippine Islands.* American Numismatic Society, New York, N.Y., 1921.

Peters, Gloria, and Cynthia Mohon. *The Complete Guide to Shield and Liberty Head Nickels.* DLRC Press, Virginia Beach, Va., 1995.

Pollock, Andrew W., III. *United States Patterns and Related Issues.* Bowers and Merena Galleries, Inc., Wolfeboro, N.H., 1994.

Snow, Richard. *Flying Eagle and Indian Cents.* Eagle Eye Press, 1992.

Stewart, Frank H. *History of the First United States Mint.* Quarterman Publications, Inc., Lawrence, Mass., 1974.

Swiatek, Anthony, and Walter Breen. *The Encyclopedia of United States Silver and Gold Commemorative Coins 1892-1954.* F.C.I. Press, Inc./Arco Publishing, Inc., New York, N.Y., 1981.

Taxay, Don. *The U.S. Mint and Coinage.* Arco Publishing Company, Inc., New York, N.Y., 1966.

Taxay, Don. *An Illustrated History of U.S. Comemmorative Coinage.* Arco Publishing Company, Inc., New York, N.Y., 1967.

Treasury Department, Bureau of the Mint. *Domestic and Foreign Coins Manufactured by Mints of the United States 1793-1980.* U.S. Government Printing Office, Washington, D.C., 1981.

Treasury Department, Director of the Mint. *Laws of the United States Relating to the Coinage: Supplement.* Government Printing Office, Washington, D.C., 1912.

Vermeule, Cornelius. *Numismatic Art in America: Aesthetics of the United States Coinage.* The Belknap Press of Harvard University Press, Cambridge, Mass., 1971.

Van Ryzin, Robert R. *Crime of 1873: The Comstock Connection.* Krause Publications, Iola, Wis., 2001.

Wilkinson, Henrietta H., *The Mint Museum of Art at Charlotte: A Brief History.* Heritage Printers, Charlotte, N.C., 1973.

Willem, John M. Jr. *The United States Trade Dollar: America's Only Unwanted, Unhonored Coin.* The Marchbanks Press, New York, N.Y., 1959.

Williams, David, *The Georgia Gold Rush: Twenty-Niners, Cherokees, and Gold Fever.* University of South Carolina Press, Columbia, S.C., 1993.

Winter, Douglas, *Charlotte Mint Gold Coins: 1838-1861.* Bowers & Merena Galleries, Wolfeboro, N.H., 1987.

Winter, Douglas, *Gold Coins of the Dahlonega Mint: 1838-1861.* DWN Publishing, Dallas, Texas, 1997.

Winter, Douglas, and Lawrence E. Culter, M.D., *Gold Coins of the Old West, The Carson City Mint 1870-1893: A Numismatic History and Analysis.* Bowers & Merena Galleries, Wolfeboro, N.H., 1994.

Yeoman, R.S. (Kenneth Bressett, Editor). *A Guide Book of United States Coins, 53rd Edition.* St. Martin's Press, New York, N.Y., 1999.

Periodicals

Guren, Jay. "Surgery Conceals Scars at O-Mint." *Coin World,* July 29, 1981. Amos Press, Sidney, Ohio.

Hettger, Henry T. "Treasury Redemption Policy Causes its Vaults to Overflow." *Coin World,* May 2, 1994. Amos Press, Sidney, Ohio.

Jacobs, Wayne L. "1870 and the Great American Silver Expulsion." *The Canadian Numismatic Journal,* January/February, 1998.

Julian, R.W. "Silver $1 Revived in 1836 with Gobrecht Design." *Numismatic News,* June 20, 2000. Krause Publications, Iola, Wis.

Lacewell, Robert M. "21 Years on 'A Great Job for a Collector.' " *Coin World,* September 23, 1987. Amos Press, Sidney, Ohio.

Lantz, Michael P. "The 1964-D Peace Dollar," *Coin World,* September 16, 1996. Amos Press, Sidney, Ohio.

Lantz, Michael P. "Ammunition Presses Worked for Coins, Too." *Coin World,* February 23, 1999. Amos Press, Sidney, Ohio.

American Memory

Many of the quotations and photographs presented in this book come from the Library of Congress's online primary source collection, American Memory **(http://memory.loc.gov).**

Image Credits

Unless otherwise noted, images are from copyright-free sources or the American Numismatic Association archives.

Title page: "First United States Mint" by Natalie Hause, courtesy of the Craig A. Whitford Collection. Frontispiece: "The Village of Secota," Library of Congress. Page 1: Wampum belt, Globe Pequot Press; strung wampum beads, Numismatic Guaranty Corporation; Maryland settlers, Library of Congress. Page 2: Hat maker, courtesy, American Antiquarian Society. Page 3: Hard-working colonists, Library of Congress. Page 5: Conversion chart, courtesy, American Antiquarian Society; Cecil Calvert, Library of Congress. Page 6: Colonial Congress document, Library of Congress. Page 10: King George III, Library of Congress; George III halfpenny, Numismatic Guaranty Corporation. Page 12: David Rittenhouse, Library of Congress. Page 13: Thomas Jefferson and Alexander Hamilton, Library of Congress. Page 14: George Washington, Library of Congress. Page 15: David Rittenhouse, Library of Congress. Page 18: "First U.S. Mint Buildings," Independence National Historical Park, Philadelphia, Pennsylvania. Page 22: Counting room, courtesy of Fred Weinberg & Co. Page 24: Coil of metal, United States Mint. Page 25: Susan B. Anthony dollar, Numismatic Guaranty Corporation. Page 28: Half eagle, Numismatic Guaranty Corporation. Page 30: City of Washington map, Library of Congress. Page 36: Both coins, Numismatic Guaranty Corporation. Page 37: Quarter eagle and half dime, Numismatic Guaranty Corporation. Page 39: Christopher Bechtler, courtesy of the North Carolina State Archives; Bechtler coin, courtesy of Hancock & Harwell; U.S. Assay Office, courtesy of the Public Library of Charlotte & Mecklenburg County. Page 41: John Hill Wheeler, Library of Congress. Page 42: Thomas Edison, The Mint Museums, Charlotte, North Carolina. Page 43: Half eagle, Numismatic Guaranty Corporation. Page 45: Templeton Reid coins, courtesy of Hancock & Harwell; "The Trail of Tears," Woolaroc Museum, Bartlesville, Oklahoma. Page 47: Dahlonega Mint building, Hancock & Harwell. Page 51: Quarter eagle, Numismatic Guaranty Corporation; "Secession Quick Step," Historic American Sheet Music, Music B 231, Duke University Rare Book, Manuscript, and Special Collections Library. Page 53: New Orleans Mint, Louisiana State Museum. Page 55: Andrew Berrett, Louisiana State Museum. Page 57: Both photos, Louisiana State Museum. Page 59: New Orleans Mint, Louisiana State Museum; Confederate half dollar, courtesy of Stacks. Page 60: Henry Stuart Foote, Library of Congress; dime, Numismatic Guaranty Corporation. Page 61: Barber half dollar, Numismatic Guaranty Corporation. Page 63: Bank scene, courtesy of The Huntington Library. Page 64: CAL. quarter eagle, Numismatic Guaranty Corporation. Page 66: Both coins, Numismatic Guaranty Corporation. Page 73: Both photos, Library of Congress. Page 74: San Francisco Mint, Library of Congress. Page 75: Engine room, Library of Congress. Page 76: San Francisco Mint, Library of Congress. Page 79: Cent, Numismatic Guaranty Corporation. Page 80: Longacre sketches, The Library Company of Philadelphia; Longacre portrait, The National Portrait Gallery, Smithsonian Institution. Page 81: Broadside, Library of Congress. Page 82: Snowden medal, David W. Lange. Page 85: Abraham Lincoln, Library of Congress. Page 86: Canadian coin, Numismatic Guaranty Corporation. Page 93: Linderman medal, David W. Lange. Page 98: Carson City Mint, Library of Congress. Page 101: Half eagle, Numismatic Guaranty Corporation. Page 104: Dalles, Oregon, mint basement, Ralph R. Keeney. Page 111: Meeting announcement, Library of Congress. Page 112: Bryan poster, Library of Congress. Page 114: Oath of allegiance medal, David W. Lange. Page 115: Transportation Building, courtesy of the Frances Loeb Library, Harvard Design School. Page 119: Carver and Washington portraits, Library of Congress. Page 120: Washington commemorative, Numismatic Guaranty Corporation. Page 122: DeWitt Clinton Ward portrait of Saint-Gaudens and clay model, Saint-Gaudens National Historic Site, National Park Service. Page 123: Denver Mint, United States Mint. Page 126: Theodore Roosevelt, courtesy, Colorado Historical Society. Page 129: William Green Russell, Colorado Historical Society; Parsons and J.J. Conway coins, courtesy of The Frederick R. Mayer Colorado Pioneer Gold Collection. Page 130: Both coin images courtesy of The Frederick R. Mayer Colorado Pioneer Gold Collection. Page 131: Magnetic Mineral Rod, Denver Public Library, Western History Collection. Page 132: Denver Mint photos, U.S. Mint. Page 133: Denver Mint photos, U.S. Mint. Page 134: Mint employee, U.S. Mint. Page 135: Denver Mint, U.S. Mint. Page 138: James Earle Fraser, the Donald C. & Elizabeth M. Dickinson Research Center, National Cowboy and Western Heritage Museum, Oklahoma, Oklahoma. Page 139: Two Moons, National Archives & Records Administration; Iron Tail, Denver Public Library, Western History Collection; Big Tree, National Archives & Records Administration. Page 140: Chain mail Liberty quarter, Numismatic Guaranty Corporation. Page 141: Elsie Kachel Stevens, Numismatic Guaranty Corporation. Page 142: One-centavo coin, David W. Lange. Page 143: William Howard Taft and troops on the ramparts, Library of Congress; Page 144: 1936-M peso and 1928-M 20-centavo piece, David W. Lange; Manila Mint interior, U.S. Mint. Page 144: Both coins and mintmark, David W. Lange. Page 145: Five-centavo coin, David W. Lange; mint exterior and staff, U.S. Mint; 1937-M 5-centavo piece, David W. Lange. Page 146: Burning building, Library of Congress; 50-centavo piece, David W. Lange. Page 147: Boy Scouts selling bonds, Chicago Historical Society. Page 148: Baker medal, David W. Lange; "Good-Bye Broadway, Hello France," Historic American Sheet Music, Music B 227, Duke University Rare Book, Manuscript, and Special Collections Library. Page 153: Dorothea Lange photo, Library of Congress. Page 154: Franklin Roosevelt, Library of Congress. Page 156: Nellie Tayloe Ross medal, David W. Lange; Page 157: Monticello, Library of Congress. Page 158: OPA volunteer, Library of Congress. Page 159: U.S.S. *Shaw*, National Archives & Records Administration. Page 160: We Can Do It!, National Archives & Records Administration. Page 161: Roosevelt dime, Numismatic Guaranty Corporation; Stalin, Roosevelt and Churchill, Library of Congress. Page 163: Lincoln Memorial, Library of Congress. Page 164: John F. Kennedy, Library of Congress. Page 168: Lincoln cents, Numismatic Guaranty Corporation. Page 169: LBJ coin, David W. Lange. Page 170: Dwight D. Eisenhower, National Archives & Records Administration. Page 172: West Point commemorative, Numismatic Guaranty Corporation. Page 173: Anthony dollar, Numismatic Guaranty Corporation; Susan B. Anthony, Library of Congress. Page 177: Mary Enos, Denver Public Library, Western History Collection.